'The Word became flesh'

'The Word became flesh'

Evangelicals and the incarnation

Papers from the Sixth Oak Hill College Annual School of Theology

Edited by
David Peterson

PATERNOSTER
PRESS

Copyright © 2003 The Editor and Contributors

First published in 2003 by Paternoster Press

09 08 07 06 05 04 03   7 6 5 4 3 2 1

Paternoster Press is an imprint of Authentic Media,
P.O. Box 300, Carlisle, Cumbria, CA3 0QS, UK
and
P.O. Box 1047, Waynesboro, GA 30830-2047, USA

Website: www.paternoster-publishing.com

The right of The Editor and Contributors to be identified as the Author of this Work has been asserted by them in accordance with the Copyright, Designs and Patents Act 1988.

All rights reserved. No part of this publication may be reproduced, stored in a retrieval system, or transmitted in any form or by any means, electronic, mechanical, photocopying, recording or otherwise, without the prior permission of the publisher or a licence permitting restricted copying. In the UK such licences are issued by the Copyright Licensing Agency, 90 Tottenham Court Road, London W1P 9HE.

British Library Cataloguing in Publication Data
A catalogue record for this book is available from the British Library

ISBN 1-84227-209-8

Unless otherwise stated, Scripture quotations are taken from the
NEW REVISED STANDARD VERSION BIBLE
© 1989, Division of Christian Education of the National Council of the Churches of Christ in the United States of America.
Used by permission. All rights reserved.

Scripture quotations marked NIV are taken from
HOLY BIBLE, NEW INTERNATIONAL VERSION
Copyright © 1973, 1978, 1984 by the International Bible Society.
Used by permission of Hodder and Stoughton Limited. All rights reserved.
'NIV' is a registered trademark of the International Bible Society.
UK trademark number 1448790.

Cover Design by FourNineZero
Printed in Great Britain by Bell and Bain, Glasgow

Contents

Foreword by Gerald Bray	vii
List of Abbreviations	xi
Introduction	xiii

1. Is Christ's Incarnation the Consummation of the Cosmic Process?   1
MICHAEL OVEY

Introduction	1
Christ as the Consummation of the Cosmic Process (*Christus Consummator*)	4
Evaluation of *Lux Mundi* Theology	15
Concluding Remarks	42

2. The Son Incarnate in a Hostile World   50
MICHAEL OVEY

Introduction	50
Christ as Co-sufferer	52
Who was Hostile to Jesus?	55
Sonship and Idolatry	76
Conclusions	81

3. The Incarnation and Christian Living   87
DAVID PETERSON

Introduction: Sharing our Humanity	87
The Pioneer and Perfecter of Faith	90
The Perfecting of Christ	93
The Perfecting of Believers	100
Conclusion: Hebrews and the Incarnation	102

4. The Incarnation and Mission   110
CHRIS GREEN

Introduction: Evangelicals and the Roots of a Guilty Conscience	110

Incarnation and Missionary Monotheism	116
Incarnation and the Missionary Mediator	122
Incarnation and the Missionary Message	124
Incarnation and the Missionary Mandate	125
Incarnation and the Missionary Model	128
Incarnation and Missionary Method	134
Conclusion: Incarnation and Mission	142

5. The Incarnation and Scripture — **152**
TIMOTHY WARD

Introduction: The Word and the Words	152
A Biblical Response: God, Christ and Words in the Bible	157
A Philosophical Response: Persons, Actions and Words	169
A Theological Response: Scripture and Spirit	175
Conclusion	179

6. The Incarnation and the Lord's Supper — **185**
CARL TRUEMAN

The Lord's Supper: A Neglected Gift	185
Luther versus Zwingli: The Lord's Supper as Incarnational Problem	187
The Positive Function of the Lord's Supper in Reformed Theology	189
Why is the Lord's Supper Necessary?	199
Conclusion	203

FOREWORD

'And the Word became flesh and dwelt among us, and we beheld his glory...' (John 1:14). These immortal words from the preface to John's Gospel have ever been the starting point for serious Christian theology. The incarnation of the Son of God is a fundamental Christian belief and one of the defining marks of our faith over against the otherwise related monotheisms of Judaism and Islam. For evangelical Christians in particular, these words have been a constant reminder that in the man Jesus Christ we have fellowship with God. The incarnation holds a central place for us, not least because it provides the necessary condition for the fulfilment of the divine plan of redemption in and through the cross of Calvary. Unlike other traditions of Christianity, which have tended to downplay the atonement, evangelical preaching has always placed this truth at its centre. As the Apostle Paul wrote to the Corinthians: 'I am determined to know nothing among you but Christ, and him crucified' (1 Cor. 2:2). It was for that purpose that the Son of God came into the world, as the old prophet Simeon reminded Mary, when she presented him for circumcision in the temple at Jerusalem: 'A sword shall pierce your heart also ...' (Luke 2:35).

It is one of the curiosities of our time that incarnational theology has come to be associated with a liberal form of Anglo-Catholicism, in contrast to which, conservative evangelicalism has often been characterised as other-worldly and theologically deficient. The charge has been that whereas liberals have preached a relevant 'social gospel', evangelicals have supposedly concentrated on 'pie in the sky when you die', ignoring the injustices of racism, poverty and inequality which have scarred the face of so many apparently 'Christian' countries. There may be some truth in this perspective, but if so, it is only because the evangelicalism in question is a diluted version of the biblical gospel so fervently proclaimed by our forbears, who in the late eighteenth and nineteenth centuries were in the forefront of social revolution.

The real difference between us is that where liberals tend to see the incarnation as a myth proclaiming the possibility of creating a new humanity here on earth, evangelicals regard it as a historical fact which bears witness to the reality that the infinite and eternal God can and does dwell among men, so that one day we may rise to dwell with him in heaven. In the historical Jesus, this divine presence remained external to his followers until after his death, resurrection and ascension. It was only when he returned to his Father, and claimed his inheritance at God's right hand, that he sent his Holy Spirit, so that we who follow him might know his indwelling presence in our lives. But the glorified Christ whom we now know is the incarnate Christ who was crucified for us. The great evangelical hymn-writers saw this clearly:

> Crown him the lord of Love
> Behold his hands and side
> Those wounds yet visible above
> In beauty glorified ...

And of course, we must not forget those majestic lines of Charles Wesley's:

> Those dear tokens of his passion
> Still his dazzling body bears
> Cause of endless exaltation
> To his ransomed worshippers ...

The risen, ascended and glorified Christ is the man who was wounded for our transgressions, and who now pleads for us at the judgment-seat of God. It is because he was fully human that we are fully saved – body, soul, mind and spirit. And it is because we are saved by his sacrifice that we can now 'walk in newness of life' here on earth, assured that we have been chosen to reign with him in eternity. The gospel is a message of inner transformation with far-reaching outward consequences. Evangelicals have always believed that changing people is the key to changing societies, and this is why we concentrate so strongly on the need for individual repentance and conversion. But this emphasis must always be understood in the context of the one to whom we are united and in whom we have died to the old life. 'I am crucified with Christ, nevertheless I live; yet not I, but Christ lives in me, the hope of glory' (Gal. 2:20). The Apostle Paul's words to the Galatians are the heart-cry of every true believer, for in us the Son of God is present, by his Spirit, in the world. This is not a hypothetical gospel of some future fulfilment, but the living and active power of the Lord at work in our midst.

By insisting that the cradle and the cross must be held together in our teaching, the contributors to this volume have demonstrated their abiding faithfulness to historic Christian orthodoxy, something which was less apparent in the work of those who claimed to be the harbingers of a new 'incarnational' theology at the end of the nineteenth century. By insisting on the need to see the whole picture, the contributors to this volume have reminded us once again of the extent to which a penal substitutionary doctrine of the atonement feeds on and feeds into historic incarnational orthodoxy. One implies the other, and together they constitute the indispensable nexus of authentic Christianity.

That this symposium should be the fruit of a theological summer school at Oak Hill College in London is a matter of particular joy to me. David Peterson and his team at the college have undertaken this important initiative on an annual basis, and in so doing have opened the gates, not only of the college, but of Christian theology, to a wider public which needs to hear these things proclaimed with intellectual depth, academic rigour and spiritual power. That they have managed to achieve this is abiding testimony to the way in which they have raised their institution to the front rank of Christian educational establishments. It can only be hoped that this volume will be the harbinger of many more to come and that the college will continue to build on the foundations so well-laid by studies such as this one.

Gerald Bray
Anglican Professor of Divinity,
Beeson Divinity School,
Samford University,
Birmingham, Alabama, USA

Abbreviations

ESV	English Standard Version
ICC	International Critical Commentary
JSNTSS	Journal for the Study of the New Testament Supplement Series
LXX	Septuagint
NIV	New International Version
NRSV	New Revised Standard Version
SNTSMS	Society for New Testament Studies Monograph Series
TDNT	G. Kittel and G. Friedrich (eds.), *Theological Dictionary of the New Testament* (10 vols; Grand Rapids: Eerdmans, 1964–74)
WUNT	Wissenschaftliche Untersuchungen zum Neuen Testament
WBC	Word Biblical Commentary

Introduction

Evangelicals are often accused of having a weak or inadequate view of the incarnation. This particularly emerges in discussions about salvation, mission and other religions. But the charge is also made in connection with our view of Scripture and our convictions about the Lord's Supper. Responses by evangelicals to such accusations seem to be few and far between. Where they have been made, for example, in connection with international congresses on world evangelisation, the results have been sometimes unsatisfying and quite controversial.

Following the pattern of dealing with great gospel issues and their implications at our Annual School of Theology, the faculty of Oak Hill Theological College decided to focus on this topic in the lectures given to clergy and other fulltime workers on Wednesday, 8 May 2002. As we read papers to one another in preparation for the School, we were amazed to discover how much the book of essays edited by Charles Gore and published as *Lux Mundi* in 1889 seemed to be foundational for understanding the charges still being made against evangelicals. Echoes of the *Lux Mundi* position are often heard in the liberal Catholic theology that pervades Anglicanism in many parts of the world today. The issue is by no means confined to Anglican circles, but it is from this particular context that the papers in this volume largely emerge.

Michael Ovey leads us to consider the influence of *Lux Mundi* in the first chapter. Michael is engaged in doctoral research on the eternal relations between the persons of the Trinity at King's College London and teaches Systematic Theology at Oak Hill. He argues that *Lux Mundi* itself presents an inadequate and distorted view of the incarnation. The basic thesis of those nineteenth-century essayists was that the Son of God took flesh as the consummation of an essentially positive natural process at work in human history. They had scant regard for the credal affirmation that 'for us and our salvation he came down from heaven'. They did not view the incarnation as intrinsically entailing the crucifixion or atonement for our sin.

Michael exposes the context from which the *Lux Mundi* theology emerged. In the late nineteenth century, there was a development of evolutionary thinking beyond the biological realm. At the same time, critical scholarship in the theological disciplines was advancing. Concern for social and political action by Christians was dominant and idealism was popular in the philosophical realm. Michael finds the *Lux Mundi* position to be exegetically inept, historically distorted and philosophically suspect. This is profoundly troubling when the ongoing influence of this position in the contemporary scene is noted.

In the second chapter, Michael Ovey pursues the idea that the incarnation took place in a hostile world. He does this in dialogue with writers like Jürgen Moltmann and Jon Sobrino, who argue that Christ died as a co-victim with the poor and oppressed of our world. In contrast with the *Lux Mundi* approach, these scholars view the cross as the outcome of the incarnation in a world ruled by sin. Acknowledging that there is some truth in this position, Michael nevertheless demonstrates its inadequacy. He does this by investigating the nature of the hostility shown to Jesus in the Gospel records. Here the rejection is expressed against the Son as the heir and representative of the Father. Jesus is treated as he is because of his unique status and identity, not simply because he is a persecuted prophet or one of the oppressed. Moreover, opposition to Jesus and his followers is often done in the name of doing good or serving God.

So the incarnation reveals Jesus as the eternal Son, who does his Father's will. It also reveals the true nature of 'the world'. Human beings harbour an unacknowledged hatred for God and want to hide from the light. They need deliverance from their slavery to sin and service to Satan. The incarnation is not in itself a saving event, but it discloses the need for salvation by Christ's atoning work. Divine kingship is rejected in the incarnation but it is definitively established through Jesus' death and resurrection. This view of the incarnation gives us a God who cares for us and identifies with us in the griefs of our existence. His grace and generosity are underscored by the fact that he experienced human victimhood and undeserved hostility for our sake and for our salvation.

Introduction

My own contribution in the third chapter is entitled 'The Incarnation and Christian Living'. Although writers such as J.A.T. Robinson have doubted the genuineness of incarnational teaching in Hebrews, I argue that their approach is exegetically weak. The incarnation is first affirmed in Hebrews in connection with the claim that the Son is the ultimate revelation of God. But the argument soon moves to the notion of redemption from sin and its consequences, particularly with reference to the fulfilment of Psalm 8 and the high-priestly work of Christ.

His perfecting through suffering, death and heavenly exaltation made him a perfectly obedient sacrifice for sin and qualified him to be the ultimate or eschatological high priest. Although the redemptive dimension to his earthly ministry is stressed, the writer also portrays the incarnate Son as our example, particularly with reference to the enduring of hostility, testing and suffering. He is the perfect encouragement to persevere in faith, because of his earthly experience and its saving outcome. Through his perfecting, those who would draw near to God and enjoy an eternal relationship with God are perfected.

Chris Green, who is Vice Principal and lectures in Pastoral Studies at Oak Hill, writes on 'The Incarnation and Mission'. He returns again to the influence of *Lux Mundi* and the charge of liberal Catholicism that evangelicals have an inadequate theology of the incarnation. Like Michael Ovey, he questions the validity of the incarnational theology presented in *Lux Mundi*, particularly with reference to its social optimism and view of the church's mission. He expounds a biblical theology of mission with respect to the incarnation and its consequences. He describes a gospel without the cross as classically defined, as no gospel at all.

In connection with the Great Commission, he addresses the issue of the Son's continuing incarnation and ministry through his disciples. Just as the incarnation and atonement are indivisible, so the incarnation must be understood in connection with the resurrection, ascension, reign and return of Christ. If Christ's humanity continues glorified in heaven, this lifts the burden of being 'the continuing form of the Messiah' from us.

Chris engages with some of the conclusions about incarnation and mission associated with the Lausanne Congress on World Evangelisation and the subsequent conference in Manilla. He is particularly critical of attempts to identify the Johannine form of the Great Commission as 'crucial' and more 'incarnational' in its purview than the Synoptic form. It is not possible to make a simple comparison between the sending of Christ by the Father and Christ's sending of disciples into the world. The incarnational model of cross-cultural mission is challenged with respect to what it implies about God and the way he communicates with his fallen world. The mission of Christians, modelled in a secondary way on the mission of the apostles, is to witness to the lordship of Jesus and call others to repentance and faith in his redemptive work.

Timothy Ward is a graduate of Oak Hill, who did doctoral research at Edinburgh University on speech acts, biblical texts and the sufficiency of Scripture.[1] He is now the assistant minister at All Saints, Crowborough. In the present volume he writes on the incarnation and Scripture. The classical doctrine of the Bible as the Word of God has been attacked in modern times because it is said to detract from the unique identity of Jesus Christ as the Word of God incarnate. Those who propound the traditional view are accused of 'bibliolatry' and of compromising God in his transcendence. Karl Barth, in particular, fears that the classical doctrine implies a second incarnation of the Word in the body of a written text.

A biblical, a philosophical and a theological response to this challenge is offered by Timothy Ward. From the Bible he demonstrates the relationship between God's person, his actions, and the words of human speakers and writers through whom he speaks. Words are a necessary medium of relationship between persons and God's words are essential for the kind of relationship with God that the Bible offers. The unique divine character of the Bible has to do with the speech-acts that God performs through its words. It has nothing to do with any particular material incarnation of those words.

Applying speech-act theory to the Bible in this way is not a philosophical misconstrual of the text. Contemporary observations about the way language functions in relationships find certain parallels in the way Scripture views the operation of God's words. Theologically, the activity of the Holy Spirit is an important dimension to the argument. By means of the Holy Spirit, the Word himself continues to speak in and through the written word. The conclusion is reached that a carefully delineated doctrine of Scripture will make clear that Christ's incarnational uniqueness is not threatened but actually served and made knowable by the permanent identity of Scripture with the Word of God.

The final chapter is contributed by Carl Trueman, formerly of Aberdeen University, now lecturer in Church History at Westminster Seminary, Philadelphia. As a visiting scholar, Carl was asked to reflect on Reformation disputes about the incarnation and the Lord's Supper and their relevance for today. Although he writes as a Presbyterian, he does so with great respect for the writings of Thomas Cranmer and expresses a genuine affinity with his Eucharistic theology.

Luther regarded the incarnate Christ as the only context in which God could be encountered as gracious and thus required Christ's humanity to be present in the Eucharistic elements. Zwingli saw no such need to find Christ present and regarded the Supper as more of a memorial and a ritual of horizontal significance between believers. Debate about the nature and significance of the incarnation was thus foundational to disputes over the meaning of the sacrament. Carl Trueman argues that Zwingli's memorialist view, which appears to be the default position for many evangelicals today, is highly reductionist. However, he is also critical of the Lutheran position and proposes that the Reformed theology of Calvin and Cranmer is more biblically and theologically satisfying.

In the latter tradition, the Lord's Supper is more than a bare memorial of Christ's Passion. It seals the benefits of Christ's death to us, nourishes us spiritually and strengthens us for greater devotion to Christ. But this theology is associated with an insistence on the fact that the localised presence of Christ's body is in heaven, not in the sacrament. As noted in chapter four, there must be a close link between the incarnation and the resurrection/ascension in our thinking about the humanity of Christ. This has consequences for any theology of Eucharistic sacrifice or view about the transformation of the elements by the Holy Spirit. Both of these issues are discussed with reference to contemporary Anglican Eucharistic theology, particularly as reflected in *Common Worship*.

Carl argues that the incarnation is negatively significant for our understanding of how Christ is *not* present, and positively significant in determining how he is present through the Spirit. Spiritual union with Christ provides the basis for enjoying the benefits which his incarnation and incarnate work have definitively achieved. The final part of this chapter considers why the Lord's Supper is necessary and how we might think of the benefits of this sacrament in relation to the benefits of preaching.

The essays in this book do not pretend to offer a comprehensive reflection on the incarnation and its meaning for us. They respond to particular charges of neglect by evangelicals and seek to examine the incarnational theology of those who have made such charges. They focus on the link between the incarnation and the cross and explore the significance of the incarnation with respect to what it reveals about God and humanity. They interact with various proposals about the significance of the incarnation for Christian life and mission. They finally examine the implications of the incarnation for our understanding of Scripture and the Lord's Supper.

The contributors hope that evangelical readers will be stirred to realise how important this area of theology is and will continue to reflect and write on the issues highlighted. They also hope that those who are critical of evangelical neglect in this area will be challenged themselves to rethink the way in which they have formulated and applied their incarnational theology. Continuing dialogue in this connection will surely enrich the whole body of Christ.

David Peterson
Principal of Oak Hill College

Notes

[1] His dissertation is now published as *Word and Supplement: Speech Acts, Biblical Texts, and the Sufficiency of Scripture* (Oxford: Oxford University, 2002).

1. Is Christ's Incarnation the Consummation of the Cosmic Process?

Michael Ovey

> Yet even expediency teaches ... that in matters of principle *the first compromise is never the last*.[1]

Introduction
Consider the way that evangelicals, perhaps especially in the Anglican Communion, have been charged with various derelictions of duty, with a kind of betrayal. The following remarks are representative but by no means exhaustive:

- You spend too little time on the incarnation and too much on the cross – your theology is distorted. There's more to it than you teach.
- You understate the incarnation and have too negative a view of human life and progress.
- You do not appreciate the value of human life and thought, our creative abilities, because you do not value the incarnation enough.
- Your God is too distant and too cold, because you do not stress the intimacy that the incarnation shows.

The common thread, of course, is that evangelical views on the incarnation are somehow defective. Many evangelicals, naturally, hear this with a mixture of bewilderment and horror. They would regard the Chalcedonian formulation of AD 451 that Jesus is fully divine and also fully human as non-negotiable,[2] and are puzzled about quite why this perception of an inadequate theology of the incarnation arises. The charge touches a sensitive point for evangelicals since it implies they do not teach the whole counsel of God, in all conscience a serious enough indictment.

Evangelicals as 'outsiders'

This charge contributes to a sense that evangelicals are not, so to speak, fully initiated. They are not among the adepts. It is small wonder therefore that some of them experience disempowerment and alienation in their interactions with some others in their denominations. They have been tacitly (sometimes explicitly) consigned to the role of perennial outsider.

The pressures and temptations such an insider/outsider social structure can create are well explored in C.S. Lewis' famous essay 'The Inner Circle',[3] which catalogues the urge to unwholesome compromise that 'outsiders' can feel. Certainly the social ramifications of a structure of this kind for evangelicals participating in a denomination may be not insignificant. For example, there may be a systematic relativisation of their contributions to debate: 'Thank you for that – but it is too partial to be truly useful.' It can result in positions of seniority tending to be closed to them: 'they are too restricted to be able to minister to the whole church.' Personal relations based on an assumption of superiority and maturity may be conducted, to use the terms of transactional psychological analysis, as parent-child relations, with evangelicals cast as perpetual children: 'Yes, I rather grew out of that.' This would tend to minimise adult-adult relations, a particularly unfortunate outcome since adult-adult relations are so strongly associated with respect and transparency.[4] To that extent, some evangelicals can sometimes find the fellowship offered in their denominational meetings but a distorted reflection of the genuinely complementarian body of Christ envisaged by Paul in 1 Corinthians 12–14.

The assumption of superiority is evident in two comments from Archbishops. Robert Runcie used to tell the joke, perhaps a trifle too often for it to be effective as humour, that the Church of England was like a swimming pool. Why? Because the noise came largely from the shallow end, referring to the Church of England's evangelicals. Rowan Williams, at the time of writing the Archbishop of Wales and the Archbishop of Canterbury designate, has remarked of evangelicalism, possibly with more genuine good humour, but with equal aristocratic disdain, that all need to bang a tambourine on occasion. It is perhaps interesting to ask what the reaction would have been had such sentiments been voiced about, say, black Christians. When senior churchmen evince such outlooks, a consciousness of isolation among evangelicals should scarcely occasion surprise. The marginalisation of evangelicals within their denominations is even a matter of note in the secular press. Consider Theo Hobson's devastating crack in a national newspaper: 'In church politics, the evangelicals are so firmly seen as the stupid party that it never even needs to be said.'[5]

The picture drawn above may not be universal evangelical experience, and it is sharply delineated. The question is, however, whether the charge about inadequate theology is true and that evangelicals are the 'stupid party'. Furthermore, we must ask why such perceptions of evangelical theology have arisen. Without an answer to these questions, it is difficult to face the accusation honestly, and this evangelicals need to do for the sake of their ministries today.

What kind of incarnation?

Accordingly, this chapter examines an account of the incarnation strongly, though not uniquely, associated with these charges, an account which portrays the incarnation as the consummation of the cosmic process. The chapter argues that this theology itself is an inadequate and distorted view of the incarnation and that those who have indicted evangelicals over inadequate accounts of the incarnation from this perspective are themselves guilty of the very charge they bring.

The current chapter should be read in conjunction with the one that follows. In the subsequent chapter, the biblical theme is developed that the incarnation was a coming of the Son of God into a world whose life, whose 'process' after the advent of sin, was hostile to him. This, of course, is a thesis at some odds with the idea that the Son of God took flesh as the consummation of an essentially positive natural process at work throughout human history.

This means that neither chapter defends the basic idea of an incarnation, as against, say, the writers of *The Myth of God Incarnate*.[6] Rather, it is taken as read that a text like John 1:14 commits Christians to an objective and substantial incarnation, not a purely mythological one. The debate, then, is over the claims of so-called liberal Catholicism, not simply theological 'liberalism'. The two are sometimes imperfectly distinguished, but for reasons that appear below, a distinction can profitably be drawn. A fuller account of liberal Catholicism emerges in the course of the chapter. For present purposes, though, it must be noted that while liberal Catholicism emerges within an Anglican context, it can be characterised as a *method*,[7] which is not restricted to Anglicanism. For that reason, the views discussed here are relevant to evangelicals who are not Anglicans.

These chapters do not give a completely comprehensive view of the incarnation. Nor do they adjudicate on whether the consummation and co-victim (the latter described in the next chapter) models are incompatible with that aspect of the Chalcedonian definition conveniently summarised as 'one person in two natures'. However, debate does arise over another area of the Chalcedonian framework – the incarnation was 'for us and for our salvation'.[8] To that extent, the question at issue is not, 'Does one accept an incarnation?', but 'What kind of incarnation does one accept?'

A key point in trying to specify what kind of incarnation one accepts is to tease out the relation between the incarnation and the passion. A notable feature of the Christ as consummation model addressed in this chapter is the independence, as it were, of the need for an incarnation from the cross.

Christ as the Consummation of the Cosmic Process (*Christus Consummator*)

We must start with the essays of the book *Lux Mundi* (1889).[9] It may surprise some that a book over a century old, and perhaps largely unfamiliar to current evangelicals, should still prove so central. It is, in fact, surprisingly significant, and the present cannot be understood without looking at this part of the past. Michael Ramsey, later Archbishop of Canterbury, described it as marking a 'new era' in Anglican theology,[10] with an alleged stress on the incarnation.[11] One distinctive characteristic of this approach is an emphasis on the work of the Logos '… in the whole created world, in nature and in man, in art and in science, in culture and in progress.'[12]

Charles Gore, the chief proponent of *Lux Mundi*-style ideas, was a profound influence on both William Temple (another Archbishop of Canterbury, who had, of course, his own distinctive emphases) and Michael Ramsey. The former especially has been strongly influential in twentieth-century theology. Avis' evaluation of Gore is equally true for *Lux Mundi* as a whole: 'a dominant, though sometimes unrecognised influence'.[13] Aidan Nichols traces the influence and line of descent from *Lux Mundi* down to the 1980s and later, for example, in the 'Affirming Catholicism' movement.[14] *Lux Mundi*, then, is both influential and representative, even if not always visible. Evangelicals who wish to grasp some of the reasons why others view them as they do must, therefore, start here at the wellhead.

The context of the Lux Mundi essays

Naturally, one must consider the context in which the *Lux Mundi* writers were working. Several major influences are at play. First, and perhaps most obviously, there is the contribution of Darwin and the thesis of biological evolution, which by this time had enjoyed increasing perceived success and acceptance through the work of men like T.H. Huxley. However, additionally, by this time evolutionary thought had been and was being extended from the biological realm to other fields of human thought. It was providing, one might say, a new paradigm in fields outside biology. 'Evolution' was therefore invoked in a number of diverse, and sometimes contradictory, causes, such as laissez-faire economic organisation, Marxism, ethnic nationalism, segregationism, and desegregationism.[15]

Secondly, by 1889 so-called critical scholarship was making itself strongly felt in English academic theology. Particularly important was the view then held by some that Old Testament religion emerged from, and was fundamentally continuous with, the pagan religions of the Ancient Near East.[16]

Thirdly, there was the need to act within the social arena, a clearly compassionate and laudable concern for Britain's poor. A 'strong' doctrine of the incarnation was felt both to justify and to require engaged social and political actions by Christians.[17] Of course, such social concern was neither initiated by, nor confined to, the *Lux Mundi* essayists. Indeed, those with much less novel theologies had earlier embraced it. Nevertheless, the lives of several of the essayists bear testimony to this social concern, which is also present in the work of William Temple.

Fourthly, there is the influence of so-called British 'idealism'. By 1889, Hegelian influences were very definitely at work in Britain and a leading idealist, T.H. Green, was teaching at Oxford in the years preceding the publication of *Lux Mundi*. His students included some *Lux Mundi* essayists. A distinctive trait of Hegelian idealism is the view that human history is a process. In this process 'Spirit' (*Geist*) is realising itself and coming to full awareness of itself. History is to that extent a unified field in which diverse events and apparent conflicts have in fact a progressive effect. Conflict provides the condition for advance. The process is in that sense essentially positive, despite events occurring from time to time which seem, in themselves, negative. In the context of the whole process, they are part of a positive progression. For Hegel, the incarnation, at least as he understood it, fitted neatly into this package, since it showed the ultimate unity between God and humanity. Grenz and Olson thus aptly summarise the conclusion of many that Hegel was a radical immanentist, for whom the world's history was God's history.[18]

Fifthly, perhaps more mutedly, there was the influence of B.F. Westcott, notably in some of his work on John's Gospel, but more particularly in an essay appended to his commentary on the letters of John, entitled 'The Gospel of Creation'. Westcott's point here was that 'the incarnation was independent of the Fall.'[19] Certainly, the circumstances of the incarnation – its shame and so forth – were due to sin, but the actual idea of it was not.[20] There was a necessity for the incarnation independent of the Fall. The Son of God would have become incarnate even if Adam had not sinned.

The content of Lux Mundi
There is a range of views within *Lux Mundi*. Having said that, the distinctive theme of the essayists is an acceptance of cosmic process.[21] Crucially, this allows some kind of co-existence with Darwinism, indeed a positive assertion that Darwinism is being applied to theology and religious studies. Evolution, claims J.R. Illingworth,[22] has 'altered our attitude to all knowledge.' He goes on:

> Organisms, nations, languages, institutions, customs, creeds, have all come to be regarded in the light of their development, and we feel

that to understand what a thing is, we must examine how it came to be.[23]

In this, as we have seen earlier, the essayists were not untypical of theorists of the time outside the biological sciences. They were simply deploying in 1889 a move made in other disciplines and areas of debate from the start of the 1860s, if not earlier. Such an extension of evolutionary thought did, however, have its opponents. Four years after the essayists publicly embraced Darwinism for theology, T.H. Huxley, highly familiar with Darwinism, attempted in his Romanes lectures to distance evolution from ethics. After defining evolution as 'cosmic process', Huxley went on to argue that social progress depended on *substituting* ethical process for cosmic process, since cosmic process was a guide not to morality, but immorality.[24] Here, Huxley was opposing just the kind of extension to ethical and spiritual values which *Lux Mundi* proposed.

Of course, the essayists were not in any case simply proposing a form of evolutionary thinking identical to that of Darwin himself or Huxley.[25] The obvious difference is that the essayists denied the process could be impersonal, let alone atheistic. Evolution is crucially leavened by idealism, such that the cosmic process is positively evaluated ethically. The advent of biological complexity is glossed as a moral good. This positive moral evaluation does not seem to be an intrinsic part of biological evolutionary theory. As we have seen, Huxley did not think so.

The significance of this is not always appreciated. It should therefore be emphasised that the essayists were not simply incorporating a scientific 'truth' into their theology. Rather they were incorporating *their version or interpretation* of a scientific 'truth', and a controversial interpretation to boot.[26]

Gore later put it this way: '[N]ature on the whole represents a progress, an advance.'[27] In this progress, inorganic material gives way to organic, organic to animal, animal to rational or spiritual. Thus, within the cosmos there is the emergence of spirit or mind. This kind of thought marks out not just the liberal Catholicism of *Lux Mundi*, but also informs the work of William Temple.[28] It bears substantial similarity to the thinking of Pierre Teilhard de Chardin, whose work has proved and is still proving highly influential both in the church and the New Age Movement. Temple and de Chardin both stress that in this process, the cosmos becomes conscious of itself as human individuals become conscious of themselves.[29]

Within this framework of development or process 'Jesus Christ incarnate is the legitimate climax of natural development.'[30] The incarnation is the natural outcome of the kind of process that God has set within the world. It is essentially continuous with the process God originally instigated in creation. This kind of incarnational thinking upholds Christ as consummation of the cosmic process.

The rationale of Lux Mundi *theology*

It is obviously important to describe the basis for this view. It must be stressed that the essayists' public self-image was that of loyal Catholics, not simply modernisers. For this reason, it is not adequate simply to describe the *Lux Mundi* school as 'liberal'. Gore's preferred term is 'liberal Catholic', which he contended should be identified with Anglicanism.[31]

John 1:9

Scripturally, *Lux Mundi* consistently appeals to John 1:9. It is not too much to say that this verse is pervasive in the essays.[32] It is, however, not exegeted at length, but rather constantly referred to, with a particular interpretation being taken, perhaps, as self-evident. 'The true light which enlightens everyone' expresses the thought that all men and women participate in the light of reason, including moral reason.

It is absolutely vital to grasp that this understanding undergirds the entire project. It forms a lynchpin in *Lux Mundi* theology and its successors.[33] This is the basis of the view that one finds truth in other religions and philosophies. Wherever human beings lived by the light of reason they were the friends of Christ. This at once justifies the appropriation of scientific achievement, philosophical truth and artistic insight on the grounds they are *Christian* truth.

Such an understanding of John 1:9 has enormous ramifications for how theology is done and constructed, the question of method. It is for this reason that Bardwell Smith is correct to insist that 'liberal Catholicism' is a theological *method* and not one necessarily confined to Anglicanism.[34] For, if this understanding is correct, the Bible itself mandates, indeed requires, accepting the alternative viewpoints and perspectives that honest and rational thinkers provide. Hence arises the claim that Gore's liberal Catholicism is, indeed, scripturally founded.[35] It then becomes *unbiblical* on this view not to look at the teaching of 'secular' disciplines, for the same Logos who became incarnate illuminates practitioners. Ramsey writes that, on the *Lux Mundi* view, 'contemporary trends of thought, like evolution or socialism, are not enemies to be fought, but friends who can provide new illumination of the truth that is in Christ.'[36] Gore writes more overtly:

> God is as truly, though not as fully, found in the disclosures of science as in Jesus Christ. It is really rebellion against the Word to shut our ears to scientific revelation.[37]

This means that the truth that is to be found in science and other areas of discourse is not just truth about the world, but theological truth, truth about God. John 1:9 is not just saying that humans have a rational faculty by which they can investigate their world. They are enlightened with respect to truth about God, a more ambitious claim.

On this basis, the Bible itself warrants a natural theology. It would be overly reductionist to say this is merely theological liberalism, precisely because there is at any rate a claim for a biblical mandate for such a natural theology. Moreover, Gore does not dispute that there is such a thing as revelation. The point is that revealed theology and natural theology do not have an absolute division between them.[38] It is just this point that was picked up in one of the earliest negative appraisals of *Lux Mundi*. Darwell Stone, an Anglo-Catholic, observed that revealed theology and natural theology were, for *Lux Mundi*, different only in degree.[39] Ramsey concedes this point.

The question at issue is whether this was as serious a fault as Darwell Stone suggested.[40] Obviously, traditional evangelical theology is much warier of allowing 'contemporary trends' to give 'new illumination', a point to which we shall return below.

Genesis 1:26ff.

To this view of John 1:9 must be added a particular understanding of the image of God in which humanity is created (Gen. 1:26ff.). There is a 'real moral likeness of man to God.'[41] On this basis, while Gore would repudiate anthropomorphism (conceiving God to exist in human terms), he does want to uphold a 'theomorphism' (that humans are shaped in God's terms), and the net result of this is that human qualities are the 'counterpart and real expression' of the divine.[42] Gore is not alone in this.[43] Again, the consequences in terms of theological method are worth considering. If human qualities are the 'counterpart' and 'real expression' of the divine, then human qualities arguably provide a guide to the divine, hence Gore's sympathy with the idea that 'good' applied to God means what it does when applied to human beings.[44]

Historically, some of the Early Fathers were claimed to support this approach. Gore cites in particular Justin Martyr, Irenaeus and Origen.[45] Thus, as the Tractarians had claimed before them, the liberal Catholic essayists felt they were not in essence innovators. The importance of the historical claim is that it supports the claim to be 'Catholic'.

Academically, the essayists were fortified by Westcott's 'Gospel of Creation',[46] which, as we have seen, argued that the Son would have become incarnate irrespective of the Fall. Their conceptions of process through the Logos present in all were also congruent with the streams of criticism in the study of the Old Testament that viewed Hebrew thought as developing from Ancient Near Eastern beliefs and practices.

Ethically, certainly for Gore, there is a question of intellectual honesty and integrity. The individual's mind cannot be subject to authority, at least of certain kinds. He writes:

> I have, ever since I was an undergraduate, been certain that I must be in the true sense of the word a free thinker, and that either not to think freely about a disturbing subject, or to accept ecclesiastical authority in place of the best judgement of my own reason, would be for me an impossible treason against the light.[47]

The choice of words is significant. The acceptance of ecclesiastical authority would be a 'treason against the light' precisely because the Logos indwells and is illuminating his reason. To refuse to act by it and accept ecclesiastical authority is to deny the sufficiency and adequacy of the light's work.

Hence, the liberal Catholicism for which *Lux Mundi* and Gore in particular stood was one where there was a 'Catholic' contact with Scripture and tradition, notably the creeds, but an openness[48] to truth coming from whatever quarter, based on the indwelling Logos – hence, the opposition to the imposition of external ecclesiastical authority, in the shape, for example, of a papal *magisterium*. It is in that sense that this Catholicism is 'liberal', free from such external authority.

The implications of Lux Mundi theology

The results of this approach are profound and serve to provide the basis for a number of stock criticisms launched against evangelicals.

First, this allows the incarnation to function as a focus of thought in some ways separate from the cross. *Lux Mundi* certainly did not attempt to deny redemption, but set this alongside, as it were, the incarnation. Hence, comes the criticism that evangelicalism distorts Christianity by over-emphasising the cross; hence, too, the thought that the Reformers held a distorted view of the faith through their focus on redemption through atonement (here the essayists were of course continuing the antipathy felt by some Tractarians for the Reformation). This perception helps generate the charge against cross-centred evangelical theology: 'there's more to it than that.' Thus, Illingworth speaks of 'partial presentations of Christianity' in post-Reformation thought and asserts that the Reformers paid 'scant attention to the other aspects of the Gospel' than soteriology.[49] Sometimes this criticism of 'partial presentation' merges into the still more serious one that the Reformers taught error: thus penal substitution is rejected by some of the essayists.[50] The implication minimally is that evangelical emphases on the cross and resurrection do not teach the whole counsel of God. Evangelicals must move on beyond a theology of the cross to something more fully orbed. Evangelicals do not teach the full *evangelium*.

Secondly, the Son appears here much more as an immanent principle guiding and indeed manifested by the world's historical process. The Hegelian influence is very strong, since Hegelianism often has a dynamic and optimistic view of the historical process, an essentially upward spiral. In Temple's thought this appears to be true of the Fall as well. He comments that Genesis 3 is a 'myth', but one which provides,

> a true analysis of all natural human *progress* [emphasis added]. Man stumbles, by the impulse of his nature, into something which, by his misunderstanding of it, is first a source of new evils, but is the condition of a hitherto impossible good.[51]

Hence in part the tendency for liberal Catholicism to see an evangelical stress on the continuing desperate state of fallen humanity as dour and pessimistic, a tendency summed up in the phrase: 'You're too negative.'

Thirdly, and largely because Christ is taken as an immanent principle universally present, the tendency is to provide an elevated place for human reason and evaluation. This can be seen in Gore's judgement that, 'philosophy was thus to the Greeks, as the Law to the Jews, a divine preparation for Him who was to come',[52] or Illingworth's, 'the history of pre-Christian religion is like that of pre-Christian philosophy, a long preparation for the Gospel.'[53] It seems that here Gore and Illingworth go beyond seeing God providentially at work in the history of Greece as well as of Israel (an uncontroversial point: see, for example, Amos 9:7). The striking thing is that there is some kind of equating of pagan works and, say, the Old Testament as vehicles of divine expression, with a difference of degree but not kind. Illingworth comments: 'all great teachers of whatever kind are vehicles of revelation, each in his proper sphere.' As such we must accept their 'verified conclusions as Divinely true.'[54] Hence, those characteristic sentiments expressed against evangelicals: 'they are so narrow', 'they won't look outside the Bible.'

There are two similar but distinct points at issue here. One is whether human reason sits *above* the Bible. For Gore the evidence is perhaps ambiguous. He is capable of referring to the Bible as 'the final court of appeal',[55] while elsewhere insisting that reason and in particular conscience must weigh any purported revelation of God.[56] This seems to run the risk that the Bible is the final court of appeal only in those areas where reason and conscience determine that it should be. In that case it is difficult to feel that Gore's adjective 'final' is in fact the *mot juste*.[57]

To the onlooker this can create an odd spectacle. The Bible will indeed be cited as authoritative for a particular proposition, but what will not be apparent is that the biblical text has been so accepted by a prior judgement of the reason. This has an important consequence. A work adopting Gore's methods in this respect will indeed have a 'biblical' look to it, in the sense that texts will be cited and there will be echoes of biblical terms and concepts. Yet it would, perhaps, be misleading to say that this simply reflects an acceptance of biblical authority, for those texts have been chosen because they appear to agree with the case being argued. They are present because they endorse opinions accepted on other grounds. Hence, Moore approves of the nineteenth-century spirit which 'would rather give up religion altogether than accept one which will not endorse and advance our highest moral ideas'.[58] The obvious question is, how would God ever be allowed to express disagreement with Moore? On Moore's methodology, disagreement would simply be denied the status of revelation.

This means that evangelicals reading works based on Gore's methods need to ask, not 'Is the Bible being cited?', but rather 'Why is the Bible being cited in the places where it is?' Is it cited because it is a decisive authority in its own right, or because it aptly expresses sentiments reached on other grounds? Clearly a useful, but not conclusive, pointer here is whether the Bible is ever allowed to critique and disprove contemporary wisdom. A problem, of course, that also arises is whether the Bible can function as a final court of appeal in those areas where the reasons and consciences of various people differ.

All this does, though, help explain some of the mutual frustration evangelicals and liberal Catholics experience in attempting to discuss, say, sexual ethics. Evangelicals stereotypically will want to appeal to biblical teaching as the final Word of God, while liberal Catholics may see that as a silencing of the voice of God in the individual reason and conscience.

The second issue that arises is the way that human reason and philosophy sits *alongside* the Bible, providing alternative and complementary viewpoints. To this extent *Lux Mundi* views of Christ as consummation allow ostensibly Chalcedonian Christology to combine with at least partial endorsement of other faiths.

Also significant here is the elevation of reason within the church. Given that the church reasons with the mind of Christ, since her members participate in him (this is argued from Jn. 1:9, at least), the voice of the church becomes insensibly blended with the voice of Christ. But note what follows. Given the developmental, progressive view of history, the voice *now* must take precedence over the voice *then*. How is the voice *now* to be identified? – perhaps by office, as with a bishop, or perhaps by a majority, as with a council or synod. In either case, the voice *now* is invested with enormous authority since it is genuinely able to discern and articulate Christ's truth. From this, to take an Anglican example, flows the idea that the Church of England can by a process of 'reception' over time discern what the will of God is on particular issues. The church comes to a consensus over time.

This reflects a very considerable problem. Majoritarian forms of church government have considerable cultural appeal, not least on ethical grounds, the argument being that people should be able to contribute to their own ecclesiastical government, just as they have a moral entitlement to do so in their political government. Furthermore, a minority on a particular issue in a political democracy is often perceived as being in duty bound to accept a majority verdict or decision. Not to do so invites the stigma of being 'undemocratic'.

The moral limits on what a majority can do in the name of 'democratic government' is a major issue in its own right within political philosophy.[59] However, the question which nags immediately here is whether the majority can make mistakes. Is it possible for the voice *now* to speak mistakenly against the voice *then*? And if it is, would the voice *now* readily spot and acknowledge its error? It is difficult to see the 'cosmic process' thesis making this an easier task for the majority. Rather, because of a prior commitment to seeing history as an upward spiral, the temptation will be continually to see the voice *then* as wrong on areas of disagreement. Church government on this kind of basis can readily carry an authoritarian tone, for all its apparent commitment to western democratic values.[60]

'Authority' is the apt term here, because the logic, spelt out by Gore in the case of scientific 'revelation', is that those who resist, or dissent from, such decisions of councils or synods are disobeying Christ. The voice of the church *now* becomes the voice of Christ. It is therefore entirely predictable on these premises that evangelicals are disdained as those who *disobey Christ*. Evangelicals are regarded as antinomian and individualist.

So the voice of the Bible becomes increasingly superfluous. This redundancy arises from the fact that:

- *either* the Bible expresses something which current reason and conscience independently legitimates (in which case we did not need the Bible to tell us);
- *or* something which current reason and conscience cannot accept (in which case the logic of the position is that it is the voice *now* which is to be preferred);[61]
- *or* something which current reason and conscience tell us cannot be definitively decided upon (in which case even if the Bible gives specific instructions, it is difficult to see it as important to enforce obedience).

There is a real difficulty for this view in thinking of the Bible telling us an important ethical truth that we do not *already* know is true or important from other material.

For these reasons, then, the liberal Catholicism of the essayists and their successors inevitably leads to a somewhat negative view of evangelical believers. This is evident in *Lux Mundi* itself. Evangelicals can be depicted as those who fail to teach the whole counsel of God and distort the gospel, as those who limit God's activity in the world, as those who fail to appreciate God's continuing goodness and as those who covertly disobey God's voice, while claiming to obey him. This might go some way to explaining the disfavour in which some Anglican evangelicals see themselves regarded. In view of the seriousness of the charges, it is worth now examining the basis on which these judgements are formed.

Evaluation of *Lux Mundi* Theology

Evaluation of *Lux Mundi* and its derivative theologies needs to be carried out in terms of its biblical basis, its historical appeal and its philosophical standing (including its ethical appeal).

Biblical evaluation

John 1:9

Starting with the Bible is not the imposition of an evangelical methodology, but rather a question of taking up the lynchpin of the *Lux Mundi* approach. It is, after all, because of an understanding of John 1:9 that the essayists justified their own inclusion of extra-biblical perspectives from science and philosophy and conscience. Is their understanding of John 1:9 justified? The text reads: 'The true light, which enlightens everyone, was coming into the world.'[62]

The *Lux Mundi* case is that light here means spiritual, moral and intellectual discernment, a light in which all human beings share. Westcott's commentary on John goes some way towards this when he comments:

> No man is wholly destitute of the illumination of 'the Light'. In nature, and life, and conscience it makes itself felt in various degrees to all.[63]

Elsewhere he comments on the light as light of all:

> ... for all of us, in so far as we have received intellect and wisdom from the Word which created us, are said to be illuminated by Him.[64]

It will, though, be noted that the *Lux Mundi* exegesis in fact tends to focus on the third of the areas of illumination mentioned in the first quotation from Westcott, that of conscience. Of course, fits readily with the idea espoused by Gore, that humans are 'theomorphic' and mirror the values and attitudes of God.[65]

In the same field of interpretation, but perhaps more strongly, we find Temple remarking:

> So it may be truly said that the conscience of the heathen man is the voice of Christ within him – though muffled by his ignorance. All that is noble in the non-christian systems of thought, or conduct, or worship is the work of Christ upon them and within them. By the Word of God – that is to say, by Jesus Christ – Isaiah

and Plato, and Zoroaster, and Buddha, and Confucius conceived and uttered such truths as they declared. There is only one divine light; and every man in his measure is enlightened by it.[66]

In a similar vein Ramsey comments on John 1:1–14:

> The divine Word has been at work in the world ceaselessly, in creation, in the processes of nature and history, giving life to mankind *and illuminating human minds with truth.*[67]

At this point one should note that this species of interpretation depends on taking 'illuminate' (*phōtizei*) in the sense of giving light so that men and women may see – as in the phrase 'he enlightened me'. This is within the possible range for the word. There are, though, other possibilities, to which we shall return.[68] For the moment we test the *Lux Mundi* construction to see whether it fits with John 1:9.

It should be said at the outset that *Lux Mundi* does not adequately discuss the context, largely because the essayists are content to invoke an interpretation (the inner light of reason and moral truth) that seems to them, apparently, self-evident. But John 1:9 shifts attention back to the light after verses 6–8 have focused on the witness of the Baptist. Verses 10–11 continue the focus on the light and speak of the light's rejection by 'the world' and 'its own'. The immediate succeeding context of verse 9 is that of an unrecognised light, nuanced by the faith of some (v. 12), but definitely not all. The recognition of the light in its coming is definitely not universal. This lack of recognition has earlier been encountered in the Prologue in verse 5, which refers to the light shining in the darkness, yet without the darkness 'grasping' (*katelaben*) it, a *double entendre* of 'understand' and 'overcome'.[69]

So the immediate context of verse 9 is that of the light's rejection, not a sharing or mirroring of the light's values in the human race. The human race is not, in this most important of senses, enlightened, a point made by Johannine exegetes at least as long ago as Chrysostom.[70] This context of rejection produces no little discomfort for a reading which suggests universal enlightenment and moral discernment, and which stresses the continuing theomorphic character of the human race such that human qualities are the 'counterpart and real expression' of the divine.[71] The divine qualities are associated with light and life. Human qualities in verses 10–11 find their counterpart not in reflecting the values of God, but in resembling the darkness of verse 5, darkness, of course, being the Johannine antithesis of light.

The thesis that men and women have an innate illumination in conscience by the light has to be treated with suspicion given also the rest of the Gospel. Temple does refer to the rejection mentioned in verses 10–11, and goes on to list factors that inhibit acceptance.[72] One is the human foible of attaching what truths they have to a purely human founder, not the light. The other is the fact of prejudice and obsession. Temple's problem is that this does scant justice to the factors John's Gospel sets out when describing human rejection.

These will be further discussed below. Suffice it here to remark, first, in general terms, Temple's account of people attaching truth to a human founder omits a highly important feature of human conduct to which Jesus adverts. Humans grant to things that they devise the force of divine authority. This is the reverse of Temple's point about attaching truth to a human founder. Rather, human constructions are given the status of 'truth'. This emerges from Mark 7:9, 13 where Jesus criticises the practice of preferring human words to those of God, having observed (v. 7) that people are 'teaching human precepts as doctrines'.[73] Temple's omission is unfortunate and significant. A consistent biblical theme is the tendency of humans to idolatry, which includes devising things that are then attributed to God.[74] This aspect does not adequately figure in Temple's discussion of suppression of the light.

Secondly, John 3:19ff. envisages rejection of Jesus by human beings because they love darkness rather than the light (v. 19) and in fact hate the light (3:20) because their deeds are evil. The terms for evil are best given a theocentric thrust (evil in the sense of being opposed to God and his Word), without excluding ideas of moral/ethical corruption before God. 'Prejudice and obsession' does not grasp the depth of the problem that John outlines, because these words do not capture the anti-God orientation to which the Gospel refers. In this way, 3:19ff. does not speak of a humanity which naturally has a community of values with God, for whom 'good' means the same as it does for God. Humans love darkness, not the light, while God does indeed love the light (Jn. 10:17), whom they hate.

In a similar vein, in John 7:7 Jesus speaks of a hatred born of Jesus' testimony that the world's deeds are evil. Here again it is not just prejudice and obsession that constitutes the problem. One may compare, too, John 16:3 where false loyalty to God is traced back to lack of knowledge of God the Father and the Son. Given that 'knowledge' language in John is so firmly linked to relationship, it is very difficult not to see John 16:3 as indicating that rejection of Jesus is the classic hallmark of lack of relationship with God. John 1:10–11 envisages just this of the world and the Son's own people. This is extremely difficult to reconcile with views of 1:9 that require the presence of the Word in the world of men and women. These passages speak of an antipathy to God while the *Lux Mundi* thesis is that humans are theomorphic, genuinely mirroring the divine in their ethical apprehensions. It may be considered unfortunate that the *Lux Mundi* interpretation has so completely inverted the teaching of John with regard to the presence of the light in human individuals.

Two objections to this analysis will no doubt be raised:

- that this argument demolishes natural revelation.
- that this argument undermines human knowledge more generally.

Each will be dealt with in what follows.

John 1:9 and general revelation
We turn to the first objection, that the considerations outlined above demolish the concept of natural or general revelation. This, though, is to misunderstand the point that is being made. In John's Gospel the terms 'knowledge' and 'revelation' regularly relate to *saving* relational knowledge, knowledge in relation to God, knowledge, indeed, of God. This is borne out classically in John 17:3 and 20:31. The Fourth Gospel teaches that humans do not 'naturally' have this knowledge (see e.g. 1:18, 3:13). If they did, of course, the incarnation would be superfluous in this revelatory aspect. Jesus,

though, seems to regard the incarnation as revelatorily necessary (e.g. Jn. 17:6 – he reveals the name of God, with the implication that it was hitherto unknown).[75]

Romans 1:18ff. and general revelation

Nor do we find a substantially different account in the seminal passage on natural revelation in Romans 1:18ff. Paul does not deny the objective fact of natural revelation (1:19), and indeed this serves to establish moral responsibility (1:20). But this is a suppressed truth (1:18), unprofitable in that sense for humans whose minds are now darkened and futile (1:21). This means that natural or general revelation in fact has a 'negative result', in Moo's phrase.[76] Moo continues:

> That Paul teaches the reality of a revelation of God in nature to all people, this text [sc. 1:18–21] makes clear. But it is equally obvious that this revelation is universally rejected, as people turn from knowledge to gods of their own making.[77]

The existence of a natural revelation is common ground between *Lux Mundi* and the teaching of Romans. The disagreement arises over the usefulness or place of that natural revelation. In Romans, the result is 'negative'. In *Lux Mundi* it is essentially positive (even if not providing complete knowledge), for it undergirds contemporary thinking that 'can provide new illumination of the truth that is in Christ.'[78]

Acts 14:16f. and general revelation

The general action of God is also to the fore in Acts 14:16f. This speaks of a God who has left a witness of himself [79] in the good he has done humanity in general providence. Yet the context shows just that this witness has not given a true knowledge of God to this audience, for they are indulging in sinful idolatry, from which Paul and Barnabas forbid them (Acts 14:15). The witness has not made the Lystrans wise. Hence, Calvin draws the conclusion that Paul and Barnabas refer to the witness of nature in verse 17 to 'deprive the Gentiles of an excuse for their ignorance.'[80] Thus again, the natural revelation has a 'negative' rather than positive result.

Acts 17:22–34 and general revelation

Acts 17:22–34 makes a similar point. It might be tempting on a superficial reading to envisage that Paul is telling the Athenians that they really have been worshipping God. They do, after all, have an altar to the unknown god (v. 23) and Paul is proclaiming the god they worship as unknown. The Athenians have also been described as 'very religious' (v. 22). On this basis, is not Paul complimenting the Athenians on their devoutness in respect of the little they do know about the 'unknown god'? True, there is more to know, but have they not responded properly in the light of the knowledge they have? Thus the argument might run.

The problem with this construction is that it disregards the flow of Paul's address and its ultimate destination. In terms of the development of his argument, Paul moves on in verses 24–5 to deal with characteristics of the worship that the Athenians, and others, offered. In verse 24 he refers to shrines and in verse 25 to service by human hands. Both aspects in fact link back to the altar, where his speech started – it is a human construction, at which human hands offer service. Verses 24–5 are therefore closely tied to Paul's opening, and reflect on the religious practice that Paul has found.

Yet Paul's observation is that the worship offered was wrong. The creator does not live in a human creation; the supreme provider does not need provision from humans. In this way, the altar to the unknown god is being negatively evaluated, for it does not refer to the real God. It suggests things about him that are the opposite of the truth that he is the creator who provides. The altar and the practices it implies have subtly inverted the relationship of human dependence on the creator that really exists, with a relationship in which God depends on humans making a house for him and human provision for his needs.

However, are these errors serious? Could it be that the sincerity and effort that the Athenians put into their religious lives means that they are in right relationship with God? The destination of Paul's argument shows that the errors are indeed serious. Paul first of all commands the Athenians to stop thinking in the idolatrous terms they have been (v. 29) and secondly speaks of a command that men and women are to repent (v. 30). This latter command is not consistent with an innocent evaluation of the 'times of ignorance'. Fault is attached. Whatever the Athenians might be expected to know of

God the creator has not been reflected in their religious practice. If anything, this has denied just those truths that relate to the creator role of God. Once again, any natural revelation has not had a positive outcome in the sense of providing a form of worship pleasing to God.

Nor does verse 22, with its description that the Athenians are 'very religious', necessarily provide a counter-argument to this. The word translated 'very religious' (*deisidaimonesterous*) can have a pejorative connotation – superstitious or bigoted.[81] Thus, the word Paul employs has a range that includes both negative and positive connotations. The pejorative meaning provides a better fit with the criticism of Athenian religion that follows, and a much better fit with the original reaction of Paul to Athenian religious practice: 'He was deeply distressed' (v. 16). The objection to such a pejorative meaning is that it would be rhetorically ineffective and inappropriate to start with such an offensive sentiment. But, as noted above, the word is not necessarily negative. On first hearing, the Athenians (who would not perhaps have the benefit of knowing about Paul's earlier negative reaction to Athenian idols) would not know it was negative. It is not rhetorically inept to start with a statement whose sting only subsequently becomes clear. This avoids both the ineptitude objection and the objection that a favourable sense to 'very religious' is inconsistent both with what precedes and what follows. For those reasons, this seems an attractive option.

Acts 17 and quotations from the poets
The Areopagus speech of Acts 17 requires attention in one further respect, the quotation from pagan poets. From one point of view, of course, these are designed to drive home the culpability of the Athenians.[82] The idea of a transcendent creator outlined in verses 24–7 was not entirely novel. The Athenians were not living consistently with truths they knew.[83] Yet, from another point of view, the question must be posed: does this not at last prove the *Lux Mundi* point? Is there not a grasping of the truth by the light of the indwelling Logos alone? After all, Paul cites two pagan poets, Epimenides and Aratus,[84] and seems to endorse what they say.

This, however, risks distorting the way in which the quotations are used. Both are used to underscore points that Paul has made earlier. Both quotations reflect the dependence of humanity on its creator and the fact that it has a relationship with him. Paul is not, though, relying on the quotations to establish the truth of these propositions. The propositions he can draw quite adequately from biblical accounts,[85] and he has already asserted the salient facts pertaining to them. To that extent, the poets do not function for him as providing an independent, hitherto unknown truth.

Nor do the poets function as independent and equal sources of truth. The thought might run: Paul knows about God's transcendence from the Old Testament, the Athenians from their poets, but it is the same truth. This again misunderstands what happens in Acts 17. Paul does not treat the poets as co-equal sources of religious truth. This is particularly evident from the use of Aratus the Stoic poet.[86] The quotation here may be an echo of Cleanthes' *Hymn to Zeus*, which had earlier spoken of humans as God's offspring. However, Aratus' quotation is shorn of certain typical Stoic associations. This is evident in at least two respects.

First, an important feature of Stoicism is its 'monistic materialism',[87] that all reality is ultimately one and ultimately material. Thus, in Stoic thought, to be an offspring of Zeus meant that one had oneself a spark of divine fire. One was in continuity with Zeus. For Zeus was an immanent principle within the cosmos and within human beings. This monistic materialism sits ill with a creator God who transcends the world and is independent of human beings in the way Paul has outlined. Paul's thought endorses the distinction between creator and created, while Stoicism blurred it.

Secondly, in Stoicism, Zeus (or God) was 'many-named' (*polyonymos*),[88] meaning that God could be named and worshipped under a variety of guises and cults. Yet it is just this polymorphic approach to worship that Paul debunks before the Areopagus: God cannot be worshipped in the way the Athenians have. Paul uses Aratus' words without Stoic ideas of monism or polymorphic worship. They have been corrected. The reason is not far to seek – they are inconsistent with characteristic biblical thoughts about the distinction between creator and created, and the way that the creator stipulates that he must be worshipped in some ways and not others. This, though, is revealing. Aratus does not function as an independent and co-equal luminary. Aratus' words are acceptable when corrected and recontextualised within biblical truth and decontextualised from Stoicism. His words are subordinated to scriptural considerations, and only then applied. The authority of Aratus' words depends on conformity to the Bible, not on something intrinsic.

For these reasons, then, biblical accounts of natural or general revelation do not have the effect envisaged by the *Lux Mundi* school. Such revelation serves to establish responsibility, not to establish human ability to find theological truth independently of the Bible and make theological judgements of equal authority with the Bible.

John 1:9 and human gifts and knowledge
We turn now to the second objection, that rejecting the *Lux Mundi* interpretation of John 1:9 disenfranchises human knowledge altogether. Again, though, this objection fails. As noted above, the *Lux Mundi* interpretation is not simply asserting that humans have an innate reason by which they may acquire knowledge of the rest of creation. It ascribes a particular theological role to that knowledge, that one can use it to know about God. However, the *Lux Mundi* interpretation is not necessary to uphold viable human knowledge of the cosmos.[89] For one may say that providence and the gifts given to humanity in creation may indeed facilitate the creation mandate. Humans by grace were given the ability to know the creation so that they could fulfil their created role as God's vicegerents in it.

Thus, Job 28:1ff. takes up the remarkable human technological skill of mining, something which distinguishes humanity in its intensity and degree. Yet, verses 12ff. set the pursuit of wisdom apart from knowledge of the physical environment and consequent management of it. Wisdom is not found in this kind of way. Instead, humanity is dependent on God speaking to tell us what Wisdom is and where she/it starts (v. 28). Job 28 distinguishes between human knowledge that is not dependent on revelation, and which we acquire for ourselves, although doubtless by God's grace in creation, and human knowledge that is 'spoken' to us. The former is real and valued. In this way there is a positive evaluation of human skills and thought that does not depend on invoking a Logos doctrine. Yet the thrust of Job 28 is precisely about the limits of such human knowledge, as distinct from knowledge that is spoken to us. The problem is that the *Lux Mundi* construction tends to elide the two, because, as Darwell Stone long ago foresaw, it has only a difference of degree between biblical revelation and other forms of human knowing.[90]

That there is a difference between what God speaks and what humans morally intuit is clear from Mark 7:9ff., referred to earlier. There, Jesus distinguishes sharply between God's command and human tradition. He does so precisely on the ground of *origin* – it is because God's command and human tradition have different origins that the activity of the Pharisees is so obnoxious.

The predictable riposte from a *Lux Mundi* position would be that certainly the 'corban' rule of verse 11 could not be attributed to the immanent Word (the incarnate Word has, after all, just repudiated it). But this does not mean that the Word does not illuminate inwardly in other areas. Such a response, though, has not grasped the extent of the problem. Had the Pharisees been asked, they would not have owned up to abrogating the Word of God, as Jesus says they in fact have (Mk. 7:8). This might be because they really do not think they have done so and have made an 'honest mistake', or because they hide their antipathy to God's laws, perhaps even to some extent from themselves. On either view, they have a problem discriminating what is in fact God's law and word from what is their own invention. They apparently have no infallible sense of divine truth that they obey correctly. As such, on any view, to authenticate something as God's Word they would have to look outside themselves, not to an inner light. The *Lux Mundi* interpretation understates just that need.

John 1:9 – other interpretations of 'illuminate'
Carson makes the point that the word 'illuminates' need not have the sense of providing enlightenment.[91] He notes that another meaning, in fact a more primary one, is 'light up', as in 'he lit up the room'. The point here, to take the example, is not that the light means that the room can see, but that the room can be seen. So in John 1:9 this would yield the sense that the light 'shows up' every man and woman coming into the world. The advantage of this interpretation is that it provides a far better fit with John 3:20, 21 and the use of 'light' language there. It is precisely the showing up function that is in view. This also avoids the difficulties of reconciling the illumination of 1:9 with the rejection of 1:10–11.

A slight difficulty with this reading is the fact that 3:20–1 primarily deals with the incarnation (v. 19) and the reactions that follow that. Arguably John 1:9 looks more generally phrased. For that reason it is perhaps worth pursuing another line, which also highlights a further difficulty with the *Lux Mundi* construction.

After all, the discomfort with *Lux Mundi*-style interpretations increases when looking at the associations of light within the Prologue. In verse 4 light is associated with creation and life. That association is all the stronger in 8:12 where Jesus is described as the light of the world (thus providing the title for the *Lux Mundi* essayists). However, the second half of the verse specifies the kind of light that Jesus is, he is the light of life, and the section as a whole speaks of a world in darkness (8:12) and facing death in sin (8:21, 24). On this basis, light and life are related to each other and stand opposite another related pair, darkness and death. This, of course, coheres with Old Testament use of light imagery. To 'give light to' can be a paraphrase of 'give life', or 'quality of life to'.[92] On this basis, the sense of John 1:9 is not that the true light illuminates in the sense of giving currently active reason and conscience to all alike, but rather that it illuminates all in providing creative life to all alike. This then adds piquancy to 1:9–12 where men and women reject the light who gives them life, and ensures there is progression and climax in verses 9–13:

- the light gives creative life to all.
- but the world that was made through him rejected him.
- even his own people rejected.
- but he gave power to become children of God.

It is true that John uses light imagery in other ways than in relation to the giving of life. Illumination of character has already been mentioned (3:20, 21). The obvious alternative example is John the Baptist, who is also described in light terms (5:35). However, even here it does not amount to an internal light of understanding, but of revelation, something external. Moreover, exactly the point about John the Baptist is that his testimony or light is not understood and accepted, for 'the Jews' do not accept the one to whom he testifies. John 5 does not speak of innate understanding, but of refusal.

For these reasons, this passage does not support the *Lux Mundi* case for innate reason and conscience of a kind that independently knows and recognises God.

Genesis 1:26 and the image of God
The other passage which *Lux Mundi* writers and their successors invoked (again rather by reference than exegesis) is Genesis 1:26, with its assertion of the creation of human beings in the image of God. Gore's point, as we have seen, is that this establishes a 'theomorphism' on the part of the human race, such that issues of reason and conscience are congruous between humans and God.

Of course, the immediate context of Genesis 1:26 does not raise issues of human reason and conscience. Rather, what is at stake is the position of humans as those whom God establishes as having dominion under him over the rest of creation. However, this does not mean that questions of rationality or personhood are irrelevant. Rather, they seem to be implied, for God's dominion forms a pattern for Adam and Eve, and that dominion is rational[93] and personal and righteous. Human dominion is within the context of God's dominion.

This, though, raises the question of Genesis 3, where human conduct stands at odds with God's dominion. This is part of the salvation-historical context into which any understanding of Genesis 1:26f. must be put. Part of the irony here is that in implicitly rejecting the legitimacy of God's dominion, Adam and Eve in consequence also delegitimate their own position as those holding dominion by the grant of God. Human conduct in Genesis 3 does not manifest the congruity of values between God and humanity, but rather that humanity has now embraced incongruous values. This sits but poorly with the 'theomorphic' estimate of Gore. It is as though there had been no Fall. To that extent Genesis 1:26 seems abstracted from its salvation-historical context.

A possible response would be that Genesis 3 is, as it were, a one off. Humans made a mistake, sinned even, but it did not change their fundamental theomorphic character. The difficulties with this answer are legion. First, as early as Genesis 6:5, the Bible signals a certain disinclination on the part of humanity to share God's values. This is instantiated in the history of Israel as she shows herself unable to keep the covenant at many points in her history, culminating in the conquest of the northern kingdom of Israel and the exile of inhabitants from the southern kingdom of Judah. In the New Testament, the Pauline depiction of humanity in Ephesians 2:1ff. as having the values of the world and the ruler of the power of the air, rather than God, suggests a humanity that is not theomorphic in the sense Gore intends.

This is not to say that the dominion mandate of Genesis 1:26ff. has been repealed (difficult in view of Genesis 9 and the Noachic Covenant). It is, though, to observe a real discontinuity between humanity as created originally and as it is now. Most importantly, though, the events of the incarnation itself show, as the previous chapter argued, that humans do not have congruity of values with God. Rather there is a covert hostility.

Purely from the point of view of church history, Gore's case at this point looks uncomfortably like a denial of original sin. This would be a curious position for a Catholic in the Church of England to assume, given that the early church condemned Pelagius' denial of original sin,[94] and the Articles of the Church of England assert original sin in Article 9.

The conclusion is that neither of the key passages establishes the anthropology that the *Lux Mundi* essayists require to make their project viable as a *biblical* approach.

Historical evaluation

We must turn now to the historical claims of the essayists. When condescending to detail, Gore, who like the Tractarians saw his Catholicism including a deep appreciation of the Fathers, adduced Justin Martyr, Origen and Irenaeus to support his thesis that the incarnation is the consummation of the natural cosmic process.[95]

Irenaeus

Gore's thesis misrepresents Irenaeus,[96] whose dominant explanation of the incarnation is that it is a recapitulation, or 'going over again' of the role of humanity in the cosmos. Christ is a second Adam who obeys and fulfils God's purposes for humanity, while the first Adam disobeyed, thereby frustrating God's purposes. Christ completed what Adam failed to do and in this way it was Adam's failure, not his laying of a foundation on which Christ

Is Christ's Incarnation the Consummation? 29

could build, that brought the incarnation. The incarnation was the result of a process going awry, not a process going right.[97]

Origen

As for Origen,[98] while one needs to be cautious about too simplistic a systematic formulation of Origen's views, one must try to set the incarnation in the context of the rest of his thought. Origen was committed to the pre-existence of 'human' souls, not least on the basis that God must always have had objects on which to exercise his eternal characteristics of goodness and power.[99] 'Pre-existence' here means the idea that souls existed before physical life on earth. God causes beings 'coeternal with himself.'[100] These human souls were originally in union with God, but their ardour and enthusiasm cooled and they fell away from God.[101] For Origen, enfleshment occurs after these pre-existent souls had fallen.[102] The exception is, of course, the 'human' soul of Jesus, also pre-existent, which cleaved perfectly to the eternal Word of God.[103] The union of human soul and divine Word thus takes place *before* the physical incarnation. The incarnation was necessary precisely because human souls had become enfleshed and needed both to have God revealed to them and to be reunited with God.[104] Here again the stress is on dealing with our sinful state, not with the incarnation of a natural process. Such process as there is has gone wrong.

Hence, Origen's overall thought does not in fact support the point that Gore claims. Human existence in the flesh is not part of a positive natural process for Origen, and the incarnation is not the culmination. Such a state is a mark of dysfunction.

The foregoing description also makes it clear that Origen's account of the nature of creation and incarnation is, to put it mildly, idiosyncratic. It should therefore be added that Origen's thinking attracted condemnation at the Fifth Ecumenical Council (Constantinople AD 553). Anathemata 1 and 4 are directed against the doctrines of pre-cosmic souls and pre-cosmic falls, while Anathema 7 is directed against the pre-cosmic union of the soul of Christ with the eternal Word.

However, given that Council's clear condemnation of Origenistic thought, it becomes puzzling that Gore should in any case cite Origen in the way he does. For Origen is not being cited as part of the history of Christian dogma, but rather as an authoritative and representative source of patristic theology which supported the legitimacy of the *Lux Mundi* view of the incarnation. Later Patristic theology distances itself from just such an uncritical use of Origen.

Justin Martyr
Turning to Justin Martyr,[105] Gore has at first glance a better case. He rightly observes that Justin uses friendship with Christ terminology of pagan thinkers.[106] The rationale for this is frequently claimed to be the presence of the rational Word in human individuals. However, once again this account needs to be significantly nuanced by other material, in fact in the same work that Gore and Illingworth cite.

First, Justin's case was not that pagan religion was born of a true knowledge of God (it will be recalled that *Lux Mundi* took a 'positive' view of pagan religion in the process of cosmic development). Rather, pagan religions were demonically inspired.[107] Whatever the indwelling Word was, it did not for Justin mean that pagan religions provided alternative valid perspectives on divine matters or additional valid perspectives. The perspective that pagan religions are demonically inspired was not, of course, unique to Justin.[108] In this, though, the early church was reflecting the teaching of Paul in particular (1 Cor. 10:20). The possibility of demonic 'inspiration' presents a significant difficulty for the *Lux Mundi* case: can humans by themselves discern the difference between demonic and divine inspiration? Since *Lux Mundi* does not advert to the demonic possibility that was so real for Justin and others, and in particular the Bible, it would be rash to conjecture what the essayists' answer would be.

Secondly, even where pagan philosophy (as distinct from religion)[109] was to Justin's mind objectively accurate, it still did not function as an independent revelation or source of truth.[110] Instead, the point was that such speculations were biblically confirmed. This goes to the relationship between propositions coming from the Bible and those derived from elsewhere. It will be recalled that the *Lux Mundi* model in principle tends to render biblical confirmation unnecessary.

Thirdly, Justin is not simply endorsing pagan thought as the independent product of the immanent work of the Logos. Justin envisages Plato as 'borrowing' from Moses.[111] The truth in Plato is attributable to his having read Moses. Justin accepts partial vision in pagan writers,[112] and therefore argues for the superiority of biblical writers[113] – it is these one ought to read. Obviously, there would be no need for the conjecture that Plato read Moses if Justin was content simply with the thought that the indwelling Logos would produce similar results in both cases. He wants to assert something more than the *Lux Mundi* position. From that point of view, Justin does not simply envisage a process in human history of the emergence of truth in which the incarnation is simply the culmination of a cumulative process.

For these reasons, then, Gore's attempt to ground his version of Christ as consummation of the positive natural process in the theology of the patristic theologians he cites must be adjudged, in the case of Origen and Irenaeus, a misrepresentation, and, in the case of Justin, suspect in its highly selective reading of his thought.

Gore and Athanasius
The problem is, however, compounded by the theologians Gore does not cite on this issue. Gore advertised himself as a man deeply learned in patristic theology.[114] One would therefore have thought it difficult to omit extended discussion of Athanasius and his seminal work *De Incarnatione* ('On the Incarnation'). In fact, *Lux Mundi* references to *De Incarnatione* fail to note that Athanasius takes the shame of the incarnation with the shame of the cross, joining what *Lux Mundi* wished to leave at least semi-detached. More significantly, Athanasius states in the opening of his work not only that the incarnation was necessary for salvation, but that the incarnation was for our salvation, and 'for this reason only'.[115] In that sense, Athanasius did not envisage a cosmic process in which the incarnation was going to happen in any event.

In fact, incarnation for the purposes of salvation fits neatly into the rest of Athanasius' theology. Other means of revelation of God have failed, as far as Athanasius is concerned,[116] and humans must know God truly if they are to be blessed. *Lux Mundi* by contrast contends for at least the partial success of other means of revelation. Our own innate sense of God and truth was insufficient for what we needed according to Athanasius, and was not leading us into progressively greater areas of truth. Our indulgence in idolatry undercut our abilities to deal with natural revelation.[117] The incarnation was not then to crown a basically successful, if fraught, natural cosmic process: it was to recreate a cosmos devastated by sin.

Gore and patristic theology
This omission of a proper discussion of Athanasius on this point tends to highlight in any event the eccentricity of Gore's citations in support of his case. Origen's condemnation has already been mentioned. But Justin, Origen and Irenaeus all, of course, predate the great trinitarian and christological discussions of Nicaea and Chalcedon, which resulted in a formulation of the incarnation in terms of its salvific purpose ('for us and for our salvation'). It is a curious feature that a movement publicly presenting itself as committed to credal orthodoxy, as liberal Catholicism was under Gore's guardianship, should not advert to this point. It could minimally attempt to make the case that the creeds of Nicaea and Constantinople and the Definition of Chalcedon are capable of an inclusive meaning (i.e. the incarnation could have other purposes than the salvific). It is clear that the *Lux Mundi* writers themselves wanted to think in terms of other purposes, but they have not shown that this was intrinsic to patristic theology.

The patristic material has been reviewed at some length. This is necessary given the liberal Catholic insistence on the authenticity of their 'Catholicism', for which patristic support is highly important. Nevertheless, after this review, it is difficult not to concur with Avis' judgement on Gore: 'He follows the Tractarians in building up proof-texts from the fathers.'[118] 'Proof-texting' readily carries the connotation of distortion and revisionism, and this connotation appears well founded in the case of the patristic evidence.

Philosophical evaluation
At this stage of the argument, it becomes clear that *Lux Mundi* approaches are not satisfactorily grounded in either biblical or patristic material. The *Lux Mundi* proposal, if it stands at all, stands as a philosophical proposal. To this we now turn.

Idealism

First, it is necessary to address the idealism in the *Lux Mundi* school and its successors. Some have suggested that the primary debt of Gore, in particular, is not to idealism, but rather to the Bible and the church's theology.[119] We have just observed how tenuous the biblical and historical claims are. It is certainly fair to comment that idealists, including Hegel, are seldom mentioned by name in *Lux Mundi*. On the other hand, Temple's *Christus Veritas* is suffused with idealism, with comparatively little treatment of evolution. Others prefer to acknowledge the presence of idealist strains, putting this in terms of influence rather than simple dependence,[120] and this seems apt. The influence, though, must be adjudged profound.[121]

The reason for this conclusion is that it is precisely the idealism that moulds the appropriation of evolution, so that the process in question is personal and theistic, not impersonal, as it certainly tended to be with, say, Huxley. To that extent, idealism is a dominant factor. However, contemporary philosophy has often remarked on the totalitarian tendencies of Hegelian historicism and its derivative schools of thought, none more trenchantly, perhaps, than Karl Popper.[122]

It will be recalled that Hegelian idealism envisaged history as a process in which Spirit realised itself. It is 'historicist' in Popper's sense,[123] that it involves an interpretation of history as a progress towards a particular self-realising fulfilment.[124] The problem Popper highlighted is that a historical event within such a framework of historicism tends to be judged by its 'success'.[125] The individual or party able to appeal to some kind of success in the displacement of other ideas or worldviews is able to argue from that success to the legitimacy and propriety of the idea, its absolute rightness, at least for the moment.

This can open the door to claiming one's own (successful) opinions carry the force of the divine mind operating within the historical process. In fact, Popper is merely the last in a long line to feel suspicious of techniques that permit one to clothe one's thoughts with divine authority. One can go back at least to Sophocles, and a scene from the *Philoctetes*, in which Philoctetes appeals to the gods while he is being captured:

> *Philoctetes:* ... must I be dragged away
> A prisoner before your eyes?
> *Odysseus:* The will of Zeus
> He is this country's king and I am
> his officer.
> *Philoctetes:* You lie, foul villain, making God's word a lie
> To shield your practices.[126]

In a similar vein, Calvin decries parallel thinking in respect of the authority of church councils as being a species of tyranny within the church, since such immanentist thinking entailed God no longer ruling his people by his inscripturated Word.[127] It is partly for this reason that examination of *Lux Mundi* thinking is so important.

An objection to the above analysis might run like this. Granted the kind of philosophy of history that Hegel (and Marx) held tends to justify by success, is it an example of the genetic fallacy to make this criticism of the 'cosmic process' ideas of the *Lux Mundi* school? In this instance, the sting of the 'genetic fallacy' charge is that one is condemning the *Lux Mundi* school because some ideas originate with Hegel: a sort of guilt by association.

However, this objection does not hold. A key feature of the *Lux Mundi* project is that the cosmic process is one in which the Word is present, and the incarnation is the consummation of this. But the cosmic process as a whole is a progress (it is positive). It is very hard here to avoid the rule of thumb that 'later means improved', and that success is an indication of legitimacy. This is particularly so within the framework of Temple,[128] where the universe realises itself in the various human consciousnesses who make it up. When human consciousnesses adopt a viewpoint, that is the cosmos realising itself. In this way, the *Lux Mundi* school adopts just those features of Hegelian idealism that prove so troubling. On this view, the 'liberal' part of the label that the *Lux Mundi* essayists adopted has a curiously ironic ring.

Popper devastatingly observes that 'lie' within this historicist framework becomes a very difficult concept.[129] To develop this point, it is worth observing that a historicist framework may well start to distort debate. The purpose of debate is to *succeed in persuasion*. If one succeeds, so that the cosmic process adopts one's position, would this adoption not in itself make the position true

Is Christ's Incarnation the Consummation? 35

(at least until the next stage of the cosmic process)? The risk here is that debate within a church or denomination that has adopted a *Lux Mundi* approach will tend towards techniques of persuasion and plausibility, rather than objective substance. This takes us to a consideration of the viability of the *Lux Mundi* method.

The viability of the Lux Mundi *method*
It will be recalled that Smith characterised the theological method of liberal Catholicism as 'open',[130] in the sense that truth could be appropriated from many quarters. The *Lux Mundi* examples are the appropriation of an evolutionary view for religion, and the feeling that biblical criticism (certainly of the Old Testament) did have something to offer the church. What falls for examination here is how it is that truth can be appropriated from both the Bible and extra-biblical sources.

Within *Lux Mundi*, this is spelled out in most detail in Moore's essay.[131] Moore questions how Christians should deal with the new truths that emerge from science, metaphysics or social and political life. He cites the story of the Caliph Omar who captured the library of Alexandria and consigned all its books to the flames, because either they agreed with the Koran (and were unnecessary) or disagreed with it (and should be destroyed as falsehood). Moore finds a better path:

> But an intelligent Christian will not ask, 'Does this new truth agree with or contradict the letter of the Bible?' but 'How does it interpret and help us understand the Bible?' And so with regard to all truth, whether it comes from the side of science, or history, or criticism, he adopts neither the method of protest nor the method of surrender but the method of assimilation.[132]

However, this important passage raises several important points. Moore talks of a truth coming from science or some other realm of human endeavour. The obvious question is, how do we know that a particular 'truth' is true? How would we establish its truth? The reason why this matters is that Moore is proposing we assimilate a particular proposition within our framework of truths. It is obviously of considerable concern to make sure that what we are assimilating is, in fact, true.

Moore appears to envisage that truths emerge from various fields fully formed and authenticated. This, though, assumes that the field of, say, psychology is capable of ascertaining definite final truth. This would be an enormously ambitious claim. We have already observed that it is not substantiated by appeal to John 1:9 or Genesis 1:26. It is worth adding that some philosophers have long regarded attaining definite 'truth' as chimerical. The Sceptics of the ancient world subjected the claim to final moral truth to severe scrutiny.[133] Their interrogation was applied to 'knowledge' attained through the 'scientific method' by David Hume over a century before *Lux Mundi* was written. Roughly contemporaneously with *Lux Mundi*, the German literary critic Fritz Mauthner was extending sceptical techniques to linguistic communication itself. Both before and since 1889, theorists have laid much greater stress on the social construction of our accounts of reality,[134] and the extent to which they are not neutral and objective, but in fact may serve some particular interest.[135] Furthermore, it is normally not the case that particular propositions are universally accepted even within a particular field of study. In the case of biblical studies, it is clearly not the case that all scholars subscribed to, say, a history of religions approach to the Old Testament. Yet the risk of Moore's approach is to absolutise a particular consensus in a particular field from a particular time as 'the truth' to be assimilated.

Of course, one can quite see that Hegelian historicism insists truth *does* emerge and is therefore available, but even here there is a paradox. For the *Lux Mundi* argument is faced with the point that what has emerged through the process, even by their own time, at least for some thinkers, is exactly a reluctance to ascribe final truth to particular propositions, including scientific propositions.

Nor, in fact, is it the case that *Lux Mundi* itself simply assimilates a 'truth', fully formed and complete. It has already been observed that the 'truth' of evolution employed in *Lux Mundi* is the interpretation or version of evolution that the essayists found palatable. They do not accept the 'truth' that Huxley for example would see in evolutionary theory, but modify it. This modification takes place on the basis of propositions that emerge not from biology simply, but from other fields of discourse, idealism and an erroneous exegesis of John 1:9. Similarly, the career of Gore in particular shows that they did not accept each and every proposition emerging from biblical criticism, for example over the New Testament. There, too, modification takes place, notwithstanding the confidence with which New Testament critics may have asserted their proposals.

However, this means that assimilation is not in fact simply the process of taking a truth from this field and a truth from that. Propositions claiming to be true need to be weighed against each other. This point is subtly evaded in Moore's remarks with his reference to contradicting 'the letter of the Bible'. That phrasing readily implies a distinction between the 'letter' and the 'real' meaning of the Bible, with the sense that the 'letter of the Bible' was not in fact what the Bible meant. The further implication is that conflicts between what the Bible says and what, for example, psychology says will reveal that the Bible did not in fact mean what we previously thought it did.

There is an important and valid point here, that current views may lead us to re-examine interpretations and find they are in fact unwarranted. But what Moore has not squarely faced is what we should do when current hypotheses and biblical teaching are in fact opposed. He has only raised the case where right understanding arising from extra-biblical material clashes with our biblical *mis*understandings, not our biblical *right* understandings.

One could, of course, assert that no biblical truth will ever clash with any extra-biblical truth, for all truth is God's truth. At one level, this is perfectly correct. But it is not helpful in the current debate, for the issue is not whether one truth from one field clashes with a truth from another field, but how propositions claiming to be true from different fields relate to each other. For example, Freud claims to furnish us with an account of the origins of religion and belief in God: it involves accepting the truth of atheism. This appears to be a straightforward contradiction of biblical teaching that involves God objectively existing. There is, therefore, a real problem to be faced: how to deal with the clash of propositions both claiming to be true. Freud would, no doubt, have wished to assert the essential truth of his proposal. There are a number of possible avenues of resolution, each of which must be discussed.

1. Always preferring extra-biblical material?

One could resolve this problem by having a rule that the extra-biblical teaching should always be preferred. In our example, this means simply preferring Freud, because he has all the benefits of knowledge unavailable to Moses. An argument in favour of this could be that any proposition arising from recent understandings is more likely to be correct than older understandings, because we must assume a growth in knowledge. On reflection, though, it is not entirely easy to see why this should be so. Why assume the Bible is always likely to be more wrong than later people who disagree with it? That disagreement might, for instance, be motivated by vested interest. One could not *a priori* exclude that possibility. In a similar vein one might accept the idea that people simply make mistakes, and that one cannot *a priori* exclude the possibility that one may make a mistake one's forebears did not. Yet if one cannot properly make that *a priori* commitment, then one cannot simply and always apply the rule that the later is to be preferred. One would have to invoke further criteria.

2. Always preferring the biblical material?

Alternatively, one could try to resolve the problem by having a rule that the Bible should always be preferred when its claims (as rightly exegeted[136]) come into conflict with other truth claims. This, of course, is a fairly traditional position, not by any means confined to Protestantism or evangelicalism. The rationale behind such a rule is that if Scripture is divinely originated, then, notwithstanding its human expression, it is uniquely authoritative. Thus, Thomas Aquinas treats the propositions deriving from the Bible as uniquely authoritative and not merely probable because they derive from a particular source.[137]

As uniquely authoritative, there is a good reason for having a rule that gives the Bible precedence. This stems from a particular form of theism, which accepts that God is uniquely knowledgeable and can communicate. In this way, truth from other fields is validated by reference to biblical truth and appropriated. Paul's use in Acts 17 of the Aratus quotation shorn of its Stoic connotations

Is Christ's Incarnation the Consummation? 39

is an example of this. This illustrates the inadequacy of envisaging that the only way of assimilating truth from outside the Bible is by making concessions over the Bible's uniqueness.

3. No set order of precedence?

On the other hand, one could resolve the problem by having no universal rule about whether to prefer biblical or extra-biblical claims to truth, but employ or permit some other procedure. This is what Moore seems to do. He addresses the question of the history of religion, which he envisages as a 'natural' history,[138] in the important sense that natural laws apply to it. The natural history of religion is,

> the result of a process with which we are familiar elsewhere, *viz*. Evolution by antagonism. The true has to be separated from the false. Immoral and irrational conceptions of God have to be thrown aside.[139]

Moore goes on to spell out how this operates:

> For among religions, too, there is a struggle for existence, in which the fittest survive. And the test of fitness is the power to assimilate and promote moral and intellectual truth, and so satisfy the whole man.[140]

Moore here employs the phrasing of evolutionary theory, the survival of the fittest, in his description of religious history. However, it should be added that the survival of the fittest refers to the improved prospects of survival for a given competitor in a given environment. It is a question of best/better adaptation to the prevailing circumstances. Moore's model is that the fittest religious ideas will be the best and truest ideas, for these are best adapted to satisfy human beings. At this point, though, two things become painfully obvious. First, the aptness of Popper's observations about Hegelian views of history, that it rewards practical success with the laurels of legitimacy and moral superiority: this is just what Moore is proposing.

This leads to the second point. Moore is making enormous assumptions about human preferences, that we prefer morally better ideas. Even within the framework of non-Christian thought this is hugely controversial, and has been so for a very long time. Plato dealt with the question of false and deceptive pleasures in the *Philebus*, but was tacitly admitting we have a problem in always choosing true and good pleasures to satisfy ourselves. In a more contemporary vein, we may think in Foucault's terms of adopting ideas because they suit our economic or other power interests, for instance.

Within the framework of Christian thought it is equally controversial and returns us to the question of Pelagianism and the corruption of indwelling sin. Paul comments that some even within the church refuse to hear the truth, having acquired itching ears (2 Tim. 4:1ff.). Their selection is based on perceived pleasure, not truth. For this reason, the survival of a belief does not necessarily indicate its truth, but may in fact be a sign of its spiritual falsehood. It is difficult to find this Pauline note in Moore, or indeed the Johannine note that humans love darkness for their deeds are evil. As will be seen in more detail in the next chapter, the incarnation shows that humans do not necessarily or even generally have an innate love of spiritual truth. It is precisely the incarnation itself that indicates the non-viability of Moore's survival model.

On this basis, Moore's model for assimilating and winnowing out truth faces considerable problems. His outline faces the very traditional difficulty of moving from the descriptive (that some ideas displace others) to the prescriptive (that good ideas always displace bad).

The implications of Moore's views on assimilation
One may add something about the profile of a Christian denomination judging truth questions on Moore's basis. It will be a denomination whose views tend to approximate more closely to the society in which it lives, or at least to the opinion formers of that society. Its agenda will tend to be set by the culture in which it lives, but with a few years' delay, as ideas percolate only with time from the culture through to the denomination. It may well tend to set considerable store on disciplines outside theology and biblical studies, perhaps feeling that the latter are antiquated sources of truth compared to the newer 'sciences'. It may start to find

Is Christ's Incarnation the Consummation? 41

legitimation for itself and its ideas from external endorsement rather than its traditional deposit of teaching. Considerable embarrassment and irritation is then felt with any members who refuse to 'modernise', for such people serve to delegitimate the denomination in the eyes of the wider world. Such a denomination will tend to find it difficult to persuade people to join it out of the culture, because it will be so palpably involved in joining them. Given a few years, the denomination will adopt their values. It will not necessarily appear 'non-prophetic' but it will tend to be prophetic on just those issues that its culture is happy to have scrutinised.

It is no surprise therefore to find contemporary denominations in the United Kingdom wedded to a *Lux Mundi* methodology experiencing dramatic drops in membership and difficulties in evangelism. Nor is the current concern over issues of, say, ecology and Two-Thirds World debt any occasion for astonishment. For, while these are legitimate objects of concern, they are concerns whose validity has been endorsed by the surrounding culture. There is an accepted sense that there is, so to speak, a case to answer on pollution. What is striking is the comparative absence of the prophetic note over issues this culture finds a good deal less congenial to have discussed – the non-viability of secularist education as a basis for a humane multicultural society; the idea that sin brings forth not just unpleasant social consequences but God's righteous anger and so forth. Above all, Moore's church will be a safe church, safe that is for slightly dated *chic*.

Ethical evaluation
It will be recalled that Gore spoke of the obligation he felt to a species of intellectual autonomy: 'I must be in the true sense of the word a free thinker.'[141] The rationale for this relates, it seems, to the indwelling Logos, which means that it would be a 'treason against the light'[142] not to be a free thinker. The drama and romantic appeal of the freestanding person of intellectual integrity is considerable. It is, though, worth briefly pursuing the 'intellectual integrity' question.

As at other points in *Lux Mundi*, this depends on the notion of an indwelling Logos who illuminates. The highly dubious exegetical nature of this has already been indicated, and the reluctance of some contemporary philosophy to accept protestations of innocence at their face value already mentioned. In the current climate of a hermeneutics of suspicion, Gore's claim to the right to be a 'free thinker' on the basis of indwelling light runs the risk of appearing self-serving. Some would see this impression confirmed by his ready invocation of this standard when the freedom in question is his, in contrast to his willingness to resort to the claims of authority over others when he was a bishop.

The obvious riposte to this is that Gore is asserting his claim to be a 'free thinker' in a Christian context. Yet here too Gore's claim is not unproblematic. Within a Christian framework, we are not free, for example, to think of God in any way we choose (consider the First and Second Commandments), nor to worship him in any way we choose (consider the worship restrictions of Leviticus).

Concluding Remarks

In an earlier generation the redoubtable evangelical teacher W.H. Griffith Thomas observed:

> the churchmanship for which Bishop Gore stands [sc. liberal Catholicism] is absolutely incompatible with that which evangelicals hold.[143]

From a different churchmanship, Darwell Stone concluded of *Lux Mundi*:

> Only we feel there is teaching which touches the vitals of the faith, against which we are bound to protest.[144]

The foregoing discussion starts to illustrate why these men thought this. We have reviewed the claims of a *Lux Mundi* theology with regard to its exegetical, historical and philosophical bases. It has been shown to be exegetically inept, historically distorted and philosophically suspect. In the areas of exegesis and history it has been notably poor at vital points in dealing with contextual questions, including questions of immediate context (Jn. 1:9); questions of biblical theological context (Gen. 1:26 in the light of Gen. 3); and questions of historical context (in patristic theology the condemnation of Origen, the full position of Justin and

Irenaeus, the place of Athanasius, the Nicene Creed and the Chalcedonian Definition).

Its claim to 'Catholicism' is rendered unsustainable since its contact with Scripture and Tradition appears so slim. Its revisionist accounts of the Bible and church history also run the risk of failing to respect in fact the views and thinking of others while vigorously championing in theory the view that the Logos was illuminating those others. To that extent, the term 'liberal' likewise acquires a highly specialised meaning.

One item remains. *Lux Mundi* and the liberal Catholic theological method associated with it have been described as representing an incarnational theology. The final irony is that the *Lux Mundi* method in fact tends to move attention away from the incarnation and onto the immanent activity of the Logos in every person outside the incarnation. It is from there that *Lux Mundi* is acquiring its new revelational truths and therefore it is there, whatever the intention, that one tends to focus, not on the career of the Logos on earth. As several commentators have remarked, *Lux Mundi* does not, in fact, have much on the incarnation. Here we return again to the *Lux Mundi* charge that evangelicals have understated the incarnation, and wryly note the irony of accusing evangelicals of betrayal. We, at any rate, must continue to turn to the incarnation, and not, as *Lux Mundi* did, away from it. It is therefore to the incarnation that we look in the next chapter.

Notes

[1] D. Stone, 'Theology and Criticism', *Church Quarterly Review* XXX (1890), pp. 195–235 (at p. 212).

[2] The relevant part speaks of Jesus Christ '… to be acknowledged in two natures, inconfusedly, unchangeably, indivisibly, inseparably; the distinction of the natures being by no means taken away by the union, but rather the property of each nature being preserved, and concurring in one person …'

[3] In C.S. Lewis, *Screwtape Proposes a Toast and Other Pieces* (London: Collins, 1977).

[4] For the tendency of groups within bureaucratic institutions to try to consolidate power by rendering their actions non-transparent see M. Crozier, *The Bureaucratic Phenomenon* (Chicago: University of Chicago Press, 1964).

[5] 'It is Time for Another Reformation', *The Guardian*, Saturday, 3 August 2002. Hobson writes with inside knowledge, but the point is the forum in which this could be said.

[6] J. Hick (ed.), *The Myth of God Incarnate* (London: SCM, 1977).

[7] See B. Smith, 'Liberal Catholicism: An Anglican Perspective', *Anglican Theological Review* 54 (1972), pp. 175–93 (at pp. 176–9).

[8] The Chalcedonian Definition was here following the Niceno-Constantinopolitan Creed 325, 381.

[9] C. Gore (ed.), *Lux Mundi*. The first edition was in 1889. The edition used here is the 'fifteenth edition' (London: John Murray, 1899), which is a reprint of the twelfth edition of 1891. The extent of reprinting is an indication of the book's circulation.

[10] A.M. Ramsey, *From Gore to Temple: The Development of Anglican Theology between* Lux Mundi *and the Second World War* (London: Longmans, Green and Co, 1960), p. vii.

[11] Ibid., pp. viii, 16.

[12] Ibid., p. 3.

[13] P. Avis, *Gore: Construction and Conflict* (Worthing: Churchman Publishing, 1988), p. 1.

[14] A. Nichols, *The Panther and the Hind* (Edinburgh: Clark, 1993), p. 132.

[15] See G. Himmelfarb, 'Varieties of Social Darwinism', in *Victorian Minds* (Chicago: Elephant, 1968), pp. 314–32, esp. p. 327.

[16] See the descriptions in R.E. Clements, *Old Testament Theology: a fresh approach* (Basingstoke: Marshall Morgan & Scott, 1978), pp. 158ff.

[17] Ramsey, *From Gore to Temple*, p. 1, sees B.F. Westcott as implementing the 'social corollaries' of the incarnation.

[18] S.J. Grenz & R.E. Olson, *20th Century Theology: God and the World in a Transitional Age* (Carlisle/Downers Grove: Paternoster/InterVarsity Press, 1992), p. 38.

[19] B.F. Westcott, *The Epistles of St John* (London: Macmillan, 1905), p. 287.

[20] Ibid., pp. 287–8.

[21] E.g. in *Lux Mundi*, E.S. Talbot pp. 97–8, J.R. Illingworth, p. 132. More specifically applied to religion, A. Moore, *Lux Mundi*, p. 49.

[22] Illingworth, *Lux Mundi*, p. 132.

[23] Ibid.

[24] Documented in Himmelfarb, *Victorian Minds*, pp. 328–9.

[25] The two did in fact have their differences. See P.E. Johnson, *Objections Sustained: subversive essays on Evolution, Law and Culture* (Downers Grove: InterVarsity Press, 1998), pp. 16–17.

26 The compatibility of evolutionary hypotheses and theism continues to be contentious. See R. Dawkins passim.
27 C. Gore, *The Incarnation of the Son of God,* Bampton Lectures (2nd ed.; London: John Murray, 1892), p. 33.
28 Temple's grades of being have slightly different terms: matter, life, mind, spirit. Cf. his *Christus Veritas* (London: Macmillan, 1924), p. 4.
29 Temple, *Christus Veritas,* p. 68.
30 Gore, *The Incarnation of the Son,* p. 18.
31 J. Carpenter, *Gore: a Study in Liberal Catholic Thought* (London: The Faith Press, 1960), pp. 44, 56. Carpenter adds that Gore accepted the presence of evangelicalism and Tractarianism in the Church of England (*Gore,* p. 58), but within a 'Catholic' framework. Pluralism in Gore thus does not seem to be a pluralism between equals.
32 E.g. in *Lux Mundi,* A. Moore p. 70; E.S. Talbot p. 96, J.R. Illingworth pp. 134, 150, 155.
33 Ramsey in his Foreword to Avis, *Gore,* p. 4, comments that both Gore and Temple 'were sure that the light which enlightens every man was present far and wide in man's reason and conscience'.
34 Smith, 'Liberal Catholicism', pp. 176–9.
35 Ibid., p. 177, fn 3, following Carpenter, *Gore,* p. 11.
36 Ramsey, *From Gore to Temple,* p. 3.
37 From 'The Adventures of Life, Lecture V', *Church Times,* 8 April 1927, p. 430. Quoted in Carpenter, *Gore,* pp. 60–1.
38 Carpenter, *Gore,* p. 48.
39 Stone, 'Theology and Criticism', pp. 214, 217ff.
40 'They [sc. the essayists] have allowed themselves a type of academic treatment of theology which is fraught with the greatest dangers.' Stone, 'Theology and Criticism', p. 234.
41 Gore, *The Incarnation of the Son of God,* p. 116.
42 Ibid.
43 In *Lux Mundi,* H.S. Holland, p. 16 and A. Moore, p. 59.
44 Ibid.
45 Cited by Gore (1892), n. 13 to p. 40.
46 The first edition of Westcott's commentary on the Johannine Epistles was 1883. Cf. note 19 above.
47 C. Gore, *The Reconstruction of Belief* (London: John Murray, 1926), p. vi.
48 This is the term to which Smith constantly, and usefully, returns in 'Liberal Catholicism'.

49 Illingworth, *Lux Mundi*, p. 133.
50 E.g. A. Lyttelton, *Lux Mundi*, pp. 218, 226.
51 Temple, *Christus Veritas*, p. 74.
52 Gore (1892), pp. 42–3.
53 Illingworth, *Lux Mundi*, p. 150.
54 Ibid., p. 145.
55 Cited by Avis, *Gore*, p. 32
56 Ibid., p. 29, commenting on the way Gore followed Bishop Joseph Butler.
57 Cf. Carpenter's comment (*Gore*, p. 91), 'once the revelation is acknowledged, reason is made the judge of its truth.'
58 Moore, *Lux Mundi*, p. 59.
59 The obvious starting point is A. De Tocqueville's *Democracy in America* (1848), vol. I, ch. 15, on tyranny of the majority.
60 Again, note the parallels with De Tocqueville's analysis of the tyrannical aspects of absolutised majoritarian forms.
61 Once again, note Moore's comments in *Lux Mundi*, p. 59. The implications of this are developed below.
62 To clear the ground, we note that Jn. 1:9 contains a notorious difficulty. Does the phrase 'was coming into the world' qualify 'the true light' (i.e. 'the true light was coming into the world') or does it qualify 'everyone' (i.e. 'everyone who was coming into the world')? This does not, in fact, affect the interpretation now under consideration, so no further discussion of this point is required.
63 B.F. Westcott, *The Gospel of Saint John* (London: John Murray, 1882; reprinted 1937), p. 7.
64 Westcott, *John*, p. 4.
65 Gore, *Incarnation*, p. 116.
66 W. Temple, *Readings in St. John's Gospel* (London: Macmillan, 1939–40; reprinted 1968), p. 9.
67 A.M. Ramsey, *God, Christ and the World* (London: SCM, 1969), p. 95 (emphasis added).
68 D.A. Carson, *The Gospel According to John* (Grand Rapids: Eerdmans, 1991), pp. 123–4 sets out the basic range.
69 Ibid., p. 119.
70 Chrysostom (fl. AD 390) 8th Homily on John. '[H]ow is it that so many continue unenlightened? For not all have known the majesty of Christ.'
71 Gore, *The Incarnation of the Son of God*, p. 116.

Is Christ's Incarnation the Consummation?   47

72 Temple, *John*, p. 10.
73 Drawing on Isa. 29:13.
74 See, for example, Acts 17:29, and the prohibition on idolatry in, for example, Dt. 4:16, which presupposes that one cannot envisage God in any way one chooses.
75 The limitations of natural revelation as founding an adequate basis for fruitful relational knowledge and hence for theological judgements are explored at length in J. Calvin, *Institutes of the Christian Religion* (1559) (trans. F.L. Battles; Philadelphia: Westminster, 1960), Book I, esp. c. 2 & 5 and Turretin, *Institutes of Elenctic Theology* (1688-90) (trans. G.M. Giger; ed. J.T. Dennison; Phillipsburg: P & R., 1992), Topic I, Questions 3 and 4.
76 D. Moo, *The Epistle to the Romans* (Grand Rapids/Cambridge: Eerdmans, 1996), p. 106.
77 Ibid. In similar vein, C.K. Barrett, *A Commentary on the Epistle to the Romans* (London: Black, 1957, 1962), p. 35.
78 Ramsey, *From Gore to Temple*, p. 3.
79 This witness phraseology is also recurrent in *Lux Mundi*.
80 J. Calin, *The Acts of the Apostles 14–28* (trans. J.W. Fraser; eds. D.W.Torrance and T.F.Torrance (Edinburgh: Oliver & Boyd, 1966), p. 12.
81 So Liddell and Scott. Calvin, *Acts 14–28*, p. 110, takes it this way.
82 'To make the Athenians ashamed', Calvin, *Acts 14–28*, p. 120.
83 J. Stott's apt comment in *The Message of Acts* (Leicester: Inter-Varsity Press, 1990), p. 286.
84 He also quotes Menander in 1 Cor 15:33 and Epimenides in Titus 1:12.
85 Notably Gen 1:26ff., Ps. 8 and, for the point about religious buildings, 1 Kgs 8:22–61, notably verse 27.
86 Fl. third century BC, from Cilicia.
87 F. Copleston, *History of Philosophy* (rev. ed.; London: Burns, Oats, Washbourne, 1947), vol. 1, p. 388.
88 See Cleanthes, *Hymn to Zeus*.
89 'Viable' here does not mean complete. Nor does it deny that any stable theory of knowledge ultimately requires, as Cornelius Van Til contended, a Christian doctrine of God as a presupposition.
90 Stone, 'Theology and Criticism', pp. 214, 217ff.
91 Carson, *John*, p. 124.
92 E.g. Ezra 9:3; Ps. 13:3; in the LXX apocrypha Sirach 34:20. Cf. Ps. 49:19.

[93] Note the patterns of ordering in Gen. 1.
[94] Council of Carthage 418, Council of Ephesus 431.
[95] Illingworth also refers in *Lux Mundi* to Irenaeus and Justin at pp. 135 and 147 respectively.
[96] Fl. AD 180.
[97] For Irenaeus' concept of recapitulation see *Against Heresies* III.21.10, 23.1; V.19.1, 21.1.
[98] Ca. 185 – ca. 253.
[99] See, for example, *De Principiis* 1.2.10.
[100] J.N.D. Kelly, *Early Christian Doctrines* (5th ed. rev.; London: Black, 1977), p. 128.
[101] *De Principiis* 2.8.3. and 2.9.2.
[102] *De Principiis* 3.5.5.
[103] *De Principiis* 2.6.3-6 esp. 6.
[104] *De Principiis* 3.5.6.
[105] Fl. AD 150.
[106] *First Apology*, 46. Illingworth, *Lux Mundi*, p. 147, uses the same passage.
[107] E.g. *First Apology*, 54.
[108] E.g., see Tertullian, *De Idolalatria*, or Athanasius, *Contra Gentes*.
[109] The distinction between Hellenistic philosophy and religion is perhaps too clear-cut for objective accuracy but does follow contours in Justin's own thinking.
[110] *First Apology*, 23.
[111] *First Apology*, 59, 60.
[112] *Second Apology*, 13.
[113] *Dialogue*, 6 & 7.
[114] See Avis, *Gore*, p. 20.
[115] *De Incarnatione* 1.
[116] *De Incarnatione* 13.
[117] *Contra Gentes* 2ff.
[118] Avis, *Gore*, p. 20.
[119] Carpenter, *Gore*, p. 85.
[120] Ramsey, *From Gore to Temple*, pp. 9–10.
[121] Contra Smith, 'Liberal Catholicism', and Carpenter, *Gore*, but agreeing with Nichols, *The Panther* pp. 134–5, and L. Smedes, *The Incarnation: Trends in Modern Anglican Thought* (Kampen: Kok, 1953).
[122] *The Open Society and its Enemies* (4th ed.; London & New York: Routledge & Kegan Paul, 1962), vol. II, p. 78.

123 Popper, *The Open Society*, vol. I, p. 8.
124 The question arises whether orthodox Christian eschatology is historicist. It is important to note that since the fulfilment of God's kingdom is achieved by his external action, not simply from within by the historical process, Christian eschatology does not reward current success with legitimacy, which is central to Popper's critique.
125 Popper, *The Open Society*, vol. II, p. 66.
126 Sophocles, *Philoctetes* (trans. E.F. Watling; Harmondsworth: Penguin, 1953).
127 Calvin, *Institutes of the Christian Religion* IV.8.
128 Temple, *Christus Veritas*.
129 Popper, *Open Society*, vol. II, p. 68.
130 Smith, 'Liberal Catholicism', p. 178.
131 Moore, 'The Christian Doctrine of God', pp. 41–81.
132 Ibid., p. 42.
133 See the accounts of Sextus Empiricus (*circa* AD 200) in *Outlines of Pyrrhonism*.
134 E.g. the work of P. Berger.
135 E.g. the works of K. Marx and F. Nietzsche, extended by M. Foucault.
136 This can include the challenges to interpretation that can arise from contemporary sciences.
137 E.g. *Summa Theologiae*, 1a.1.8.
138 Moore, *Lux Mundi*, p. 49.
139 Ibid.
140 Ibid.
141 Gore, *Reconstruction*, p. vi.
142 Ibid.
143 W.H. Griffith Thomas, 'Bishop Gore's Open Letter', *Churchman* 28 (1914), pp. 487–500 (at p. 500).
144 Stone, 'Theology and Criticism', p. 229.

2. The Son Incarnate in a Hostile World

Michael Ovey

> The cross is proof positive that given half a chance man will murder his maker.[1]

Introduction
'God is dead. God remains dead. And we have killed him.'[2] This comment of Nietzsche's 'madman' is no doubt designed to work on many levels. Part of its subversive force comes from the way it parodies such a distinctive feature of the Christian faith: the Son of God died and was murdered by the humans he had created. That murder to which the incarnation led seems very revealing, for it suggests that the incarnation was an entry into a hostile world.

The previous chapter examined the view that in the incarnation Christ is consummation of the cosmic process, and found it wanting. This chapter aims to examine biblically the theme that the incarnation occurs in a hostile world and to consider what this reveals. That revelation is both of God, who becomes incarnate under these conditions, and also of humanity, which rejects him. The bulk of the discussion is on this second area of revelation. This involves interacting with a second current incarnational theology, the view that in the incarnation Christ essentially reveals himself as one who is co-victim, especially with the oppressed.

The previous chapter posed the question, What kind of incarnation does one accept? It related that question to the kind of links there are between the incarnation and the passion. It is time to return to this issue in more detail. Several basic possibilities present themselves as to what those links might be:

1. Jesus' death is simply disconnected with the incarnation. The incarnation does not intrinsically entail the crucifixion. The incarnation is independent of the passion. Such is the *Lux Mundi* position described in the last chapter and rejected. This view might be entertained because Jesus was, so to speak, on an *incognito* visit and this got out of hand, as people sincerely trying to protect God's honour made an honest mistake.

2. Jesus dies a co-victim death.
   This thesis is associated with the ideas of Jürgen Moltmann, Jon Sobrino and others. On this view, the incarnation is intrinsically connected to the cross. The connection, however, is that the Son lived in a world which is unjust to so many of its citizens. As a citizen of this world, his was an essentially *common* death, the natural outcome for one living in his social location. Cowardly judges and malicious authorities are part of the experience of many. The thesis that Jesus died as co-victim is examined in this chapter and found wanting.

3. Jesus dies a unique death.
   The thesis adopted in this chapter is that Jesus was killed in some sense *knowingly*. People *at some level* knew who he uniquely was and did not like it. This means the incarnation intrinsically implies the cross, because it is who Jesus is that prompts the opposition and crucifixion.

To put the issue more bluntly, what value do we give to the claim that people did not recognise Jesus. True? Self-deceptive? Downright false? The reason this is so significant now is that it makes an enormous difference to whether one thinks the primary human problem is lack of information, or something more than that. This will hugely influence both how we evangelise and how we pastor.

To investigate this further we must look more closely at:

- the thesis that the link between incarnation and passion is one in which Jesus was essentially co-sufferer;

- the nature and extent of hostility to Jesus;
- the implications of the kind of hostility that Jesus met.

Christ as Co-sufferer

Description

A crucial contribution has been made here by Moltmann, whose work has proved highly influential, notably with writers from a liberation theology context in Latin America, such as Sobrino.[3] One must here recall the enormous concern felt by Latin American theologians over poverty and political oppression. Naturally, we may recognise the validity of the concern without feeling obliged to endorse uncritically the incarnational theology which they have occasioned.

In terms of influence, the major philosophical contribution, as with the *Lux Mundi* school, is 'Hegelian evolutionary theory',[4] but mediated through Marx's views of class conflict. However, again like *Lux Mundi*, biblical terminology is retained. A key image here is of 'Christ our Brother',[5] but particularly our brother in that he shows solidarity with us in our sufferings. It should be noted that, in contrast to the *Lux Mundi* approach, the incarnation is taken very closely indeed with the cross. The cross is the natural capstone of Jesus' experiences in the incarnation, in the same kind of way that the lives of many poor and oppressed end with some final act of violence by the authorities. One should say that the cross is the outcome of an incarnation in a world 'situ-ated in sin'.[6]

Jesus has a concrete experience of injustice *as one of* the poor and oppressed.[7] Hence Sobrino can comment:

> In Jesus' case, his universal love was translated into a decision to be 'with' the oppressed and to be 'against' the oppressors, precisely so that his love could be 'for' all of them.[8]

The stress is very much here on incarnational solidarity with the poor and oppressed. They are sinned against, so that events like crucifixion happen to them, perpetrated by the rich and powerful. Hence arises the view that Jesus' death is a typical death, an ordinary death, at least ordinary for one of the oppressed.

Many find this approach attractive and helpful. In the hands of Moltmann, it is a way of addressing what is for him perhaps the central theological question, that of theodicy, the justice of God. Thus, God cares about and repudiates the crimes of the twentieth and twenty-first centuries. The incarnation and passion show just that. Jesus is a member of a conquered race, in a backwater area, of lowly social status. In the passion he dies a death reserved for the refuse of the Roman Empire, and in Jewish tradition associated with being accursed.

This understanding of the incarnation and cross fits naturally with a particular understanding of the Exodus as a key salvation-historical event.[9] The importance of the Exodus in salvation-history is undeniable. The Exodus does, though, tend to be understood by these writers simply in terms of a political order that God overthrows. It is that, but it is also an event that stands for liberation from a different kind of bondage, namely bondage to sin, the world and the devil.

Discussion

Two points should be made at the start of any evaluation. First, obviously the theodicy question is a real one, vividly presented in Europe by the Holocaust, and visible daily in the poverty of some parts of Latin America. Secondly, equally obviously, there are important elements of truth in the idea that Jesus shares our condition and experience (cf. Heb. 2:17–18; 4:15–16).

However, it is much less clear that this theme of Jesus as co-victim provides the sole or major explanation of the incarnation. This chapter started with a brief reference to the idea that the incarnation was for Jesus an experience of hostility. It is certainly true that hostility features in the co-victim scheme. Nevertheless, that hostility has a particular character. For hostility here tends to be directed against Jesus as a member of the oppressed classes, with any hostility directed against God tending to be attenuated. The result, to put it a little crudely, is that the incarnation and passion disclose the problems between human beings, not between humanity and God, except in the derivative sense that God minds about the way humans treat each other.

Possible effects of this attenuation are worth pondering. For the oppressed it can perhaps cloud the issue of their own direct relationship with God and any hostility that lurks there, perhaps even creating the impression of innocence before God in this direct relationship. For the oppressor, too, his or her problem may become fundamentally shaped in terms of treatment of other humans, rather than attitude to God. God tends to appear as a third party trying to redress matters within human affairs. Donald Macleod captures some of the concerns here with typical lucidity: 'Moltmann's passion for theodicy betrays him into being obsessed with suffering almost to the exclusion of sin.'[10]

Of course, biblical ethics are indeed enormously concerned with the treatment of one human being by another, but it would be inadequate to say that biblical ethics and norms are concerned exclusively with this horizontal dimension. The obvious example is the very considerable amount of material in the Old Testament that deals with worship, both in terms of the prohibition on idolatry and also in the regulation of the cult. Furthermore, actions against fellow-humans are sometimes given a theocentric nuance.

Thus, oppression of the widow and the orphan is regarded as an insult to the Creator (Prov. 14:31), while in Psalm 51:4 David describes his sin as being against God. Uriah and Bathsheba are not mentioned in the body of the psalm, and Bathsheba only in the superscription. This is truly remarkable given that David has used power singularly oppressively against them, by his abusive exploitation of the woman Bathsheba and his murder (through others) of Uriah the Hittite. Yet this almost stereotypical account of the abuse of the weak and vulnerable by the powerful is construed as a direct crime against God. The Lord is depicted as the injured party too, not just an interested third party with sympathy.

Misgivings are compounded on this point by the way in which the conflict in Exodus is developed. Exodus 3:7ff. does feature God's compassion for his people, and liberation theology is right to note this. Yet the narrative progresses to make it clear that there is also a direct confrontation between Pharaoh and God. Pharaoh disclaims any obligation to obey God (Ex. 5:2), and this perspective helps frame the contest that follows.[11] This aspect is reinforced by the way Pharaoh appears as one set against the creational and covenant values of God. He is, for example, opposed to the multiplication of Israel.[12]

The outcome of this attenuation of the sense of hostility against God is unfortunate. With it readily comes a weakened view of the propitiatory nature of Christ's death, for God correspondingly has less to be propitiated about, so to speak. With it too can come a tendency to envisage social amelioration in terms of relief of poverty and redistribution of political power as solving humanity's most fundamental problems. On this basis, while the cross retains a deep symbolic value and a real role as exemplar, its salvific effect may be understated.

It is clear at this point how significant the question of hostility to Jesus and its nature has become. Earlier, the point was made that the incarnation reveals something both about God and humanity in relation to God. The co-victim thesis is a hypothesis about what the incarnation reveals of God, but involves certain positions about humanity. The two foci of revelation cannot be easily separated. Certainly, the question of hostility to Jesus and its nature requires further investigation, but while this investigation will bear directly on what the incarnation reveals of humanity, it will also carry implications for what is revealed of God.

Who was Hostile to Jesus?

Synoptic material
The traditional starting point for a 'high' incarnational Christology is John's Gospel, and it is certainly true that the Synoptic accounts do not start with a clear affirmation of an incarnation in the way that John does in the Prologue. Nevertheless, the Synoptic accounts do provide distinctive views of incarnational questions and the humanity and divinity of Jesus. In particular the Synoptics, like John, face us with questions about the reaction of human beings to the incarnate Son and questions about the purpose of his coming. Accordingly, consideration starts with Synoptic accounts of reactions to the incarnation and the coming of the Son, before moving to John.

The Parable of the Tenants in the Vineyard (Mk. 12:1–12)
We commence with a parable which deals very much, not simply with Jesus' identity, but with reaction to that. The parable comes at a telling point in Mark's narrative. The confession of Peter and,

later, the transfiguration has taken place. In addition, while Jesus has entered Jerusalem in triumph in Mark 11, he has repeatedly warned about the sufferings of the Messiah. This parable serves both to introduce and to interpret those sufferings; hence, the importance of the parable for present discussions. It can act in part as a test of the adequacy of an explanation of Jesus' passion in purely co-victim terms.

Next, it must be noted that the parable is told against the chief priests, scribes and elders (11:27; 12:1, 2), the people who would most firmly see themselves as friends of God.

Within the parable itself, the setting is of rightful but disputed dominion or ownership. The tenants do not criticise the owner for being oppressive in his dealings with the tenants, let alone simply for being a landlord. His sending of the servants to collect the rent points to his dominion. The tenants want that dominion ended and their actions are depicted as illegitimate.

Vitally, the son is killed here, not because the tenants make an honest mistake ('We know he claimed to be the son and heir but we thought it was not true'), nor because they see the peasant simply as a vulnerable peasant whom they can oppress as they perhaps do with others ('We wronged him, but not because he was the son and heir'). Instead, he is murdered precisely because they do recognise him (v. 7). They envisage his death as establishing their own dominion. They think, by removing him, to take his place.

Jesus stresses that these actions and attitudes will issue in judgement, for, as the quotation from Psalm 118:22f. indicates, God establishes what humans have rejected. Hooker comments that the quotation seems out of place,[13] but Cranfield is surely right to stress that the quotation functions as a warning.[14] The warning is not simply about divergence but about diametric opposition between the wishes of God and the standards of humans ('the builders'). The chief priests, scribes and Pharisees are being warned that in opposing Jesus they are in effect opposing God, the 'owner' in the parable, whose plans are so signally rejected by his tenants. There is no indication of any real congruity of values between tenants and landlord, despite the dependence of the former on the latter. In this way, the quotation from Psalm 118 fits poorly with the 'theomorphic' contention of *Lux Mundi* noted in the previous chapter, at any rate for the 'tenants'.[15]

The unit finishes with a slightly ironic touch: 'they looked for a way to arrest him' (v. 12, NIV). This underscores the truth of the parable: the religious leaders behave in the kind of way the tenants do, knowing that Jesus has depicted them as 'the tenants'.

The character of the coming of the son here requires comment. The coming of the vineyard owner's son corresponds to the coming of Jesus in the incarnation. However, the coming of the vineyard owner's son is not a coming that is the natural outcome of a process that the owner intends and desires. Rather, it is a result of breakdown. To this extent, the Parable of the Tenants in the Vineyard is manifestly inconsistent with the thesis examined at length in the previous chapter, that Christ comes as consummation of the natural process.

Nor is the coming of the son and his experiences any more compatible with the other model, described above in this chapter, that of Christ as co-victim. The son is not just murdered in precisely the same way and for the same reasons as the servants the owner previously sent. There is something unique about his treatment. He is treated the way he is, not just because he comes to vindicate his father's rights. That is something the servants also do. His treatment is the result of who he is, his father's heir. The murder is the outcome of his unique identity, not because he is simply another instance of the vulnerable classes.

One must further add that the reason why the unique identity of the son matters so much in the parable is that the tenants are directly hostile to the owner. It is not even that the son in himself excites hostility ('We like the owner, but we can't stand his son and heir'). The hostility is in the first instance against the owner and only derivatively against the son. That hostility is not born of the owner's insistence that the tenants treat each other or even their workers in a particular way. It is his dues as owner, symbolised by the produce he claims (v. 2), that is the bone of contention. The co-victim model does not adequately capture this direct hostility, nor its basis in the illegitimate urge to usurp ownership.

Uniqueness in the son's suffering in the Parable of the Tenants in the Vineyard?
However, the claim that the son is treated uniquely needs to be carefully nuanced. The son here is unique in some ways, but not others.

There is a commonality between the treatment of the son and the treatment of the servants (e.g. v. 5). The reference here, of course, is to the treatment of the prophets. In this way, the parable locates Jesus in the salvation-historical stream of *rejected messengers of God*. It is easy to overlook quite how strongly the Synoptic material in particular stresses that the prophets suffered rejection.[16] Allied to this is the treatment of John the Baptist, with whose fate Jesus is linked.

A related strand here is the suffering of the righteous at the hands of the wicked.[17] The wicked attack the righteous almost, it seems, because of that very righteousness, as is made explicit in the deuterocanonical Wisdom 2:12–20. The righteous man of Wisdom 2 is opposed and persecuted because he upholds the law of God and points out that the wicked's actions are sinful (v. 12). To that extent, the enmity of the wicked is in a God-centred framework. One may compare too Psalm 83:1–5, where the opposition to the people is presented ultimately as an attack on God, who has covenanted to protect the people of Israel: 'against you they make a covenant' (NRSV).

In these respects, then, as rejected prophet and as rejected righteous man targeted by the wicked, one could say Jesus is co-victim, but this is not entirely general. In terms of the text, where Jesus' sufferings are explained in terms of commonality, that commonality centres primarily on him in these categories, rather than his position as sharing in the fate of those oppressed by the world's economic and political systems.

This is a significant distinction. Both messenger of God and righteous man receive their definition by their orientation to God, the messenger of God as one who proclaims the word of God in its sovereign force and the righteous man as one who lives under the sovereignty of that word. Both are opposed by those who deny the sovereignty of that word in at least some respects. It is, one might say, the way messenger and righteous man represent God's claims that presents the problem. This means that something is lost when Jesus is depicted in co-victim terms simply as one who suffers with the oppressed. What is lost is the direct antipathy felt towards God.

Uniqueness in the Son's sufferings – the import of Psalms 2 and 110
We now turn from the Parable of the Tenants in the Vineyard to consider more generally the unique aspects of Jesus' experiences

in the incarnation. Psalms 2 and 110 are of considerable significance here. Psalm 2 is applied to Jesus right at the start of his public ministry in his baptism, where it is combined with Isaiah 42:1.[18] This tends to provide a context in which Jesus' life and ministry are to be viewed. Psalm 110 is, of course, frequently cited in the New Testament[19] and applied by Jesus to himself in the Synoptics.[20]

Both psalms speak of an opposition to God's chosen ruler, and this is a unique capacity. With respect first to Psalm 2, its application to Jesus at his baptism is rightly seen in terms of fulfilment of Old Testament promises of kingship. Yet the very basic point must be added that Psalm 2 envisages a kingship that is vigorously resisted and contested by the 'nations' (v. 1) and the kings of the earth (v. 2). It is certainly true that the opposition will be unsuccessful (v. 4), but the dominion of the Lord's anointed is opposed ('Let us burst their cords asunder …' v. 3). The application of Psalm 2 to Jesus at the baptism hints not just at kingship, but at opposed kingship. This theme is all the stronger given the combination with Isaiah 42:1, since, as Carson notes,[21] Jesus is linked to Isaiah's suffering Servant.

Again, in Psalm 110, the first three verses concern a kingship that is appointed by God (v. 1), clearly opposed,[22] but vindicated (notably v. 2). Given that Psalm 110 is so important for grasping the New Testament's interpretation of Christ, any account of Christ's work that does not deal with the hostility which the psalm so emphasises must be deemed defective.

However, the character of this opposition to God's king is not yet entirely clear. It is true that Psalm 2 has suggested a motivation in the wish to be free of God's rule (v. 3 and its reference to 'cords' and 'bonds' being burst asunder), but naturally one asks whether this is overt. It seems unattractive to argue that a religious Jew of Jesus' day would have openly approved the sentiments of Psalm 2:3. It is, then, to the character of the opposition to God's king that attention turns.

The character of opposition in the Synoptic Gospels
The actual opposition to Jesus is strikingly presented in terms of irrationality. Thus, in Mark 2:1–12 the paralytic's physical healing is intimately related to the declaration of his spiritual forgiveness.

The physical healing therefore provides strong authentication for the reality of the forgiveness and the authority to grant it. Yet, this rational inference appears in the long term to be refused. Again, the refusal to deal honestly with the question about John the Baptist in Mark 11:31–3 does not bode well for rational consideration of the claims of Jesus. Yet, most troubling of all is the way Jesus' exorcisms are attributed to his own unclean spirit,[23] providing a graphic depiction of good being categorised as evil.

Matthew's version of this is perhaps especially illuminating. Matthew contains the objection that Jesus' exorcisms are demonically inspired on two occasions, 9:34[24] and 12:24. The repetition tends to add emphasis and significance,[25] and the extended comment after Matthew 12:24 confirms this. What is perhaps striking about Jesus' response to the Pharisees in 12:25ff. is his analysis of their motives. He does not see their non-recognition as an honest mistake, nor the product of a cautious scholarly scepticism towards religious claims, nor even the product of an unfortunate, if understandable, 'hermeneutics of suspicion'. Instead, he analyses their words as being the products of evil hearts (12:34, 35). The Pharisees' abuse of Jesus 'revealed their true nature.'[26] The response says something about them. What is more, it is implied that they are themselves blasphemers (or running enormous risks of becoming so), even though their surface rhetoric presents them as defenders of God against evil.

Capel Anderson ably brings out this aspect of the characterisation of Jesus' enemies in Matthew.[27] Using the term 'Jewish leaders' as a blanket term she points out Matthew's repeated depiction of their 'evil nature' – 'a group of wicked hypocritical enemies of Jesus'.[28] Here, 'hypocrites' is a particularly important description.[29] By it a strong outward/inward distinction is asserted: outward righteousness and inward wickedness.[30]

However, two points should be made in respect of this hypocrisy. The first is that it is not just a hypocrisy of pretending to be moral when one is not. It is linked to pretending to be a friend of God who obeys him and defends his honour when one is not. This is clear from Jesus' application (Mt. 15:8, 9) of Isaiah's prophecy (Isa. 29:13) to those he describes as hypocrites (Mt. 15:7). The presenting issue of this inward distance and alienation from God is the treatment of his word. The inner reality of their actions is the abrogation of God's word (Mt. 15:6), corresponding to their inner hearts. Hypocrisy in this sense tends to acquire a particular nuance: outwardly a friend of God but inwardly disobedient and at enmity with God.

The second point is that in this inner character, enmity to God, the hypocrites are in continuity with those who persecuted and killed the prophets (Mt. 23:31ff.). Just as the incarnate Son is in continuity with the servants of God in the Old Testament, so are Jesus' contemporaries in continuity with those who despised God's servants and the words from God they pronounced.

For these reasons, opposition seems to cluster around the inner nature of 'the Jewish leaders'. It is their evil natures that generate opposition, even though this nature is covert, for the public presentation is to 'worship with their lips'. The unfortunate thing is that Jesus' actions and words consistently bring this particular kind of hypocrisy into the open.

The extent of opposition in the Synoptic accounts
But how widespread is this hypocrisy of pretending to be God's friend but inwardly standing opposed and disobedient? This is significant for two reasons. First, it bears on the question whether hostility to Jesus in the incarnation was a purely local phenomenon or a more typical reaction for humans in general. This is a peculiarly acute question for the present because it helps shape how one understands, say, professed indifference to Jesus. Secondly, if this particular kind of hypocrisy and opposition is indeed only local, then to what extent is Matthew (and other Gospel accounts) anti-Semitic?

These questions must be answered at a number of levels. One starts with the issue whether opposition is basically restricted to the latter parts of the Synoptics and the events of the passion. In fact, on reflection, the Synoptics are dominated by the spectre of opposition.

After all, Matthew's birth narrative features Herod's attempt at murder (Herod not being strongly marked as an 'orthodox Jew'), and this attempt is based not on the ordinariness of Jesus but is related specifically to his kingship. This is evident both in the repeated use of kingship vocabulary (Mt. 2:1, 2, 3, 4), and in the relevant quotation from Micah 5:2 which deals with the Messiah as ruling.

Mark 2:1–12 tells of the healing of the paralytic, one of the earliest miracles Mark records. Yet this healing raises the question of rejection, since it is so clearly tied to the identity of Jesus as one who can forgive sin. That identity is questioned. This possibility of rejection is tied to suspicions of blasphemy, the charge to which Caiaphas so joyously returns in Mark 14:64.

In Luke 2:34, at the presentation, Simeon prophesies about opposition to Jesus, instantiated only a chapter or so later in Luke 4:16–30 as Jesus' sermon culminates in his description of the prophet's typical fate, rejection (v. 24) and his own subsequent rejection (vv. 28f.). Here, though, Jesus' rejection is not simply in terms of being a prophet, but in terms of one who has come to fulfil the prophecies of Isaiah.

These things, happening so early in the Synoptic accounts, frankly cast something of a shadow over the life and ministry of Jesus. The astute reader of a Synoptic account has anxiety as Jesus heals on the Sabbath, cleanses the Temple and so forth. The Synoptic accounts of the incarnation are coloured from very early on with the theme of rejection and opposition.

Nor is it a satisfactory response to this to suggest that this is only in terms of the ministry of Jesus, not the incarnation in itself. First, the incidents with Herod and Simeon both raise the issue in Jesus' infancy, not when his ministry is under way. They prove, though, to be typical. Herod's opposition foreshadows the kingship motifs of the entry into Jerusalem (Mt. 21:5), the ironic acclamations of the Roman guard (Mt. 27:29) and the crucifixion under the equally ironic title 'This is Jesus, the king of the Jews' (Mt. 27:37).[31] Simeon's words, likewise, are words of prophecy which are fulfilled. Secondly, the Synoptic Gospels focus so largely on the ministry and the passion that an account of the incarnation that tends to isolate the theological meaning of the incarnation from these things itself starts to become 'unincarnational', in the sense of not dealing with the incarnation as it actually took place.

This is an important point to make. The incarnation is an event in space and time, and the historical contours need to be respected in understanding it. The historical contours that the Synoptics develop deal very largely with the ministry and passion and resurrection. As noted above, the Synoptics do not have extended discussion of the concept of an incarnation. They rather give an account of the events of the incarnation, or more accurately a selection of them. That selection ties the incarnation closely to the cross because the events surrounding the cross are told at such length, and because significant amounts of the material dealing with the ministry pave the way for the passion, notably in their depiction of opposition.[32] Any theology of the incarnation which tends to isolate it from Jesus' ministry and passion is defective because it risks being an account of the incarnation abstracted from history, an idealised version of the incarnation rather than a real one.

However, given that opposition themes are quite persistently present, we move to the question of the identity of that opposition. It may be thought that Jesus' opposition was really 'the scribes and the Pharisees'. In fact, the political breadth, so to speak, of opposition should not be understated. Herod's response has already been mentioned, but one finds other areas where opposition seems wider. Thus, the Pharisees go hand-in-glove with the Herodians in Mark 3:6, in a fine example of co-operation between religious and state authority, again notably early in the account. There is, of course, near the end of the accounts also the ecumenical achievement of the crucifixion as pagan Romans and Jewish priests at last find some common ground. This latter factor makes one wary of too ready an assumption of anti-Semitism: opposition is beyond ethnic Israel. Psalm 2:1–2 and Psalm 110:5–6 prepare us for this with their references to the nations and kings of the earth, phrases suggestive of the Gentiles.

This leads to yet another dimension of the question of opposition. Given that opposition is quite persistent, and across the 'political spectrum', what social depth does that opposition have? After all, the language of Psalm 2:2 and Psalm 110:5 is of kings and rulers, while Mark 12:1–12 is told against chief priests, scribes and elders. This inevitably poses the question whether the opposition comprises simply those in power, in particular in that time and place.

Some caution is required here. First, the disciples and the women at the tomb are not depicted simply as foes in the way that, say, 'the Pharisees' are. Nevertheless, the desertion of Jesus by his friends is clear, particularly in the case of Peter. Moreover, even Peter can be charged with reflecting Satan's values rather than God's.[33] Secondly, there is some generalising material. Luke 4:28 depicts a general reaction against Jesus' teaching in the synagogue at Nazareth,[34] while Matthew 27:25 depicts 'all the people' (*pas ho laos*) accepting responsibility for Jesus' murder. This verse needs enormous care. Carson rightly observes that the charge of anti-Semitism is misplaced here.[35] In particular one must ask whether the people of Jerusalem are being treated as representative of general human attitudes or as being different from general human attitudes. In fact, surrounding material points to similarity between Jews and Gentiles. The pattern of Matthew 27:27–44 strongly figures mockery and cruelty aimed at Jesus. Those involved include the soldiers of Pilate (27:27ff. – at least representing the Gentiles), as well as passers-by (27: 39f.), and the Jewish hierarchy (27:41ff.). This mockery, then, appears to go beyond racial divisions and is deeper than just the ruling classes.

Nevertheless, these seem perhaps slender indications. Accordingly, we must turn to John's Gospel to explore further the common nature of opposition to the incarnate Son.

Material from John's Gospel

The world and 'the Jews'
Perhaps the first thing that should strike us in reading John's Gospel in relation to this hostility against Jesus is the correlation between 1:10 and 1:11. We approach 1:10 having been informed of the dependence of 'the world' on the Word, for verses 1–4 show the Word is creator of all. 'The world' therefore has an inevitable relationship with the Word. Yet in 1:10 we find 'the world' not knowing the eternal Word through whom it came to be. 'Knowing' is a highly important concept in John, denoting not just an intellectual knowledge, but relational knowledge, and it is in such relational knowledge that eternal life is to be found (e.g. Jn. 17:3). 'World' too is a rich Johannine term, used in the Gospel to suggest humanity, created, yet, as the Gospel progresses, in an evil orientation and domination.[36] The statement of 1:10 is therefore devastating. It is describing a created humanity which does not know or recognise its creator, is therefore alienated from its

true identity as created by that creator, and estranged from the life that sustains it.

Yet, 1:11 is, if anything, still more troubling, for this says the same thing about the Word's own people, God's peculiar possession.[37] They act like 'the world'. Thus begins the Johannine tendency to see Jesus' treatment by 'the Jews' as exemplifying his treatment by 'the world'.

There is, therefore, a certain irony in the thought, still sometimes voiced, that John is an anti-Semitic Gospel, with the idea of a differentiation drawn by John between Jews and other people groups. The whole point of the Jews as a corporate character in the Gospel is that they act typically like the world, we humans generally, rather than being in some way different.[38] A.T. Lincoln makes the point neatly: '"the Jews" are the representatives of the unbelieving world.'[39] All this is perhaps most explicit in John 8:23, where the Jewish opponents of Jesus are given the character designation 'of this world'. In this Gospel to be 'of' something or someone is to denote one's character, one's tendency, even one's destiny.[40] This presentation of 'the Jews' as representing 'the world' perhaps reaches its apex when the chief priests (who are heavily identified with 'the Jews') claim that their only king is Caesar, that emblem of human power not submitted to God (19:15) – here, 'the Jews' side with 'the world'. In this way, one of the important features of John is his universalising tendency with respect to the treatment of the Jews. This means that 'the Jews' in John serve to illuminate 'the world'.

John is therefore not anti-Semitic in the sense of discriminating against the Jews by saying their negative treatment of Jesus is unique.

Treatment of Jesus by groups within the Gospel focuses in large part on his claim to be the Son. The sonship of Jesus has rightly been seen from the early history of the church as of the greatest significance in revealing God to us.[41] However, the narrative progresses to show the reality of 'world' and 'own people' rejecting the Son. The idea that people want Jesus dead on account of this sonship is a recurrent feature. This is set out in John 5:18. They wish to kill him because he claimed to be God's own Son. This dominating motif is brought forward finally in John 19:7 as the reason why Jesus should be killed: 'We have a law, and according to that law he ought to die because he has claimed to be the Son of God' (NRSV).

It is worth adding that it is once again Jesus' unique status that is in view in this indictment. He is not being treated like this simply because all people of his race and social class are mistreated by the authorities (although granted mistreatment might in fact be the norm).

However, the chief priests' statement reeks of irony. On one level, it is perfectly true, Leviticus 24:16 does indeed lay down a divine law about blasphemy. Yet there is another level of meaning. No doubt the chief priests should be subject to God's law, but is God's law in fact the only law at work in their lives and in the world? Here it is necessary to review how John treats not just Jesus, but how he depicts and analyses the world and the Jews.

Who is 'the world' / 'the Jews'?
Here we look in particular at the Tabernacles material of John 7–8. The material starts and ends with a hidden Jesus, hidden at the beginning in Galilee away from the Jews in 7:1 and hidden again in 8:59. In the intervening material, Jesus emerges as one who brings the water of life (7:28), as one who is the light of life (8:12) and as God's own Son, notably in that he knows God (8:55), teaches his word (7:16, 8:28, 45) and does his will (8:29). A consistent theme here is that Jesus is, in fact, a law-keeper.

However, in the course of John 7–8, the Jews emerge as the converse: they want to bring death, not life (7:1, 8:59), they do not know God (8:55), they do not do God's will (7:19, 52) and are opposed to the truth (8:45), because, ultimately, they are not sons of God. A theme here is that the Jews are law-breakers, exemplified in Jesus' charge in 7:19 that they break the law of Moses by wanting to kill him, and Nicodemus's implied charge in 7:51 that they break the law about due judicial procedure.

In this way, sonship is at the heart of the dispute between Jesus and the Jews in this material. Both claim to be sons of God. It is true that the claim of the Jews has an ethical (doing God's will) rather than ontological (relating to substance) import. They are good sons because they are good law-keepers is perhaps the way to put it. Yet, although Jesus' claim has an ontological dimension, it also has an ethical one. He is son not merely ontologically, but also ethically.⁴² Jesus' point is that his sonship includes the ethical dimension (hence the stress in John 7–8 on Jesus' keeping the Law and doing the will of his Father), whereas they are not sons even in the ethical sense.

Who is the world's 'father'?

Instead, their sonship has a different lineage. They are sons of the devil (8:44), whose characteristic is to bring death and lies. The nature of Jewish rejection, and thus 'the world's' rejection, is at last laid bare. Not ignorance, but nature, in that they and the rest of we humans are 'of' the devil. That 'ofness' is demonstrated by the fact that we want to obey him, not God. It is his 'Law' to lie and to kill.

This series of oppositions can be set out thus:

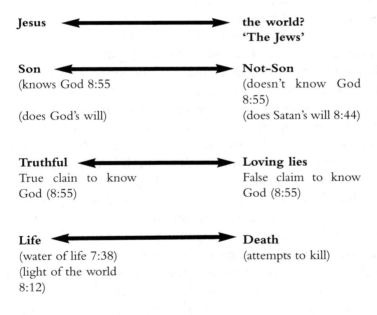

It is no surprise, then, to find the chief priests pointing to a law about killing someone who claims to be God's son and is. It is Satan's law that such a one be put to death, precisely because Jesus is telling the truth (8:45). This is a far cry from Jesus as the consummation of a positive natural process. John underlines how tragically natural the rejection was for humanity. Equally, it is the Son's unique identity that provokes the rejection, not his status simply as one of a particular class.

'Ignorance' texts?

However, is this quite enough? Are there not texts which imply some kind of ignorance? Several are at stake, Luke 23:34, Acts 3:17 and 1 Corinthians 2:7–8. The reason why this is such an important point in Anglo-Saxon culture is the influence of forensic ideas of responsibility. The maxim of English law is *actus non facit reum nisi mens sit rea* – the act does not make the person culpable unless the mind is also culpable. One becomes blameworthy for an action if one *intended* it. If one does an act in ignorance, so the theory goes, then one cannot fully intend it in this sense.[43] Given this part of our own cultural background, the question of ignorance is therefore highly significant.

It is convenient to take Luke 23:34 with Acts 3:17 since they are both Lukan texts. Leaving aside the question of Luke 23:34's authenticity,[44] the essential thought of the verse is also present in Acts 3:17. Both use ignorance language about the murder of Jesus.

However, in both cases it scarcely amounts to simple ignorance. Contextually, both come at a point where there has been ample attestation to Jesus' identity through word and deed. In fact, Peter has made just this point in his earlier speech in Acts 2:22. In terms of content, Luke 23:34 is a prayer for forgiveness, the remission of sins, while Acts 3:17 is followed almost immediately (v. 19) with a command to repent, which pre-supposes the commission of sin. Both texts therefore acknowledge the presence of sin in those who are described in terms of ignorance. The ignorance is culpable. That culpability is strongly affirmed in the Pentecost 'sermon' in Acts 2, not just in verse 22 already mentioned, but also in the murder terminology of 2:23, paralleled in 3:15. Acts 4:10 further points the finger at the rulers, elders and priests, who understand Peter's speeches as indicating their guilt (cf. 5:28).

These ignorance texts, then, need to be taken in this framework and point rather to thinking that cannot know because it is so warped, rather than an ignorance that would excuse in an English court of law on the grounds there was no *mens rea,* no guilty intention.

This assists with the third text, 1 Corinthians 2:7–8. The passage certainly deals with the lack of understanding of the rulers of this age. Yet this is in the context of a contrast established in 1 Corinthians 1 between the wisdom of the world and the wisdom of God. God's wisdom appears as folly, no doubt, to the world (1:21, 25) and the world's wisdom is folly to God (1:20). The world's wisdom appears as unable to come to know God (1:21a) and it is thus no surprise to find it cannot grasp the significance of the cross. It is ignorance to that extent.

Nevertheless, this ignorance that is the outcome of worldly wisdom is also negatively evaluated. God has so ordained these things about the inability of worldly wisdom because he wishes to remove boasting (1:29, 31), that characteristic and culpable attitude of human self-assertion in independence of God. In this way, the association of human wisdom, and the ignorance it perversely generates, is with pride and self-assertion.

In this way, these texts do not assert a simple lack of understanding that would suggest moral innocence. Rather, they reflect the culpable ignorance of a distorted and corrupted understanding, a self-deception along the lines of Romans 1:18ff., where Paul speaks of men and women suppressing the truth. The self-deception of Romans 1:18–32 has real 'noetic' effects. But notwithstanding this, responsibility remains, for God is wrathful about us as a race which suppresses the truth (see v. 18). With this in mind we must return to John and his diagnosis of the opposition to Jesus.

John's diagnosis of the opposition to Jesus
This section will argue that Jesus envisages the world as estranged from his Father, doing evil, but cloaking that knowledge from itself and in fact claiming to be God's friend, or 'son'. He understands his treatment by the world as flowing not from a sincere desire to serve God, but from a desire not to have its true nature exposed. Clearly such a synthesis requires substantiation, so we turn to a more detailed consideration of key Johannine passages.

1. John 3:19–21

> And this is the judgment, that the light has come into the world, and people loved darkness rather than light because their deeds

were evil. For all who do evil hate the light and do not come to the light, so that their deeds may not be exposed. But those who do what is true come to the light, so that it may be clearly seen that their deeds have been done in God.

Here one finds a parallel to the thought of John 1:10, but expanded and explained. The Light, the Son, comes, but is rejected. Instead, people prefer darkness, a perverse and destructive preference given the associations in this Gospel between darkness and death.[45] Still, the grounds for this preference are here explored: people's deeds are evil (Gk. *phaula*, v. 19). It is worth recalling at this point how strongly 'doing evil' is theocentrically defined in the Bible. To 'do evil' is not simply a case of breaching a moral code, but breaking the will of the living God and thereby offending him. The people love darkness because their lives are opposed to God. Opposed, that is to say, to the Father who sends Jesus the Son.

John 3:20 specifies this hatred a little more closely. It deals not just with an instinctive antipathy of darkness for light, but the motivation is the avoiding of exposure, avoiding being revealed for what one is. However, it needs to be stressed here that two things are at stake. One is the 'coming to the light', which in the framework of John refers to believing in Jesus. Not coming to the light (v. 20), but preferring darkness (v. 19), deals with rejection of Jesus. The second thing at stake is attitude to God, the Father who sends Jesus. It is this that is picked up in 'doing evil' (v. 19).

The order between these two aspects that John draws out here is important. The rejection of Jesus is grounded on the attitude the world has to his Father. Jesus is rejected because he reveals what that attitude to God truly is. This is an absolutely cardinal point in the analysis John provides here: *people do not wish to be seen for what they are, for they are enemies of God.*

This provides a slightly different perspective on opposition to Jesus. It is not just his claims about who he is, but what that means for who we are. Something similar is picked up in John 7:7, as Jesus tells his brothers about the world's hatred for him.

2. John 7:7

The world cannot hate you, but it hates me because I testify against it that its works are evil.

The Son Incarnate in a Hostile World 71

This statement comes towards the beginning of the Tabernacles material and serves to introduce a prominent theme of John 7–8, that Jesus speaks of his opponents' character. The world hates him, he says in this instance, because he testifies about its identity and character, that its deeds are evil. This point is anticipated in 3:19–20, where the Gospel speaks of the world's deeds being shown up by the Son for what they are. It is then expanded in John 7–8, as Jesus testifies that his interlocutors are law-breakers, do not know God and are children of Satan. These points are instantiated in their treatment of Jesus, condemning him without the due process the Law enjoins (7:51f.), lying about their relationship with God (8:41 as opposed to 8:44), and trying to kill Jesus (8:59). It is the exposure of this reality that Jesus points to as causing hatred. The world does not want to know, it seems, that it is anti-God. Jesus goes further in John 16:2–3.

3. John 16:2–3

> They will put you out of the synagogues. Indeed, an hour is coming when those who kill you will think that by doing so they are offering worship to God. And they will do this because they have not known the Father or me.

In 15:18–27 he has further explained the world's hatred. Here, though, he speaks of the hatred of the world for his followers. It hates his disciples because they have been taken 'out of' the world (15:20). The 'of' language once again deals with character and nature, so that here Jesus speaks of his followers as those who no longer, through Jesus' gracious choice of them (15:19), share this character. It hated him first, and does so because it does not 'know' the one who sent him (v. 21), and in hating him, shows that it hates the Father who sent him (15:23). As with 3:19–20 and 7:7, the attitude to God and the attitude to Jesus are closely entwined.

However, and this is perhaps the twist, the opposition to Jesus is carried out under the pretext of serving God (16:2). This is a profoundly destabilising comment. It means that an internal subjective conviction that one is serving God may be misleading. The sentiment 'I'm sure God would like this and I'm sure I'm treating him lovingly by doing this' is not in itself a guarantee that that is true. In a sense, this lesson is implicit from the instruction of the

Old Testament that God is not to be approached and worshipped as we think fit and appropriate, but as he has revealed he should be approached. Thus, in Numbers 16 Korah and his clan want to approach God, but not on the terms he has stipulated.

Rather, the guarantee that one is indeed serving God is accompanied by something more objective – whether or not Jesus is acknowledged and honoured as Son, for this is God's will about how he himself is to honoured (Jn. 5:23). Jesus goes on (16:3) to trace the mismatch between the claim to honour God and the reality back to a question of the 'knowledge of God'.[46] These actions are in fact done because they do not 'know' God (16:3), with all that not knowing God entails.

This means that opposition to Jesus and his followers is done in the name of doing good. People will claim to be honouring God, or perhaps honouring some ultimate ethical value. The point about 'son' here is that it speaks of one who is a 'friend of God', who does God's will. In that sense it speaks of one able to trust in their own righteousness. Hence even atheists can, paradoxically, mount the claim to be 'sons of God', for they too can make the claim to 'righteousness' before some ultimate value, whether that value be 'intellectual integrity'[47] or the need to stop exploitation by an unscrupulous priestly caste.[48] It is intriguing to note the *ethical* structure of much atheist discourse. Yet in fact, opposition to Jesus reflects a hatred of God, a refusal to do his will and a repudiation of goodness. But, it must be stressed, this is an *unacknowledged* hatred. It is hidden at the general surface level about which Jesus is speaking.

An unacknowledged hatred
These texts leave us seeing ourselves as having unacknowledged and carefully hidden springs of action. These relate to our race's antipathy to God and our consequent compulsion to eliminate his Son who brought just this antipathy into the open. This is, of course, enormously contentious. Two objections must be considered.

1. Is atheism an exception?

The obvious question arises whether atheism forms an exception to the points made above. Reformed and other theologians have been keen to analyse atheism not simply in terms of the arguments adduced in support of such a position (although that has been done), but also the motivations and aims behind the arguments. This should not be misunderstood or misrepresented as an attempt to avoid the arguments. Rather, a straightforward denial of God to a consistent theist tends by itself to eliminate the prospect of dialogue, a point made elegantly by Thomas Aquinas.[49] They have left nothing to discuss. To that extent, an analysis of the motivations of atheistic argument serves actually to further the cause of dialogue, because one can discuss at least the motivations for the position.

At this point, it must be remembered that the Bible itself does not discuss 'theoretical' atheism. It does, though, advert to a 'practical atheism', those who say 'there is no God'[50] and act accordingly. However, the biblical analysis focuses on the attractions of the attitude. Thus, Psalm 10:4 speaks of one in whose thoughts there is no room for God, but, from such a person's viewpoint, this is good, for it means there is no ultimate accountability for his actions (Ps. 10:11).[51] One attraction of atheism is that it removes constraints. Hence, Calvin deals with atheism in terms of those who 'deliberately befuddle themselves' so that ultimately 'they shut him [sc. God] up idle in heaven.'[52] In like manner, Turretin takes similar biblical material and poses the question, Who is an atheist? One who does not want God to be.[53] Both these theologians are relating the atheist question to Romans 1:18ff. and the issue of suppressed knowledge. Atheism is construed as one more way in which the knowledge of which Paul speaks is suppressed.

Such an analysis of atheism leaves it essentially similar to the unacknowledged hatred of which John speaks. It is not the issue that arguments in favour of atheism are believed. Rather, the question is what has rendered these arguments believable.

2. Is the thesis of unacknowledged hatred reductionistic?

It is naturally tempting to respond to the thesis that there is unacknowledged hatred of God by insisting that it is reductionistic, and possibly even uncharitable, insisting on a 'cynical' reading of human efforts.

At this point it is necessary to clarify in what ways 'reductionist' is a serious objection to a particular theory. We must distinguish between legitimate and illegitimate reduction. Legitimate reduction attempts to explain particular phenomena at more fundamental levels of explanation. For example, one 'reduces' depression in a particular person to an explanation not simply in terms of them as a person, but as a person whose moods are affected by a chemical imbalance. In that sense, it is a proper search for underlying causes. Illegitimate reduction can be characterised as a procedure that may purport to do that but actually causes particular features of the phenomena under investigation to disappear. Thus, some ethicists argue strongly against the idea that all my actions can be explained in terms of animal instincts for which I am not responsible. It is felt that such a 'reduction' eliminates something important about the nature of a 'person'.

Given this distinction, does the thesis of unacknowledged hatred appear reductionist in this illegitimate sense? Several considerations arise. First, the claims to sincerity by those opposed to God and Jesus are not eliminated. Rather, as John 16:2,3 indicate they are indeed accepted as phenomena but not endorsed at their own valuation. Secondly, there are excellent reasons for not accepting one's human valuations of one's own sincerity: there is an underlying conundrum in that those who claim to honour God end up murdering his Son. This alone prompts the thought that human claims to sincerity may not be transparent. Thirdly, a related point, the incarnate Son prompts us to this kind of reduction, for example in his Synoptic teaching on hypocrisy.

This last consideration also applies to the charges of cynicism and uncharity. If one accepts that Jesus' analysis is uncharitable and cynical, then it seems also necessary to endorse the thought that he is not the perfect revealer of God. Clearly, at this point, one has an account of the incarnation that is outside the bounds of orthodoxy. One might then have good reason to accept the sincerity of 'the world' but much less reason to envisage Jesus as the Son who speaks the truth God gives him. This is the problem that Jesus leaves us with in both Synoptic and Johannine material. If he is indeed what he says, the Incarnate Son, then one must take with the utmost seriousness his teaching on 'hypocrisy' (the Synoptic category) and the 'son of Satan' (the Johannine category).

Implications of the thesis of unacknowledged hatred
With these objections answered, we must return to some of the implications of the idea that humans naturally harbour an

unacknowledged hatred for God. This is enormously important for pastoral work. Take apologetics. The model of apologetics that envisages Christian and non-believers meeting intellectually on a neutral rational common ground seems misconceived. There may be common ground in that both are claiming to be acting and thinking rationally. There may well be common ground in discussing matters which are not directly related to the issues of 'knowing' God, but what Jesus teaches here is that the claim to act and think rationally masks a fundamental commitment not to think rationally where that would expose our antipathy to God.

Similar considerations arise with evangelism. This understanding rules out the traditional English appeal to Revelation 3:20, with its understanding that the response of faith is one that I make independently and autonomously, precluding God's grace preceding and enabling this, illuminating my heart by the work of his Holy Spirit (cf. 2 Cor. 4:6).

With regard to ethics, this thesis underlines how far from the truth is any simple application of the *Lux Mundi* principle that humans are theomorphic, such that human values are a 'counterpart and real expression' of the divine.[54] It is clear from this thesis that one cannot merely argue from 'our experience' to the moral rightness of a particular course of action. Thus, the method apparently adopted by Rowan Williams in his essay, 'The Body's Grace', is more than a little suspect. He writes of the possibilities of grace in one-off heterosexual extra-marital encounters:

> Yet the realities of our experience in looking for such possibilities suggest pretty clearly that an absolute declaration that every sexual partnership must conform to the pattern of commitment or else have the nature of sin and nothing else is unreal and silly. People do discover … a grace in encounters fraught with transitoriness and without much 'promising'.[55]

Aside from the problematic status of the term 'our experience',[56] Williams seems here committed to treating human experience and self-perception as self-interpreting when it is exactly this that is thrown into question by the incarnation and the attitudes it evokes.

Lastly, it is also clear that this thesis has implications for interfaith debate and sits but poorly with the thesis of a general human spiritual progress over the years.

Sonship and Idolatry

The preceding argument leads us to think about the incarnation in two ways. First, it is a revelation about sonship. It reveals that Jesus is Son of God and that the world is not son, but idolatrous. Secondly, it manifests God's sovereignty overcoming human sin.

Revelation

Revelation of Jesus the Son
To begin with, the incarnation reveals Jesus as the eternal Son, which is, of course, his consistent claim, explicitly or implicitly. His death is specifically linked to this in John 19:7 and opposition to him clusters around this concept from John 5:18 onwards. One can envisage this sonship as having two aspects. As 'son' he does his Father's will, for this is a characteristic of a 'good' or true son. Jesus stresses just this 'ethical' sonship (e.g. Jn. 4:34 and 6:38). In this way he is a true Israelite, indeed a true human being. He therefore reveals true humanity.

However, John 5:19ff. in particular carries further implications about Jesus' sonship, that he is the divine and eternal Son of God. This claim is of singular significance not just for the identity of Jesus, but also for the identity of God. For if Jesus is Son, then God must be Father, specifically, the Father-of-Jesus.

It is right to say that Jesus comes as a revealer in the incarnation, but he does not reveal simply himself. His revelation of himself brings with it his revelation of his father. John 8:26 stresses that Jesus speaks the words given him to say by the one who sent him; these words relate, *inter alia*, to his sonship. However, Jesus can also say in John 17:6 that he has made God's name known. This is at first glance a somewhat puzzling statement: did not Moses make God's name known?[57] The answer, of course, is that Jesus makes known Yahweh as Father, his Father.[58]

This personal identity of the First Person has rightly been emphasised in some recent trinitarian theology, because it shows that personal relationship is not alien to God, unlike the god of

Aristotle, nor is personal relationship epiphenomenal for God, thereby tending to devalue it, nor is personal relationship something for which God depends on the world, thereby making him dependent on creation. Instead, personal relationship is intrinsic to God and eternally present. This matters for our appreciation of our own relationship to him, in prayer for example, and our understanding of relations with others.

This revelation is, moreover, one that only the Father and Son can ultimately make, and the Father has chosen to do so through the Son's incarnation. Hence the importance of the incarnation and hence, too, Jesus' remarks in John 14:6f. If we are to think of God as Father, it can only be so through seeing Jesus as his Son. Jesus does not say, 'No-one comes to God except through me.' He does say, 'No-one comes to the *Father*.' It is for these reasons that defence of the incarnation has been so important: in defending Jesus as the incarnate Son, we uphold God as Father.[59]

Trinitarian theologians since the Nicene period (and before) have insisted on the importance of this point: that the eternal reality of God is known in his identity as the Father of the Son. It is trite, but important, to observe the difficulties in the way of knowing God. Aside from considerations of hostile bias on our parts as subjects who attempt to know, there is the question of the knowability of the object of knowledge. How can finite beings know an infinite God?[60] Is it not safer to reside in an apophatic theology that says simply 'God is not this' or 'God is not that'? Hilary of Poitiers recognised these points, but saw such 'negative' knowledge of God as essentially pre-Christian.[61] Christian knowledge of God goes beyond these negative propositions, because God has made himself known as Father through the revelation of his incarnate Son. This, for Hilary, is the saving knowledge of God, the distinctively Christian knowledge.[62]

The logic of this is that a theology that insists on the unknowability of God, or which says that all we have from the incarnation is a questioning of our human systems, undercuts the incarnation, for the incarnation is the revelation of the Son. It is not an act of humility, contrary, perhaps, to appearances, to insist on the hiddenness when that amounts to a refusal to let him bear witness to himself. Rather, as Hilary of Poitiers insists,[63] when we are baptised into the threefold name of Father, Son and Spirit we are baptised into the reality of God, not into an idolatrous conception, nor a mask behind which the real God lurks but lurks unknown. In this sense, the incarnation, wonderfully, is the eternal God making himself truly, but not exhaustively, known in space and time.

Revelation of the non-sonship of the world
However, the converse of this is that Jesus reveals something else: that the world is not a son. This means that God is not 'Father' to the world, not in this sense.[64] John 8 in particular is dedicated to drawing out the representative character of the world. 'The Jews' claim to be sons but are not; they purport to do God's will, but do not. Jesus, one might say, acts in a typically prophetic fashion, denouncing the sins of the world. His fate, naturally, is that of other prophets who do just that. The acid test in Jesus' view for being 'of' the world, and thus no son of God, is refusing to accept him as son of God. Jesus' life illustrates not just that the world is not son, but that it readily cloaks just this truth from itself. It has delusions about sonship.

Two points must be stressed here. First, the world has a double delusion about sonship. It thinks it is a 'son of God', but is not. It thinks it is not a 'son of Satan', but is. The world in that way has suppressed knowledge not merely of who God is (Rom. 1:18ff.), but also of who it is. Secondly, a fatal consequence of that delusion may also be the idea that it does not need the saving work of the Son. It is this attitude that is evinced in John 8:33. 'The Jews' there insist they do not need to be set free from slavery since they have never been slaves.

As it happens some of the essayists in *Lux Mundi* cloud just this issue. H.S. Holland[65] justifiably stresses the relationship of humans as created by God, and uses the terms of sonship to describe this creative relationship.[66] Disastrously, however, he envisages that faith is essential sonship emerging into consciousness of this fact,[67] so that he can write, 'Faith is the discovery of an inherent sonship.'[68]

It must be stressed what a difference this makes to doctrines of salvation. On Holland's view, what is needed is a realisation of what one is, of one's current relationships, a pattern oddly reminiscent of some strands of Gnosticism. What this obscures is the New Testament idea of adoption. Adoption implies a change of status from being not-son, to being son. What has also been omitted is precisely the other sonship that Jesus is at such pains to teach and to which his experiences in the incarnation testify, that the world is a 'son of Satan' (paraphrasing Jn. 8:44). The omission is, though, serious. It is all too easy to move from the proposition that God is father *qua* creator to the idea that all is well fundamentally with human relations with God: the relationship is fundamentally intact. It is no surprise, then, to find A. Moore writing in *Lux Mundi*[69] that the incarnation reveals God as Father, but the fatherhood is 'the One Father of humanity'.[70] This is exactly the proposition the incarnation denies.

Idolatry and sonship
The consequences of the error made in *Lux Mundi* and similar writings are far-reaching. Calvin stresses that the knowledge of ourselves and of God is 'joined by many bonds'[71] such that the one affects the other. To postulate something about ourselves can affect our conception of God. Anthropology and theology are linked. However, what 'the world' naturally postulates of God is that he is its father. In doing so the world attributes something to God, a relationship in which he exists and is shaped, so to speak, and the world tends to postulate an affinity between it and God. God resembles it.

It is just this affinity that Gore draws on as he speaks of humanity and its values as a 'counterpart and real expression' of the divine.[72] It should be added that there is indeed a biblical principle associated with this, the principle of 'like father, like son' which is such a feature in John 5 and 8. The risk, then, of attributing sonship to the world is that this dubious anthropology breeds an idolatrous theology, one in which God is indeed conformed to the imagination of humans, contrary to Acts 17:29.

The dangers facing 'the world' at this point are very great. It has been stressed that the world, while in fact being a 'son of Satan', tends to see itself as 'son' towards God, so that it imagines its own values are indeed naturally those of God. It will therefore clothe with divine status not the will of its supposed father, God, but the will of its real father, Satan.

The incarnation, however, exposes just this. It reveals not our sonship of God, but our lack of it. The Son's assumption of humanity does not make us automatically children of God. The treatment of Jesus by the world shows that that certainly has not happened, for if it had, then the world would love Jesus. This is Jesus' own reasoning in John 8:42. The lack of love displays that the world is no son of God even after Jesus has taken flesh, although the world continues to be creationally dependent on God. This means, of course, that the incarnation is not in itself a salvific event. It does disclose the need for salvation. The incarnation implies the cross and reveals the need for it.

The true Son, Jesus Christ, breeds a true theology. Again, this is a point insisted upon by Nicene trinitarian theology, that in seeing the Son we see the Father.[73] This again emerges from the Johannine theme of like father, like son. This question of what kind of sonship is revealed in the incarnation depends strongly on the notion that a 'son' does his father's will. This naturally leads on to another area, that of sovereignty.

Sovereignty

The incarnation can be characterised as a sovereign act. As divine Son of God, he vindicates in his incarnation God's rule in this world in all kinds of ways: over nature, over 'super-nature' with the exorcisms, over sin and death, over David as his greater son, over the temple he cleansed, but notably over humanity. He does come as king, and enters his royal city in that capacity. Athanasius captures this sovereign aspect as he speaks of the incarnation in terms of a king taking up residence.[74]

This divine kingship is, of course, rejected, forming a continuity with the rejection of God's rule in Eden and the rejection of God as king by Israel in 1 Samuel 8:7. In John 19:15 the priests say they have no king but Caesar, when, of course, one of the Passover hymns includes the phrase 'We have no king but thee.'

The incarnation is a sovereign act in another way, too. Jesus' life is what human life should be like, lived obediently under God. He succeeds where Adam has failed. In Irenaeus's terms he recapitulates creation by supplying the defects of Adam. In this sense, he shows himself very much to be not 'of' this world (Jn. 8:23), and we know from John 15:19 that to be 'not of this world' is to elicit this world's hatred. Here Jesus is in continuity with the persecuted prophets and the righteous of the Old Testament who suffer for their obedience to God. He is also in continuity with his disciples and later Christians who suffer not just for their class or race or gender (although that is no doubt true), but for their confession.

Seeing Jesus' life as life under the sovereignty of God leads to a final point. The Father's will for his life is expressed in part in the Old Testament and a vital thrust here is that the Old Testament predicts the suffering and rejection of the Messiah (Lk. 24:26f., 45–7). Jesus understands himself this way, applying Psalm 69:4 to himself, that he is hated without a cause, without a legitimate rational cause that is to say. The same Psalm speaks (v. 9) of zeal for God's house consuming the psalmist, again applied to Jesus (Jn. 2:17). Jesus' incarnate life is nothing if not zealous for God and such zeal in a world like ours is calculated to lead to rejection. In that sense, incarnation and passion are linked, indissolubly. Incarnation and cross go together, a cross where the true Son deals with the penalties merited by false sons by bearing them himself. So, the incarnation shows a sovereign God who deals with his people's sin and who has indeed come to serve, and not to be served (Mk. 10:45).

Conclusions

This survey of some of the material on the incarnation has noted the biblical stress on the world's opposition to the incarnate Son and seen it rooted in the world's very pretensions to sonship while being covertly hostile to God. Both the Christ as consummation and Christ as co-victim theses fail to capture this, thereby, unfortunately perpetuating the cloak cast over the world's true motivations, resisting God's sovereignty. This is especially unfortunate with the Christ as consummation thesis since it tends to elevate human authority in precisely those areas where it is most suspect, all under the rubric of honouring God – a procedure unnervingly reminiscent of Jesus' depiction of the world in John 16:2.

More generally, this description of an opposed incarnation highlights Jesus as hero. Inveterate and unmerited hostility, deserted by friends, often misunderstood by them, he emerges at times as an isolated and desolate figure, as predicted by Isaiah 53, most visibly so on the cross, but also persistently throughout his ministry. With this comes a deeper appreciation of his obedience to his Father and his love for his undeserving people.

Furthermore, it was noted above that part of the attraction of the Christ as co-victim thesis was its pastoral import. It gives us a God who cares for us and identifies with us in the grief of our existence. Is this lost in the account of the incarnation that sees it in the context of covert human hostility to God? Emphatically not, because the incarnate Son shares the burdens of our existence, and becomes incarnate knowing not merely human victimhood, but also undeserved human hostility to God. This latter point underscores his grace and generosity. It certainly does not diminish it. The conclusion then is that presenting Christ as co-victim is not a magnification of the incarnation, but a diminution.

We find too this view of the incarnation affects the contours of our salvation. Nietzsche continued his discussion of the murder of God thus:

> How shall we comfort ourselves, the murderers of all murderers? What was holiest and mightiest of all that the world has yet owned has bled to death under our knives,—who will wipe this blood off us? What water is there for us to clean ourselves? What festivals of atonement, what sacred games shall we have to invent?[75]

Again here we see the link between incarnation and cross. For with such a world doing such deeds, it cannot cleanse itself but salvation must indeed be by grace alone, and must be a salvation which deals with objective guilt before and against God, not just a sense of alienation from and oppression between humans, true though those categories may also be.

In terms of our own theology, the concept of the incarnation manifesting the world's hostility to God undercuts accommodationism, in the sense of allowing natural theology or thought an equal role with Scripture. The world's hostility to the incarnation reveals our profound need to sit under the Word of God, not alongside it, let alone over it. That, naturally, should be reflected in our own internal deliberations within our churches and denominations, our relations with other faiths and secular faiths, our evangelism and apologetics.

Strikingly, Jesus makes us see opposition in the light of opposition to him. This challenges – am I opposed because I mirror Jesus or because I am obnoxious? This warns, implicitly – if the world loves me and endorses me, is it because I do not mirror Jesus? This reassures – if the world opposed the incarnate Son, it will oppose his servants. But God has foreseen this, and his Son tells us, as Nietzsche failed to grasp, that he has already overcome the world (Jn. 16:33).

Notes

1. R.C. Lucas, in an unpublished sermon.
2. F. Nietzsche, *The Gay Science* (1882) Book 3.125. A recent edition is edited by B. Williams (trans. J. Nauckhoff and A. Del Caro; Cambridge: CUP, 2001).
3. In particular, J. Sobrino *Christology at the Crossroads* (London: SCM, 1978). He stresses the local nature of the theology to the extent that one is doubtful whether he would claim that his ideas are straightforwardly applicable in a West European context.
4. D.F. Wells, *The Search for Salvation* (Leicester: Inter-Varsity Press, 1978), p. 134.
5. Sobrino, *Crossroads*, p. 106, commenting on the New Testament term 'first-born'.
6. Ibid., p. 202.
7. Ibid., p. 124.
8. Ibid., p. 125.
9. Cf. G. Gutiérrez, *A Theology of Liberation: History, Politics and Salvation* (rev. ed. London: SCM, 2001 [1973]) and R. Alves, *A Theology of Human Hope* (Indiana: Abbey Press, 1969). Note the helpful analysis of liberation theological treatments of the Exodus in Wells, *Search*, pp. 134–5.
10. D. Macleod, *Jesus Christ is Lord: Christology Yesterday and Today* (Fearn: Mentor, 2000), p. 151.
11. Note, for instance the motif that Pharaoh shall 'know' about God (Ex. 7:3, 17) and Pharaoh's confession of sin against God (Ex. 10:16).
12. Ex. 1:10, 16, 22. Contrast Gen. 1:28; 12:2.
13. M. Hooker, *The Gospel According to St. Mark* (London: Black, 1991), pp. 276f.
14. C.E.B. Cranfield, *The Gospel according to St. Mark* (rev. ed.; Cambridge: CUP, 1977), p. 369.
15. If the theomorphic contention was sound with respect to the tenants they would honour and respect the son, for the father clearly values the son and the theomorphic contention requires they share his values.

16. Mt. 5:12, 23:29–36; Lk. 11:45–52. Cf. Acts 7:52.
17. Pss. 10:8; 11:2; 37:12, 14, 32; 52:1; 64:4; 94:4–5.
18. Mt. 3:17, Mk. 1:11 and Lk. 3:22.
19. In fact, one of the most frequently cited texts.
20. Mk. 12:36; Mt. 22:44 and Lk. 20:42f.
21. D.A. Carson, 'Matthew', in *The Expositor's Bible Commentary*, vol. 8 (Grand Rapids: Zondervan, 1984), p. 109.
22. Verses 1 and 2 speak of enemies, verse 3 mentions troops and battle. There is a war against God's king.
23. Mt. 9:34; 12:24; Mk. 3:22–30; Lk. 11:14–22. Cf. also Jn. 8:48, although the circumstances are different.
24. Mt. 9:34 is not universally present in the manuscript evidence, but Carson 'Matthew', p. 234, and R.H. Mounce, *Matthew* (Peabody, MA: Hendrickson, 1991), p. 89, both note that Mt. 10:25 tends to presuppose it and that the absence relates to one manuscript tradition.
25. For this role for repetition see J. Capel Anderson, *Matthew's Narrative Web: over, and over, and over again* (JSNTSS 91; Sheffield: Sheffield Academic Press, 1994).
26. R.T. France, *The Gospel According to Matthew* (Leicester: Inter-Varsity Press), p. 210. Cf. Carson, 'Matthew', p. 293.
27. Capel Anderson, *Narrative Web*, pp. 98ff.
28. Ibid., p. 98.
29. Frequently repeated (6:2, 5, 16; 15:7; 22:18; 23:13, 15, 23, 25, 27, 29; 24:51), with the general words of the Sermon on the Mount (ch. 6) gradually exemplified in the particular cases later in the Gospel.
30. Capel Anderson, *Narrative Web*, p. 104. Carson, 'Matthew', p. 349, speaks of a 'show'.
31. Carson, 'Matthew', pp. 573, 576, for the ironies here.
32. The birth narratives do not form an exception given the ominous notes of opposition. The Gospel of John does have the 'cosmic' perspective of the Prologue, but this too features opposition and the balance of the Gospel is again orientated towards the week preceding and including the crucifixion.
33. Mk. 8:33; Mt. 16:23.
34. 'All' (Gk. *pantes*) in the synagogue.
35. Carson, 'Matthew', p. 571, points out that Matthew is well aware that the first disciples were Jews and that this is not to be applied to later church-synagogue relations.

36 See, for example, R. Brown, *The Gospel According to John*, vol. 1 (London: Geoffrey Chapman, 1971), p. 509.
37 Cf. Ex. 19:5.
38 This is not to deny that they should be different.
39 A.T. Lincoln, *Truth on Trial: The Lawsuit Motif in the Fourth Gospel* (Peabody, MA: Hendrickson, 2000), p. 19.
40 See L. Keck, 'Derivation as Destiny: "Of-ness" in Johannine Christology, Anthropology, and Soteriology', in R.A. Culpepper and C. Clifton Black (eds.), *Exploring the Gospel of John* (Louisville: Westminster John Knox, 1996), pp. 274–88.
41 In the pre-Nicene period, Tertullian in *Contra Praxean*, Hippolytus in *Contra Noetum*. In the Nicene period Athanasius in *Contra Arianos* and Hilary of Poitiers in *De Trinitate*. All see Jesus' sonship as establishing God's eternal character as Father.
42 This is a crucial part of John's presentation of the trinitarian relations of Father and Son: the Son does the Father's will and is no independent 'rival'. See especially 5:19–30. If he were 'independent', so as to constitute a 'rival', this would imperil biblical monotheism.
43 There are in fact various qualifications that this would need to give a complete account of, say, English homicide law. There is, for example, a concept of culpable negligence.
44 It is not universally present in the textual evidence.
45 E.g. 8:12.
46 The lack of knowledge of God has been brought forward in John 7–8 as one contrast between 'the Jews'/'the world' on the one hand and Jesus on the other. See 7:28f. (where this elicits attempted violence, ironically verifying Jesus' comments) and 8:55.
47 E.g. David Hume.
48 E.g. Mikhail Bakunin or Emma Goldman.
49 *Summa Theologiae*, 1a.1.8.
50 Pss. 14:1, 53:1.
51 Cf. Ps. 36:1.
52 Calvin, *Institutes*, I. 4.2.
53 Turretin, *Institutes of Elenctic Theology* (1688–90) (trans. G.M. Giger; ed. J.T. Dennison; Phillipsburg: Presbyterian & Reformed, 1992), Topic 3 Q. II.ix. He is adapting Owen.
54 C. Gore, *The Incarnation of the Son of God* (Bampton Lectures; 2nd ed.; London: John Murray, 1892), p. 116.

55 R. Williams, 'The Body's Grace' (London: LGCM, 1989), p. 7. Delivered in 1989 as the Michael Harding Lecture for the Lesbian and Gay Christian Movement, but confirmed by Williams 2002 as still representing his position.
56 Williams does not advert to the methodological problem created by the fact that many do not share his experience, but might even draw the contrary conclusion from their experience. At this point one wonders whether the phrase is anything more than a rhetorical cloak for 'Me and my friends'.
57 Ex. 3:13ff.
58 Space precludes dealing with the proposition that we must now revise the 'Father-Son' terminology because of alleged patriarchalism. Suffice it to say that these are biblical terms and are embedded in biblical themes of fatherhood and sonship. For a fuller discussion, see D. Bolonick, 'Revelation and Metaphors: the Significance of the Trinitarian Names, Father, Son and Holy Spirit', *Union Seminary Quarterly*, 1984, pp. 31–42.
59 For this reason the Nicene theologians saw the Arian heresy as an attack, not simply on the Son, but on God.
60 Posed by Hilary of Poitiers (fl AD 360) *De Trinitate* I.6.
61 Although confirmed by Ex. 3:14, which he construed as dealing with God as uncreated, self-existent being.
62 Hilary, *De Trinitate* I.10.
63 Hilary, *De Trinitate* II.1ff.
64 The next section deals with the point that God could be called 'Father' in his capacity as creator.
65 In the essay on 'Faith', in *Lux Mundi*, pp. 1–40.
66 E.g. p. 9.
67 H.S. Holland, 'Faith', in *Lux Mundi*, p. 10.
68 Ibid., p. 11.
69 A. Moore, 'The Christian Doctrine of God', in *Lux Mundi*, pp. 41–81.
70 Ibid., p. 55.
71 Calvin, *Institutes* I.1.1.
72 C. Gore, *The Incarnation of the Son of God*, p. 116.
73 Jn. 14:9. The references to the revelation of the Father by the Son based on this verse are legion in the defenders of the Nicene Creed (and indeed before: see Tertullian, *Against Praxeas*).
74 *De Incarnatione* 9.
75 Nietzsche, *The Gay Science*, Book 3.125.

3. The Incarnation and Christian Living

David Peterson

> By his work he created a new dimension and channel for the fusion of obedience, confidence, hope and fidelity, because he pioneered this road.[1]

Introduction: Sharing our Humanity

Apart from John's Gospel, Hebrews may be the next most obvious place to look for incarnational theology in the New Testament. This 'word of exhortation' (13:22) begins with a wonderful affirmation of the pre-existence of the Son of God, which is the necessary framework for any expression of incarnation. In 1:2–3, the Son is described as the one through whom God created the world. Moreover, he is 'the radiance of the glory of God and the exact imprint of his nature', who 'upholds the universe by the word of his power'. The writer then applies a number of Old Testament texts to Christ (1:6–12), which proclaim him as the object of angelic worship, the one whose throne endures for ever, who is involved in laying the foundations of the earth and will bring it to an end in his own good time. This glorious Son is then described as having been made 'for a little while lower than the angels' (1:9), as the writer interprets Psalm 8 with reference to Christ. Perhaps the strongest statement of incarnation paralleling John 1:14 is to be found in Hebrews 2:14–15:

> since therefore the children share in flesh and blood, he himself likewise partook of the same things that through death he might destroy the one who has the power of death, that is the devil, and deliver all those who through fear of death were subject to lifelong slavery.

Doubts about the genuineness of incarnational teaching in Hebrews

Acknowledging the presence of this pre-existence theology in Hebrews, however, some scholars have also drawn attention to what they call adoptionist terminology. For example, having made purification for sins and sat down at the right hand of the majesty on high he has '*become* (Gk. *genomenos*) as much superior to angels as the name he has inherited is more excellent than theirs' (1:3–4). Again, in 2:9, he has been crowned with glory and honour '*because of* (Gk. *dia to*) the suffering of death'. In 5:5–6 he has been *made* (Gk. *genēthēnai*) high priest and in 5:9 has *become* (Gk. *egeneto*) 'the source of eternal salvation' as a result of his learning obedience through what he suffered and 'being made perfect'.

Adoptionism and incarnationism are usually held to be opposite extremes in Christology. However, J.A.T. Robinson argued that Hebrews holds them together without apparently any sense of discomfort or discrepancy. The Son of God is not a heavenly figure coming in from the outside, but rather 'Jesus was never anything but like his brothers', and 'it is only by maintaining his identification with them to the limit that, as their leader or foreman (2:10), he can be made perfect and thus enable them, in all their numbers, to become partners (3:14) in his relation of sonship.'[2] Jesus was a man who received 'a call to the unique role of living as God's son or personal representative'.[3]

Robinson's approach is engaging but exegetically weak. His arguments can be answered by a careful look at the texts that he highlights.[4] For example, we should note the contrasting tenses in 2:14. The children 'share' (stative use of the perfect tense, *kekoinōnēken*) blood and flesh, but the Son 'partook' of the same things (aorist tense, *meteschen*), 'that through death he might destroy the one who has the power of death'. At a particular point in time, the transcendent and pre-existent Son described in 1:1–4 'accepted the mode of existence common to all humanity',[5] so that he could achieve for us what no other human being could achieve. As a result, 'the children' come to 'share in a heavenly calling' (3:1) and to 'share in Christ' (3:14).[6] If the author of Hebrews and the readers presumed it was merely a human Jesus who died for them, what need would there be to stress so forcefully the humanity and human experience of Jesus (2:10–18, 4:15, 5:7–8,

12:2–3)? Indeed, it might be imagined that defeating the devil and breaking the power of death was something only God could do! The writer's use of the adverb 'likewise' (2:14, Gk. *paraplēsios*), meaning 'in just the same way', underscores the total involvement of the Son in the human condition. It anticipates 2:17 ('he had to be made like his brothers in every respect [Gk. *kata panta*]') and 4:15 ('one who in every respect [*kata panta*] has been tempted as we are, yet without sin').

Understanding the language of 'becoming'
There certainly are expressions that look like an adoptionist Christology in Hebrews, but the idea of the Son 'inheriting' and 'becoming superior' is not inconsistent with incarnationalism. As the one appointed 'heir of all things' (1:2), the Son must make 'purification for sins' and be enthroned 'at the right hand of the Majesty on high' (1:3), to enter into that inheritance. This is necessary so that his people – the 'many sons' (2:10), who are called Christ's 'brothers' (2:11–12), and 'the children' God has given him (2:13:14) – might be redeemed to share 'the world to come' with him (2:5–18). In the whole segment from 1:4 to 2:16, the Son *becomes* 'for a little while lower than the angels' (2:7, 9),[7] to fulfil the divine plan of redemption, and then by resurrection, ascension and enthronement, *becomes* 'as much superior to angels as the name he has inherited is more excellent than theirs' (1:4). Christ's status as heir is manifested and exercised in his exaltation to 'the right hand', 'a transcendent position that guarantees his brethren their inheritance and a share in a "heavenly calling".'[8]

The theme of the opening paragraph (1:1–4) is repeated in the writer's application of Psalm 8: 4–6 to Jesus in 2:5–9. It was specifically 'because of the suffering of death' (Gk. *dia to pathēma tou thanatou*) that he was 'crowned with glory and honour'. As in Philippians 2:6–9, death appears as the ultimate expression of the Son's humiliation and the ground of his exaltation. In both passages there is an affirmation of incarnation and in both New Testament documents the implication is that 'Christ *becomes* through exaltation what he by nature already *is* from eternity – Lord all.'[9] However, it is as *man*, albeit God incarnate, that he is exalted. Moreover, this whole process is 'for us and for our salvation.' He fulfils Psalm 8 as the true man or last Adam, enabling us to share in his dominion over sin, death and the devil (2:10–15; cf. Rom. 5:12–21; 1 Cor. 15:42–9). Our destiny as human beings is fulfilled by becoming those who 'share' in Christ (3:14, Gk. *metochoi tou Christou*) through faith.

There is a further interesting application of a psalm to Jesus in Hebrews 10:5–10. The words of Psalm 40:6–8 find their ultimate fulfilment on the lips of Jesus as he 'comes into the world' (10:5, Gk. *eiserchomenos eis ton kosmon*). His obedience, which led him to sacrifice himself for us in death, was lived out in the body that God prepared for him. In this human body, he would say, 'Behold, I have come to do your will, O God, as it is written of me in the scroll of the book.' Considering where Hebrews began, with those strong affirmations of pre-existence, this passage speaks in a Johannine way of the Son's entry into the world as his entry into a bodily life. Without pursuing this matter in any more detail, it seems clear to me that 'the author of Hebrews presents the human life of Jesus as unambiguously real and as set between and continuous with the Son's eternal pre-existence and his eternally permanent life with God since his resurrection.'[10]

The Pioneer and Perfecter of Faith

My main concern in this chapter is not simply to prove that there is incarnational theology in Hebrews, but to highlight its place in the writer's argument and to explore its pastoral value for us today. The expression 'pioneer and perfecter of faith' in 12:2 is an excellent starting point for unpacking this.

Christ as our example

Hebrews 12 begins with a reference to the 'cloud of witnesses' (Gk. *nephos martyrōn*) mentioned in chapter 11. These are those who have 'received witness' or acknowledgement from God because of their faith (11:2, *emartyrēthēsan*, cf. 11:4–5, 39). They stand in Scripture as witnesses to the nature and possibilities of faith for later generations. We are not to picture them as onlookers, cheering us on in 'the race that is set before us', but rather see them as those to whom we look for encouragement.[11]

In addition, the Christian has the supreme encouragement that springs from contemplating Jesus. Use of the personal name Jesus in 12:2 (cf. 2:9; 3:1) suggests that the focus should be on his experience as a human being. The parallel between his incarnate experience and ours here has to do with enduring hostility, suffering and shame, and not growing weary or faint-hearted because our hope is set on the joy of God's kingdom (12:2–3).[12] We are to run with endurance the race that is set before us, looking to Jesus, who entered God's rest by the pathway of suffering, shame and disgrace, and is now 'seated at the right hand of God'. Believers are summoned to run the race that is set before them, considering Christ's own experience, and his present glory.

The word 'pioneer' or 'founder' in 12:2 (Gk. *archēgos*) recalls 2:10, where the same word is used in the expression 'pioneer of their salvation'. Much debate has taken place about the translation of this Greek word because it is used elsewhere with the sense of originator/initiator/author (e.g. Acts 3:15), but also with the sense of leader or pathfinder (e.g. Acts 5:31).[13] The athletic metaphor and the comparison of Jesus' experience with that of believers in 12:1–4 suggests the primacy of the leadership motif. Christ is forerunner and example for his people in the life of faith (cf. 6:20, where *prodromos* unquestionably means 'forerunner').

Faith in 12:2 should be understood with reference to Hebrews 11 as something exercised by the cloud of witnesses, pre-eminently by Jesus himself, and also by us. The writer does not strictly speak of Jesus as 'the pioneer and perfecter of our faith' (NRSV). He is the pioneer and perfecter of *faith* in its absolute sense (12:2, *ton tēs pisteōs archēgon kai teleiōtēn Iēsoun*). He is 'the perfect example – perfect in realisation and in effect – of that faith we are to imitate, trusting in him'.[14] He is the supreme pioneer and the perfect embodiment of faith. 'He has realised faith to the full from start to the finish.'[15]

The imitation of Jesus is not a theme with which some evangelicals seem comfortable. Perhaps it is felt that this approach can obscure the need for complete dependence on Christ alone for salvation. But it is a biblical theme and needs to be taught and lived as Hebrews directs. At the same time, we need to acknowledge that Christ himself makes faith possible: saving faith is elicited and sustained by the work of Christ, which is proclaimed and made available to us in the gospel.

Christ as the ground or source of faith

It was noted above that the Greek word *archēgos* can have the sense of originator/initiator/author. The context of 2:10 suggests that Christ accomplishes something unique by his death and exaltation on behalf of others (cf. 2:9, 14–15, 17). His death was more than an identification with us in our mortality, showing us how to die. As 'the pioneer of *their* salvation' (2:10), he accomplished a deliverance for his people which they could not accomplish for themselves.[16] He leads us along the path to glory and is able to save us completely because he has already secured for us 'an eternal redemption' in his death and exaltation (9:11–12). So the sense of 'source' or 'author' of their salvation must be included in our reading of 2:10 (ESV 'the founder of their salvation' seems to encapsulate both senses of 'leader' and 'author'). Similarly, in 12:2 the notion of originator/initiator/author should be included in our understanding of the expression 'the pioneer and perfecter of faith'.

We also need to see the link between the perfecting of Christ, which will be discussed below in connection with 2:10, 5:9 and 7:28 (where the verb *teleioun* is used) and the notion of Christ as the perfecter of faith in 12:2 (where the cognate noun *teleiōtēs* is used). As pioneer and perfecter he constitutes 'the new ground, content and possibility of true realisation of faith in God. By his work he created a new dimension and channel for the fusion of obedience, confidence, hope and fidelity, because he pioneered this road.'[17] Jesus is the one who has given faith its perfect basis by his high-priestly work. 'Although he was Son, he learned obedience through what he suffered and being made perfect he became the source (Gk. *aitios*) of eternal salvation to all who obey him' (5:7–9).[18] Christ's passage through suffering and shame to the glory of the Father's right hand opened the way for us to follow in his footsteps. But he himself was perfected and obtained perfection for us by his *unique* self-offering to God (10:5–10, 14). We are not simply saved by following his pathway of obedience and suffering. Faith in Christ as the unique saviour and high priest is essential and foundational, but such faith commits us to the pattern and pathway of his own faith.

Since Christ has given faith a perfect basis by his high-priestly work, his faith and what it achieved both for himself and for others, becomes a greater incentive for faith on our part than the faith of the Old Testament believers. His faith is thus qualitatively and not just quantitatively greater than theirs. This reflection on what it means for Jesus to be pioneer and perfecter of faith leads us back to consider what is meant by the perfecting of Christ and the perfecting of believers in Hebrews. This exploration will reveal something more of the significance of the incarnation for us.

The Perfecting of Christ

In 2:10, 5:9 and 7:28, the writer speaks about the perfecting of Christ and in 7:19; 9:9; 10:1, 14; 11:40; 12:23, he refers to the perfecting of believers. The Greek verb *teleioun* ('to make complete, whole, adequate') is used throughout in a 'vocational', rather than a purely formal, or a narrowly cultic sense.[19] Although a vocational reading of this terminology suggests an element of personal consummation, the perfecting of Christ is not simply 'the personal consummation of Christ in his humanity'. Arguing this way, Westcott concluded that the incarnation 'brings to each human power and each part of human life its true perfection.'[20] But Jesus is perfected as 'the pioneer of their salvation' (2:10), 'the source of eternal salvation' (5:9), and as the Son who is high priest after the order of Melchizedek (7:28). He is 'qualified' or 'made adequate, completely effective' in these redemptive roles by the experience of his earthly testing, crucifixion, resurrection and enthronement.[21]

The broad perspective
The context of 2:10 suggests that Jesus' perfecting has something to do with his ascension and crowning with glory and honour, as the one destined to rule over 'the world to come' (2:5–9). By this means, God leads or brings (Gk. *agagonta*) 'many sons to glory' (2:10). His perfecting must also include the suffering of death, which is the ground of his exaltation (2:9) and the means by which he 'tastes death' for everyone. The significance of his death is further explained in terms of robbing the devil of his power, delivering his people from lifelong bondage (2:14–15), and making atonement for their sins (2:17). His perfecting must also involve the whole incarnate experience by which he 'became' a merciful and faithful high priest (2:17, Gk. *genētai*). That priestly

ministry involves making atonement 'for the sins of the people' and helping them to persevere in the face of suffering and temptation because of his own earthly testing (2:18; cf. 4:15; 5:7–8; 7:25).

This last perspective is anticipated in 2:10 by the use of the plural *dia pathēmatōn* ('through sufferings', NRSV), unfortunately rendered in the singular by NIV, ESV. The writer insists that there were 'sufferings' *through* which Jesus had to pass,[22] to be perfected as 'the pioneer/founder of their salvation'. The preceding verse puts the emphasis on 'the suffering of death' (*to pathēma tou thanatou*, lit. 'the suffering which consists of death') as the ground of his exaltation. By the end of the chapter, however, it is clear that his suffering involved the whole sequence leading to his crucifixion, by which he was tested or tempted and prepared for that obedient offering 'without blemish' (cf. 9:13–14). In 5:7–8, Jesus' suffering includes at least the events in Gethsemane. In 12:3, the hostility that Jesus endured against himself was certainly a form of suffering and cannot be restricted to the actual process of crucifixion. Although the focus in 13:12 is on the redemptive achievement of his suffering, there is an exhortation in 13:13–14 which suggests a wider agenda. The writer 'naturally dwells on the painful condition by which the triumph was prepared because he wishes to encourage his readers to endurance in suffering.'[23]

Learning obedience

The perfecting of Christ as 'the source of eternal salvation' in 5:7–10 is related to the process by which 'he learned obedience through what he suffered'. The expression 'Son though he was' (Gk. *kaiper ōn huios*) makes it clear that he was Son of God already during the period of his earthly ministry and was not raised to that status by his ascension-enthronement.[24] As noted previously, the suffering of the Son included at least the events in Gethsemane. 'In the days of his flesh' could be a general reference to the whole period of his incarnate life and the words 'with loud cries and tears' suggest an application 'to other prayers and times of peculiar trial in the Lord's life.'[25] The loud cries of Jesus on the cross could be included (cf. Mk. 15:34, 37), though it is doubtful that these involved prayer to be saved 'from death' (5:7). Only the Gethsemane traditions offer us a clear picture of Jesus under the dread of death and seeking escape from it (cf. Mt. 26:38–9; Mk. 14:34–6; Lk. 22:41–4; Jn. 12:27–8).

Jesus the Son of God was tempted or tested 'in every respect as we are' (4:15, Gk. *kata panta kath' homoiotēta*), 'yet without sin'. Recalling the wording of 2:17, that the Son had to be 'made like his brothers in every respect' (Gk. *kata panta homoiōthēnai*), the writer affirms again that he shared fully in the struggles of human existence (2:18 suggests that this dimension was included in the meaning of 2:17). However, Hebrews 5:7 illustrates this claim in one particular way, focusing on the temptation to swerve from doing the will of God because of the suffering and anguish involved. This had a pointed relevance to the situation of the readers (10:32–9; 12:1–4; 13:12–14). Jesus' prayer to 'him who was able to save him from death' corresponds with the prayer in the Gospel narratives for 'this cup' to be removed. When Hebrews mentions that 'he was heard because of his reverent submission' (NIV, NRSV, Gk. *eulabeia*), the allusion is to the words by which he rededicated himself to doing the will of his Father ('yet not what I will but what you will'). Jesus was not simply delivered from the fear of death because of his reverent submission, but was brought through death, resurrection and ascension to the Father's side.[26] This is the sequence of thought in 5:7–10. It was by learning obedience in this way that he was perfected as 'source of eternal salvation' and 'high priest after the order of Melchizedek'.

As divine Son in the sense outlined in 1:1–2; 5:5, it might be expected that he would be exempt from the discipline of having to learn obedience through what he suffered (5:8). He needed no educative correction. Learning obedience was not necessary because he was disobedient, but his obedience needed to be 'proved' through testing. His humanity was total and authentic, but as one 'without sin' (4:15; cf. 7:26) he needed to continue faithful and blameless throughout his trials. Various experiences of suffering and temptation prepared him for the ultimate act of obedience. The cross was the consummation of that process and the final expression of his sinlessness. His obedient self-offering in death made it possible for us to be definitively cleansed from sin (9:14), sanctified (10:10) and perfected (10:14).

It is sometimes argued that a sinless Jesus seems less than fully human. How could he save sinners unless he shared in the human condition by sinning?[27] But Christ was perfected as 'the source of eternal salvation' and 'high priest after the order of Melchizedek' (5:9–10). He is our redeemer, not simply our example, in the struggle against sin. He is the second or last Adam (cf. Rom. 5:12–21; 1 Cor. 15:45–9). Adam had no history of sin before he was tempted and fell, but his humanity was real. By his faithfulness even to death, Christ fulfilled the ideal of Psalm 8 and made it possible for us to enjoy with him the dominion that Adam lost (2:2–9).

As well as the redemptive aspect of his learning obedience through suffering, the Son needed to experience 'just what obedience to God involved in practice, in the conditions of human life on earth.'[28] He needed to acquire 'a practical comprehension and an appreciation of suffering which was indispensable for him to sympathise as priest with those who are his brothers.'[29] Put another way, 'what Christ experienced was not a development of moral character but a full acquaintance with the entire range of human existence and depravity, i.e. his brothers' (and sisters') very situation.'[30] This is an important aspect of Christ's priesthood in Hebrews. The writer does not simply focus on 'making purification for sins' (1:3), providing atonement (2:17) or securing 'an eternal redemption' (9:12), by means of his sacrificial death and entrance into the heavenly sanctuary. As 'a merciful and faithful high priest', he 'lives forever' (7:23–5) and is ever able to help those similarly tested (2:18) and to provide mercy and 'grace to help in time of need' (4:16). The theme of Christ the faithful high priest is developed in 3:1–6. This forms the basis for an exhortation to faithfulness in 3:7–4:13. The theme of Christ the merciful high priest dominates the section 4:14–5:10. The challenge of 4:14–16 arises from the preceding argument but also serves to introduce a new paragraph (5:1–10), where the focus is on his qualifications for priesthood.

There is certainly an exemplary dimension to his learning obedience through what he suffered. He needed to habituate himself to obedience, 'that he might exhibit to us an instance and an example of subjection even to death itself.'[31] This perspective finds expression in 12:1–11 and 13:13, as we have already noted, and is suggested in the immediate context by the addition of the words 'to all who obey him' (5:9). 'If we then desire that Christ's obedience should be profitable to us, we must imitate him, for the Apostle means that its benefit shall come to none but to those who obey.'[32] Salvation is obtained by trusting in the once-for-all work of Christ, but saving faith is expressed in an obedient faithfulness like his (cf. 3:1–6).

Without doubt, the ascension-enthronement of Jesus is stressed in 4:14 and in the linking of the two psalm citations in 5:5–6. This is one reason why some commentators identify the perfecting of Christ with his heavenly exaltation and exclude the suffering and testing of Christ from the process. The writer's comment in 5:8 is regarded as a parenthesis, explaining the reverence or godly fear of Christ in 5:7. All this is regarded as a preliminary to his perfecting by heavenly exaltation in 5:9. So, for example, David A. deSilva has argued on linguistic grounds that 'having been perfected' in 5:9 (Gk. *teleiōtheis*) means '"having been brought to the final goal" of that journey described in 5:7–8, namely having entered the divine realm from which advantageous location he can secure divine benefits for his loyal clients.'[33] Those who argue on theological grounds that Christ became our high priest at the incarnation, when his human nature was created and united with the divine in the person of the eternal Son of God, speak of Christ's resurrection-ascension as the perfecting of his humanity through glorification.[34]

In response, I would stress again that Jesus' perfecting was 'through' or 'by means of sufferings' (2:10), and that the *teleiōtheis* at the beginning of 5:9 explains the necessity for the Son's learning obedience through what he suffered in terms of his qualification to become 'source of eternal salvation' and 'high priest after the order of Melchizedek'. Jesus' incarnate life was not simply designed to acquaint him with the human situation, but to prepare him for the climactic act of self-sacrifice by which he secured an eternal redemption for us. His exaltation as a man enables him to be the eternal high priest (7:23–8), whose sacrifice is forever able to save those who draw near to God through him (cf. 9:11–14, 23–6; 10:12–14, 19–23). The focus is not on the perfecting of his humanity per se.

In 5:7–9, we catch a glimpse of how Christ in his humanity 'realised to the uttermost the absolute dependence of humanity upon in God in fulness of personal communion with him, even through the last issues of sin and death.'³⁵ Again, in 10:5–10, we read of Christ presenting his body as a living sacrifice to God, realising perfectly in his own life the obedience that fulfils the ideal of sacrifice in Psalm 40 and achieves a definitive sanctification of believers. However, the focus in Hebrews is on the death or 'blood' of Jesus as the means by which our salvation is achieved. It is not correct to conclude with writers like Westcott that the perfecting of Christ is 'the personal consummation of Christ in his humanity'.³⁶ The need for atonement and a reconciling priestly ministry is made the foundation of everything in Hebrews, and 'the incarnation is defined solely by relation to it.'³⁷ Christ is perfected as saviour and high priest, not simply as man.

Perfected as Son and High Priest

With the language of perfection, Hebrews does not focus on the changes involved in the 'being' of Christ, but on the process by which he saves and perfects his people.³⁸ His perfecting as Son in 7:28 is clearly related to his sacrificial death and his resurrection-ascension, as 'a priest for ever, after the order of Melchizedek' (7:15–27). The link between his divine sonship and his high priesthood is made in several ways by the writer (cf. 1:1–3; 3:1–6; 4:14–15; 5:5–10; 7:3, 15–28). His perfecting as Son involves the fulfilment of his redemptive role through incarnation, suffering death, resurrection and ascension, enabling him to reign in glory with those he has redeemed. This takes us back to the point made earlier, that Christ's status as Son and heir is manifested and exercised in his exaltation to the right hand of God:

> Christ is the heir of the universe by reason of his divine nature, and all things are subject to him because he is God, and yet, there is the role played by his humanity and by his historical acts of salvation in the actual realization of his dominion over the cosmic universe, an idea which shows affinity to Colossians 1:16–20.³⁹

His high-priestly office involves his blood shedding, his entrance into the heavenly sanctuary by resurrection-ascension (9:11–12) and his continuing work of 'intercession' (7:25), by which he makes salvation available to those who draw near to God through him. Just as his enthronement 'at the right hand of the Majesty on

The Incarnation and Christian Living

high' marked the consummation of his work as Messiah and the full manifestation of what it means for him to be Son (1:3–4), so it marked the consummation of his work viewed from a sacerdotal point of view and the full manifestation of what it means for him to be heavenly high priest (8:1–2; 9:23–8; 10:11–14).

Christ did not 'become' high priest simply by virtue of his resurrection-ascension. The writer's use of the Day of Atonement imagery stresses that Christ's sacrifice on the cross and his entrance into the heavenly sanctuary are part of the same priestly action (cf. 9:11–14, 23–8; 10:19–21). His designation as high priest after the order of Melchizedek (5:10) was in Psalm 110:4 (cited in 5:6), which revealed at a particular point in time the will of God for the Messiah. But this text does not mean that he became high priest at his ascension. Son though he was in his earthly ministry (1:2; 5:8), his heavenly enthronement marked the consummation of his messianic work and the proclamation of his sonship to all, as he entered into his inheritance and fulfilled Psalm 110:1. Similarly, that enthronement marked the consummation of his priestly work and the proclamation of his eternal high priesthood, in fulfilment of Psalm 110:4. 'Christ is always, from the moment he was priest at all, a priest after the order of Melchizedek.'[40] Only such a position can adequately link his earthly and his heavenly ministry as priest: 'The Son exhibited and authenticated himself as a priest in the performance of his priestly functions',[41] namely in his sacrificial death and entrance into the heavenly sanctuary.

In short, then, the perfecting of Christ as Son and high priest involved his proving in temptation, his redemptive death to make a once-for-all atonement of sin, and his exaltation to glory and honour at the Father's right hand.[42] Thus perfected or qualified, he opens the way for his 'brothers' or 'children' to share his glory and continues to provide them with the necessary help to persevere in their calling and reach their heavenly destination (cf. 4:14–16; 7:25; 10:19–25; 12:1–4; 13:12–15). To insist that the primary sense of Christ's perfecting is his vocational qualification, rather than his moral perfection or 'the personal consummation of Christ in his humanity', is not to approach Hebrews with preconceived ideas about the incarnation, but rather an attempt to reflect the balance in the writer's presentation.

The Perfecting of Believers

As with the perfecting of Christ, the verb *teleioun* ('to make complete, whole, adequate') is used in a 'vocational', rather than a purely formal, or a narrowly cultic sense with reference to the perfecting of believers (7:19; 9:9; 10:1, 14; 11:40; 12:23). The perfecting which Christ makes possible because of his own perfecting has to do with our relationship with God and not with the perfecting of our humanity in a purely moral sense. There is clearly a cultic dimension to this, but also a sense of eschatological consummation or glorification (as the apostle Paul would describe it).[43]

The writer introduces this theme by arguing that perfection was not available through the Levitical priesthood (7:11, where the cognate noun *teleiōsis* is used). More broadly, he asserts that 'the law made nothing perfect' (7:19), since law and priesthood are so intimately connected (cf. 7:12). This leads to the assertion that in Christ 'a better hope is introduced through which we draw near to God' (7:19). That better hope is based on the better priesthood of Jesus, by which he inaugurates a better covenant, based on better promises (7:20–8:6).

Drawing near to God is an important notion in Hebrews, closely linked to the concept of perfection. In 10:1 the writer observes that the sacrifices of the Mosaic Law, 'that are continually offered every year', can never 'make perfect those who draw near'. This text implies that some approach to God was possible under the first covenant because of the provisions of God himself. However, the priesthood, sacrificial system and the sanctuary were only 'a shadow of the good things to come instead of the true form of these realities' (10:1; cf. 8:1–6; 9:1–10). People were not perfected as worshippers or as those who would draw near to God. 'The certainty of the actualisation of the drawing near is now stronger and surer and more complete than in the OT and later Judaism.'[44]

The terminology of drawing near to God (Gk. *engizein* in 7:19 and *proserchesthai* in 4:16; 7:25; 10:1, 22; 11:6; 12:18, 22) can be applied quite narrowly to prayer (as in 4:16), or more generally to a relationship with God (11:6), understood in terms of approaching God as the great king, entering his courts and living in his presence.[45] The 'better hope' of the New Covenant by which we draw near to God is based on the once-for-all sacrifice of Jesus, his heavenly exaltation and his continuing work of intercession for us as heavenly high priest (7:25; 10:19–22).

There is a sense in which we have already come to our goal of meeting with God in heaven and being perfected through the blood of Christ. In 10:14, the Greek emphatically asserts that, 'by a single offering he has perfected for all time (Gk. perfect tense, *teteleiōken*) those who are being sanctified'. The terminology of perfection itself quite naturally suggests some eschatological or ultimate adjustment to our situation. However, 10:14 clearly locates this perfecting in the past with respect to its accomplishment and in the present with respect to its enjoyment. In 12:22–4, the Greek again asserts that 'you have come' (Gk. perfect tense, *proselēlythate*) to the heavenly city, to God the judge of all, and to 'the assembly of the firstborn who are enrolled in heaven', who are also called 'the spirits of the righteous made perfect' (Gk. perfect, *teteleiōmenōn*). This perfection or consummation of believers in an eternally secure relationship with God is made possible by 'the sprinkled blood' of Jesus, the mediator of a new covenant (12:24).

However, it is also true that Hebrews urges us to 'keep on drawing near to God' (4:16; 10:22, Gk. present tense, *proserchōmetha*). This means constantly realising in the present the benefits of Jesus' finished and continuing work (cf. 4:14–15; 7:25; 10:19–21), but also realising in advance the benefits of the perfection which he has made possible for us by his high-priestly ministry. Whereas the provisions of the Mosaic Law could not 'perfect the conscience of the worshipper' (9:9),[46] 'the blood of Christ' can 'purify our conscience from dead works to serve the living God' (9:14). Consequently, believers can continue to 'draw near with a true heart in full assurance of faith, with our hearts sprinkled clean from an evil conscience and our bodies washed with pure water' (10:22).

This focus on the purification of the conscience from the guilt of sin, to enable a new devotion or service to God, is portrayed as the fulfilment of the promises of the New Covenant in Jeremiah 31:31–4. Jesus inaugurated this covenant and made its benefits available by the obedient offering of himself in death (cf. Heb. 8:6–13; 10:15–18). So the perfecting of believers involves purification or cleansing from sin and a definitive sanctification of hearts and lives in a new obedience to God (cf. 10:10, 2913:12).⁴⁷ However, 11:39–40 and 12:23 suggest that perfection ultimately involves arriving at the heavenly Jerusalem, where Jesus has gone before as forerunner (6:19–20). He has opened the way for us to enter God's presence and enjoy the life of that unshakeable kingdom and heavenly assembly by his sacrificial death, resurrection and ascension (12:22–9), that is, by his own perfecting as our saviour and high priest.

The language of perfection is used in Hebrews to express the writer's inaugurated eschatology. By his perfecting, Jesus has accomplished all that is necessary for the perfecting of believers. The glory that is to come is only an unfolding of what has even now been achieved through the sacrifice and heavenly exaltation of our saviour. DeSilva rightly concludes that this teaching should impel Christians forward on their pilgrimage, 'preventing them from succumbing to the contrary motions of drifting off, falling away or turning away.'⁴⁸ They are to be sustained by the knowledge of what Christ has already accomplished for them and the fact that they have already begun to enjoy it. The perfecting of their conscience allows them to keep drawing near to God and to keep meeting with his people, so that they might be encouraged to serve him in the obedience of everyday life, as they wait for the final 'day' to appear (10:19–25; cf. 3:12–15).

Conclusion: Hebrews and the Incarnation

Hebrews begins with a reference to the ultimate revelation of God in the person and work of the Son (1:1–4). Having spoken 'at many times and in many ways' by the prophets, in these last days he has spoken to us 'by his Son' (cf. Jn. 1:1–18). This note is sounded again in 2:1–4, when the writer warns about paying closer attention to what we have heard. The message declared by the Lord Jesus is more significant than the revelation given through Moses and declared by angels. It also carries with it a greater penalty for neglect, later explained in terms of 'a fearful expectation of judgement and a fury of fire that will consume the adversaries' (10:26–31). The Son of God is called the divine apostle in 3:1–6, worthy of more glory than Moses, 'as the builder of a house has more honour than the house itself', or as the son of a house has more honour than a servant in that house.

In the flow of the argument, such references suggest that the Son is the ultimate revelation of God, not simply in his speaking, but in his incarnate life, his sacrificial death and his heavenly exaltation.[49] Revelation and redemption are closely linked in 1:1–4 and in 2:1–18. What was 'declared at first by the Lord' was 'the great salvation' he would accomplish. To fulfil Psalm 8 for us and restore the dominion lost by Adam's rebellion, the Son was made 'for a little while lower than the angels' and then was 'crowned with glory and honour', exalted again 'because of the suffering of death'. By this means he revealed the incredible grace of God and his absolute sovereignty over sin, death and the devil.

The significance of the Fall and its consequences is teased out when the writer emphasises the need for Jesus to share our flesh and blood, to die the death that would 'destroy the one who has the power of death, that is, the devil, and deliver all those who through fear of death were subject to lifelong slavery' (2:14–15). Moreover, the Son needed to be made like us 'in every respect', so that he might become 'a merciful and faithful high priest in the service of God, to make propitiation for the sins of the people' (2:17). The redemptive purpose of the incarnation is powerfully asserted in such verses. However, there is a related purpose to the incarnation which is highlighted in 2:10, 18; 4:15; 5:7–10; 7:26–8; 9:14; 10:5–10; 12:1–4; 13:12–14.

His perfecting 'through sufferings' made him the perfectly obedient sacrifice for sin, able to provide a definitive purification, sanctification and perfection for believers. It also made him the ultimate or eschatological high priest, who lives for ever to intercede for us (7:25) and administer to us the benefits of his once-for-all work sympathetically. This enables us to draw near to God with confidence in the present, seeking mercy and grace to help in time of need, holding fast the confession of our hope without wavering (4:14–16; cf. 10:19–23). We are challenged to follow the example of Christ in his suffering and in the testing of his obedience, but also to look to him as the source of endurance and renewing grace (3:1–6; 12:1–4). He is both the founder and perfecter of faith. Thus, we may be glorified with Christ (2:10), share the 'rest' of the new creation with him (4:1–10), and enjoy the fellowship of the heavenly Jerusalem (12:22–4), 'the city that is to come' (13:14).

Notes

1. P.J. Du Plessis, TELEIOS *The Idea of Perfection in the New Testament* (Kampen: Kok, 1959), p. 226.
2. *The Human Face of God* (London: SCM, 1973), pp. 158–9. A similar position is argued by J.D.G. Dunn, *Unity and Diversity in the New Testament An Inquiry into the Character of Earliest Christianity* (London: SCM, 1977), pp. 222–3, 259–61.
3. Robinson, *The Human Face of God*, p. 159.
4. A more thorough critique is provided by J.W. Pryor, 'Hebrews and Incarnational Christology', *Reformed Theological Review* 40 (1981), pp. 44–50.
5. W.L. Lane, *Hebrews 1–8* (WBC 47A; Dallas: Word, 1991), p. 60. There is no semantic difference between the verbs that refer to the 'children' and to the Son in 2:14. Both roots describe 'a full participation in a shared reality'. The distinction lies in the different tenses of these verbs.
6. Gk. *metochoi* in 3:1, 14, is a present participle, meaning 'partakers, sharers', from the same verbal root as *meteschen* in 2:14.
7. Robinson, *The Human Face of God*, pp. 159–60, argues that *brachy ti* in 2:7, 9, cannot be a temporal expression, since Ps. 8:6 makes a qualitative statement about humanity's status in the created order, 'little lower than the angels'. However, Lane, *Hebrews 1–8*, p. 48, rightly observes that Hebrews interprets the two lines of the Psalm without reference to the synonymous parallelism of Hebrew text. 'From the perspective of the psalmist, to be made "little lower" than a heavenly being is to be "crowned with glory and honor". But for the writer the two members of the parallelism expressed two phases in the life of the Lord. He explains that the first line concerns Jesus' temporary abasement, while the second speaks of the subsequent exaltation and glorification.'
8. H.W. Attridge, *The Epistle to the Hebrews* (Philadelphia: Fortress, 1989), p. 40. Attridge, p. 47, insists that, 'the implication that Christ became the Son at some point should not be pressed. The focus, here as regularly in Hebrews, is not on the inauguration of Christ's position, but on the fact of its superiority. Christ within the supernal world has a higher position than any other member of that world because he is in possession of a special "name".'
9. O. Hofius, *Der Christushymnus Philipper 2:6–11* (WUNT; Tübingen, 1976), p. 93 (my translation).

10. R. Williamson, 'The Incarnation of the Logos in Hebrews', *Expository Times* 95 (1983–4), p. 7. This is a helpful article, though I cannot agree with his conclusion that Hebrews describes Christ as the Logos or Word of God in 4:12. It seems to me that the word in this context is the gospel, which has been the focus of attention in 4:1–7 as 'the message they heard' (4:2, *ho logos tēs akouēs*).
11. Cf. F.F. Bruce, *The Epistle to the Hebrews* (London: Marshall, Morgan & Scott, 1964), pp. 346–7; Attridge, *Hebrews*, pp. 354–5.
12. However, the writer immediately draws attention to a difference when he says, 'In your struggle against sin you have not yet resisted to the point of shedding your blood' (12:4). He does not expect that every believer will have to suffer death for the sake of Christ and the gospel.
13. Cf. D.G. Peterson, *Hebrews and Perfection. An examination of the concept of perfection in the Epistle to the Hebrews* (SNTSMS 47; Cambridge: Cambridge University, 1982), pp. 57–8, 171–3.
14. B.F. Westcott, *The Epistle to the Hebrews* (3rd ed.; London: MacMillan, 1914), p. 397.
15. J. Moffatt, *A Critical and Exegetical Commentary on the Epistle to the Hebrews* (ICC; Edinburgh: Clark, 1924), p. 196. Bruce, *Hebrews*, p. 351, says Jesus is presented as 'the one who has blazed the trail of faith and as the one who himself ran the race of faith to its triumphant finish.'
16. In 9:27–8, Christ's death is related to the fact that all must die, but its unique purpose to 'bear the sins of many' is stressed.
17. Du Plessis, *The Idea of Perfection*, p. 226.
18. On my translation 'although he was Son', see note 24 below. In this passage again there is an emphasis on the uniqueness of Christ's work on behalf of his people, but also an indication of the need for those who would benefit from his salvation to follow in his footsteps ('to all who obey him').
19. Cf. Peterson, *Hebrews and Perfection*, pp. 22–3, 46–8, where I show how the terminology is used in Greek literature for the perfecting of someone in a particular role or calling (cf. Lk. 13:32). Against Lane, *Hebrews 1–8*, pp. 57–8, the cultic use of this verb in the LXX does not justify the conclusion that Hebrews means that Christ was specifically 'consecrated' to his priesthood (*Hebrews and Perfection*, pp. 26–30, 96–103).
20. Westcott, *Hebrews*, pp. 66–8.
21. Moffatt, *Hebrews*, pp. 31–2; Attridge, *Hebrews*, pp. 83–7.

[22] *Dia* with the genitive case in 2:10 indicates a passage 'through' sufferings, whereas *dia* with the accusative case in 2:9 indicates that 'the suffering of death' was the ground or reason for his crowning with glory and honour. It is less likely that *dia* with the genitive case in 2:10 is used instrumentally ('by sufferings'), since this would narrow the perfecting to suffering alone.

[23] Westcott, *Hebrews*, p. 443.

[24] NIV, ESV unhelpfully render 'although he was a son', ignoring the flow of the argument from 5:5. If Ps. 2:7 is used in 1:5; 5:5 with the ascension-enthronement particularly in view, it will mean that Hebrews envisaged that event as inaugurating a new 'situation' for Christ, by virtue of his incarnation and sacrifice (cf. Rom. 1:3–4). It is now as the triumphant man of Psalm 8 and messianic priest-king of Psalm 110 that he reigns. It was when he was enthroned as the Christ that his unique and essential relationship to God as Son was decisively manifested.

[25] Westcott, *Hebrews*, p. 128.

[26] I have discussed this issue and details of comparison with the Gospel narratives more fully in *Hebrews and Perfection*, pp. 86–92.

[27] So, for example, R. Williamson, 'Hebrews 4:15 and the Sinlessness of Jesus', *Expository Times* 86 (1974), pp. 4–8. Cf. my response in *Hebrews and Perfection*, pp. 188–90.

[28] Bruce, *Hebrews*, p. 103.

[29] C. Spicq, *L'Épître aux Hébreux*, vol. 2 (Études Bibliques; Paris, 1952), p. 117 (my translation).

[30] J.M. Scholer, *Proleptic Priests. Priesthood in the Epistle to the Hebrews* (JSNTSS 49; Sheffield: JSOT, 1991), p. 188.

[31] J. Calvin, *Commentaries on the Epistle of Paul to the Hebrews* (trans. J. Owen; Edinburgh, 1853), p. 123. Calvin (p. 108), however, says that the Son of God had no need of such training himself. Without it, 'we could not otherwise comprehend the care he feels for our salvation.' This last statement is true, but the preceding one weakens the sense of 5:8.

[32] Ibid., p. 125.

[33] D.A. deSilva, *Perseverance in Gratitude. A Socio-Rhetorical Commentary on the Epistle "to the Hebrews"* (Grand Rapids/Cambridge: Eerdmans, 2000), p. 199. Earlier attempts to argue this case are noted and critiqued in Peterson, *Hebrews and Perfection*, pp. 66–73, 98–103, 119–25.

[34] Cf. A. Cody, *Heavenly Sanctuary and Liturgy in the Epistle to the Hebrews*.

The Incarnation and Christian Living

The Achievement of Salvation in the Epistle's Perspective (St. Meinrad, Indiana, 1960), pp. 81–2, 97, 101–3, 173.

35 Westcott, *Hebrews*, pp. 66–7.
36 Ibid., pp. 49–50.
37 J. Denney, *The Death of Christ* (London: Tyndale, 1964), p. 121. Denney argues that, 'the atonement, and the priestly or reconciling ministry of Christ, are the end to which the incarnation is relative as the means.' It is 'the atonement which explains the incarnation' (pp. 131–2).
38 Against, M. Silva, 'Perfection and Eschatology in Hebrews', *Westminster Theological Journal* 39 (1976), pp. 60–71, who restricts the perfecting of Christ to 'some type of change *in his human nature*' at the resurrection, cf. Peterson, *Hebrews and Perfection*, p. 70.
39 Cody, *Heavenly Sanctuary and Liturgy*, p. 108.
40 A.B. Davidson, *The Epistle to the Hebrews* (Edinburgh, 1882), p. 150. Cf. Peterson, *Hebrews and Perfection*, pp. 191–5 (Appendix B 'When did Jesus "become" high priest?').
41 Davidson, *Hebrews*, p. 151. Cf. G. Schrenk, *TDNT* 3, pp. 274–9.
42 Cf. O. Michel, *Der Brief an die Hebräer* (Meyer Kommentar 13th ed.; Göttingen: Vandenhoeck & Ruprecht, 1975), p. 224.
43 Cf. 2:10 ('to glory', *eis doxan*), in the light of 2:5–9 ('crowned with glory and honour'). DeSilva, *Perseverance in Gratitude*, pp. 199–204, separates too easily the cultic element from the element of consummation. However, my argument is that the vocational reading of perfection ties these two dimensions more obviously together. Cf. Peterson, *Hebrews and Perfection*, pp. 126–67.
44 H. Presiker, *TDNT* 2:331.
45 I have explored the use and meaning of this terminology more fully in *Hebrews and Perfection*, pp. 78–9 (especially notes 33–4), 112 (especially note 49), 128–9.
46 The Greek of 9:9 reads literally, 'perfect the worshipper with respect to conscience' (*kata syneidēsin teleiōsai ton latreuonta*).
47 DeSilva, *Perseverance in Gratitude*, p. 202, rightly observes that the perfecting of those who approach God through Jesus signals at one stroke the cleansing and consecration of the worshipper, the accomplishment (completion) of two rites in the Mosaic Law 'designed to bring an object to an appointed goal (cleanness, holiness).' However, he fails to develop the link between this accomplishment and the promises of the New Covenant about a new heart-obedience. The

achievement is more than a bringing of humanity 'back to its proper, divinely appointed state of enjoying face-to-face fellowship with God'.

[48] DeSilva, *Perseverance in Gratitude*, p. 204. 'Their center of gravity is thus fixed on God and the gathered worshipping community', though deSilva fails to note that the sphere of Christian worship or service in Hebrews is the world and the function of the church gathering is essentially edification. Cf. D. Peterson, *Engaging with God A biblical theology of worship* (Leicester/Downers Grove: Apollos/ InterVarsity Press, 1992), pp. 228–60.

[49] In contrast with *en tois prophētais* (lit. 'in the prophets') in 1:1, the words *en huiō* (lit. 'in the Son') in 1:2a suggest a revelation in word and deed because of what follows in 1:2b–4.

4. The Incarnation and Mission

Chris Green

> Modern Anglican theology owes many of its characteristics to the central place held within it by the incarnation ... Furthermore, the doctrine of the Incarnate Christ as the Logos gave a constant impulse towards relating the incarnation, wherever possible, with contemporary movements in thought or social progress ... The question is now being asked in retrospect: is there an inevitable loss in theological perspective or proportion if the incarnation is allowed to become the centre of theology?[1]

Introduction: Evangelicals and the Roots of a Guilty Conscience

The birth of liberal theology across Europe and North America in the late nineteenth century produced a range of versions of the thought that humankind is improveable and improving. As Michael Ovey has noted in chapter 1, the form it has taken in the Church of England is called liberal Catholicism, and the essays published in 1889 as *Lux Mundi* marked its arrival.[2] Centre stage, as the group's chosen name indicated, was the placing of liberal theology in Catholic vestments. But to achieve the aim of being demonstrably in line with authentic Anglicanism they knew, as Manning and Newman had known before them when they introduced those Catholic vestments, that they had to displace Reformed theology from its position in the written formularies of the denomination. In so doing, they articulated a charge that has been made frequently since:

> The Reformers, from various causes, were so occupied with what is now called Soteriology, or the scheme of salvation, that they paid but scant attention to the other aspects of the gospel. And the consequence was that a whole side of the great Christian tradition, and

one on which many of its greatest thinkers had lavished the labors (sic) of a lifetime, was allowed almost unconsciously to lapse into comparative oblivion; and the religion of the incarnation narrowed into the religion of the atonement. Men's views of the faith dwindled and became self regarding, while the gulf was daily widened between things sacred and things secular; among which latter, art and science, and the whole political and social order, gradually came to be classed.[3]

That is, the consequences of the Reformers' theology has been a defensiveness and small-mindedness in which the only concern of the church has been the salvation of souls, and what people do with the remainder of their lives and minds, and what happens in the body politic, is an irrelevance.

This assessment is by no means neutral. We should first remember that it was part of the explicit aim of the earlier nineteenth-century Tractarian movement to reclaim the allegedly lost aesthetic dimension of Christianity; lost, we should note, by the anti-aesthetic and anti-medieval Reformation. Liberal Catholicism emerged just as pure Anglo-Catholicism was entering the doldrums, and took the rewriting of theology and history further. It was the task of *Lux Mundi* not merely to justify the very possibility of theology in the face of the applied sciences, but to adopt and sanctify their conclusions. This was particularly the issue with the social optimism produced by the powerful application of Darwinian evolutionary theory to the whole range of public life, from economics to eugenics.[4] In claiming that evolution was the outworking of the plan of the saving, creative Logos, liberal Catholicism was a natural child of its optimistic age. It was also a response to the discoveries of critical biblical scholarship, which demanded a more questioning approach to traditional views, and was a parallel attempt to that of F.D. Maurice, who published *The Kingdom of Christ* in 1838. The idea began to emerge in British theology that God was at work beyond the churches, bringing in his kingdom by means other than merely the proclamation of the gospel. *Lux Mundi* therefore wanted to work out a new and more sophisticated understanding of God and his world, couched in the language, though not the thought, of orthodoxy, and attempting to be within the framework of an all-embracing worldview that was allegedly lost at the Reformation. The Reformers were therefore a necessary target, for they stood for a once-for-all, and biblically controlled view of theology. It was this combination which so 'grievously shocked' *Lux Mundi*'s first readers and made them think the authors had adopted 'a rationalistic and pelagianising tone'.[5]

Lux Mundi's accusation would certainly have surprised the many reformed contributors to the arts and sciences in the seventeenth century, for whom the Reformation had done precisely the opposite of what *Lux Mundi* alleged. Their theology provided an affirmation of the goodness and reality of the created order, and the importance of everyday life outside the cloister walls. A whole new theology of the value of everyday life and work was ushered in, so that the music of Bach, the paintings of Rembrandt, the founding of the Royal Society, the poetry of Milton and Spenser and so on all presuppose a reformed understanding of the world to exist.

On the particular charge of lack of political engagement, one should compare the ambition of the pilgrims in America. They were, one commentator has contended, the first group in history to believe that 'one could intentionally and organizationally make changes in one's community',[6] and that view was wholly built on the theology of the magisterial Reformation.[7] Within that, of course, confident evangelism had a primary place. 'The seal of the colonists of Massachusetts Bay had on it a North-American Indian with these words coming out of his mouth: "Come over into Macedonia and help us"',[8] but it was set in a theologically driven political agenda. *Lux Mundi* misrepresented what happened, because one of the great gains of the Reformation was that there was no longer a sacred/secular divide.

Nor is it a fair comment, for it ignores the fact that the presenting issue for both sides of the Reformation was not the incarnation (on which both were agreed[9]), but justification. Furthermore, Calvin's view of Christ's work, for instance, is not 'narrowed into the religion of the atonement', but the affirmation of Christ as the great prophet, priest and king.[10] That said, of course, for Calvin the incarnation is unthinkable without the cross. It is not that he ignores the incarnation; but he explicitly denies that Christ came in the flesh for any other purpose than redemption, and that to want to know what would have happened had we not sinned is foolish. 'It is as if (God) were purposely setting bars about our minds so that whenever Christ is mentioned we should not in the least depart from the grace of reconciliation.'[11] To say that this narrows the incarnation is utterly unjustified. *Lux Mundi* needed to make the charge, however, as background for the view that the incarnation is related to the atonement as merely one among many aspects of Christ's becoming man, the chief of which was to affirm us in our progress and bring us to our intended evolutionary goal of Godlikeness. He showed us what could further be done if we were to strive hard enough.

Nevertheless, the charge took hold. In part, this was because the stresses that produced the revisionism of *Lux Mundi* had triggered a similar defensiveness among evangelicals, who were as disturbed by Darwin, critical scholarship, and the social gospel of F.D. Maurice, although less willing to surrender. While it was never the case that evangelicals had opted out of social engagement, their refusal to compromise on a supernatural gospel and their dislike of many of the intellectual trends that marked late Victorianism made them look isolated and naïve. Various myths began to circulate, such as their alleged blindness on slavery or poverty, or their ignorance of the scientific progress being made,[12] and defensiveness began to enter the mindset.

The charge still echoes today, something like, 'Evangelicals (i.e. the Reformers in modern dress) have a such a high view of the cross that they have virtually ignored the incarnation; and since the incarnation is the ground of Christian mission, they narrow mission down to evangelism.' Or as the missiologist David Bosch wrote bluntly, 'Protestant churches, by and large, have an under-developed theology of the incarnation.'[13] And despite the undeniable fact that when one examines the evidence evangelicalism passes those tests,[14] it still hits enough of a nerve for it to rankle.

To be clear, though, we should distinguish between two aspects of the accusation that evangelicalism is by nature a privatised form of faith. It is certainly the case that between the late nineteenth century and the mid-twentieth-century evangelicalism faced an onslaught of various secular forces, within as well as outside the established churches, and that the tendency in those circumstances was to retreat. Faced with a form of the gospel that was anti-supernatural and regarded political action as a justifiable way to extend God's kingdom, the initial response was to stress the supernatural and revelatory nature of the faith (hence the major debates over inerrancy and infallibility), and the need for a trust in Christ rather than mere action. Evangelicals thus took a defensive stance. However, this crisis reaction must not be confused with the normal position of evangelicalism, which has stressed public engagement as well as private devotion. The liberal Catholicism the evangelicals encountered first of all redefined the past by misrepresenting the Reformed theology they aimed to usurp, and then denied key theological tenets – thus forcing evangelicals to defend them even at the risk of appearing defensive, negative and quaint. That evangelicals today still feel they should apologise for their historic lack of political and social engagement is a mark not of the accuracy of the accusation, but of the successful rewriting of history.

There are, frankly, two theological agendas here, with two very different and incompatible views of Christ's incarnation and the church's mission. In the face of classic orthodoxy, *Lux Mundi* saw the world as a basically good, if flawed place and human beings on an upward curve, checked by sin but shown their potential in Christ.[15]

Charles Gore's preface to the tenth edition of *Lux Mundi* states:

> The real development of theology is ... the process by which the Church, standing firm in her old truths, enters into the apprehension of the new social and intellectual movements of each age; and because 'the truth makes her free' is able to assimilate all new material, to welcome and give its place to all new knowledge, to throw herself into the sanctification of each new social order, bringing forth out of her treasures things new and old, and showing again and again her power of witnessing under changed conditions to the catholic capacity of her faith and life.[16]

That phrase 'the sanctification of each new social order' is seminal for much subsequent understanding of mission, and not only in the Church of England.

It is striking, if not scandalous, that such social optimism could survive the worst moments of the twentieth century and still be observed today. The last century has shown successive waves of political thought that should have called for denunciation rather than smug 'sanctification', and even to say such doctrines within living memory of the swastika sounds very unpleasant. Nevertheless, the idea that, deep down, people are basically good and society is basically on an upward path towards the kingdom of God can still be discerned. In *Lux Mundi* the classic doctrines of original sin, the curse on the world, the uniqueness of Christ, and the nature of the incarnation have been completely redefined for us, even if the language remained. The value of the incarnation for us today is to show us of what we might be capable, and for the body of Christ – the church – to continue the upward drive. Incarnation thus melted into ecclesiology with no remainder; the mission of the church is one of communal spiritual and social improvement. The reformed understanding of a creation and humanity locked in a sin prison to which only God has the key was necessarily abandoned, and the need for the atonement faded.

From a particularly Anglican view, the impact of *Lux Mundi* has been enormous, and from an evangelical viewpoint, devastating. Archbishop Michael Ramsey carefully tracked the history and growing influence of liberal Catholicism in his seminal study *From Gore to Temple*. He was in many ways, of course, the product and proponent of the same trajectory that has continued through Archbishop Runcie up to today.

Part of the evangelical weakness of response has been the lack of attention paid to liberal Catholicism. Pure liberalism, in the sense of a denial of the miraculous or of a core credal tenet, has been opposed on a number of occasions. But liberal Catholicism, which has made it possible to affirm the creeds, redefine their meaning, capture the ecclesiastical high ground and from there to condescend to evangelicals and make us feel theologically inept, has been largely ignored.[17]

Evangelicals must, then, respond to this charge better. We need to consider a series of questions. What was the mission of the incarnate Jesus – if it is proper to talk of his having one mission? How does that relate to the overarching mission of God? Granted an orthodox reading of the incarnation, death, resurrection, ascension, reign and return of Christ what *is* the mission of the incarnate Jesus today?

Incarnation and Missionary Monotheism

Monotheism and the world

The Old Testament's view of God can be well described as 'complex monotheism'. It is monotheist because 'the Lord our God, the Lord is one'.[18] It is an absolute monotheism, because the one God is a creator, ruler and saviour, all terms that admit no rival or equal without compromise. This monotheism sets Israel in a unique role towards the nations, for she is the uniquely saved possession of every nation's sole ruler and creator. So Psalm 33 is focal when it says,

> Let all the earth fear the LORD;
> let all the inhabitants of the world stand in awe of him.
> For he spoke and it came to be;
> he commanded and it stood firm.
> The LORD brings the counsel of the nations to nothing;
> he frustrates the plans of the peoples.
> The counsel of the LORD stands forever,
> the thoughts of his heart to all generations.
> Happy is the nation whose God is the LORD,
> the people whom he has chosen as his heritage (Ps. 33:8–12).

Despite a minority view that Israel should have been outwardly evangelistic towards those nations,[19] most theologians of mission have observed that Israel's task was to be a light, attracting people by the glory of her covenantal life,[20] and witnessing by her obedient worship to the significance for all nations of her unique status. The long-promised renewed nation, monarchy, priesthood and legislature would be the further delight of the whole world. Monotheism thus posed Israel a question. What was her view of the surrounding nations if all their gods are idols and all their laws subject to comparison with hers?

Yet that monotheism is complex, because even from the outset there is a dialogue within God: 'let *us* make man in *our* image'.[21] A relationship begins to emerge between God and his Son,[22] or God and his Spirit,[23] and this becomes even more explicit when the prophets outline a relationship between God, his Spirit and his Word, or between God, his Spirit and his Servant.[24] Clearly, the

God who had covenanted with them was to be understood in a complex and interpersonal way, and his final revelation would be needed to reveal the way this complexity could be resolved.

When the New Testament Christians understand and pray to Jesus as God in human form,[25] it is this God they have in mind, with the inevitable claims for a worldwide importance. If it is the world's creator and ruler who has become a man, and he has done this to save the world as well as Israel, then the Old Testament's promises have been fulfilled. And this incarnation shows a complex monotheism too, for this incarnate God prays to and hears from his Father, and is anointed with and promises his Spirit.

Incarnation and ministry

Jesus began his public ministry by defining it in the terms of Isaiah's promise,

> The Spirit of the Lord is upon me,
> because he has anointed me
> to bring good news to the poor.
> He has sent me to bring release to the captives
> and recovery of sight to the blind,
> to let the oppressed go free (Lk. 4:18, quoting Isa. 61:1, 2).

Luke evidently intends us to read this as programmatic for Jesus, and so we should expect to see him invest those four categories of 'poor', 'captives', 'blind' and 'oppressed' with some theological weight. It is no surprise, then, that Luke shows Jesus healing the blind and being with the poor.[26] But what is a surprise is that the other two categories disappear. In Luke, the only prisoner who is ever affected by Jesus' ministry is Barabbas, and although we probably should read his story as a reflection on the crucifixion, as an innocent man dies as the penal substitute for the guilty, Luke does not make a linguistic link to 4:18 at that point. That focus lies elsewhere, because his story has explained that those who are 'released' or 'set free' are those who are 'oppressed' by sin, and whose freedom comes by way of 'forgiveness (*aphesei*) of their sins'.[27]

This is entirely of a piece with the original context of Isaiah 42:6–7 and 61:1–2, where the experience of being 'poor', 'captives,' 'blind' and 'enslaved' was the nation's experience in Babylon, where they were exiled for their sin.[28] The significance of the Exile was broader than simply the nations directly involved, however. The gathering together of the renewed nation of Israel both prefigured and made possible the ingathering of all the nations, and in Isaiah that is particularly identified as the work of the Servant:

> Listen to me, you islands; hear this, you distant nations: Before I was born the LORD called me; from my birth he has made mention of my name. He made my mouth like a sharpened sword, in the shadow of his hand he hid me; he made me into a polished arrow and concealed me in his quiver. He said to me, 'You are my servant, Israel, in whom I will display my splendour.' But I said, 'I have laboured to no purpose; I have spent my strength in vain and for nothing. Yet what is due to me is in the LORD's hand, and my reward is with my God.' And now the LORD says – he who formed me in the womb to be his servant to bring Jacob back to him and gather Israel to himself, for I am honoured in the eyes of the LORD and my God has been my strength – he says: 'It is too small a thing for you to be my servant to restore the tribes of Jacob and bring back those of Israel I have kept. I will also make you a light for the Gentiles, that you may bring my salvation to the ends of the earth' (Isa. 49:1–6, NIV).

In the broad biblical sweep, the Exile is a judgement in history on a nation for its sins. More importantly, it is a demonstration in history of the coming judgement on all humankind for its sins, and Judah's loss of her land is a demonstration of humankind's more important loss of its Edenic Garden.[29] We must take care not to confuse picture with reality. Humankind's greatest problem is the loss of paradise by the Fall, and the placing of Israel in her land, her subsequent rebellion and loss of that land, and her recovery of it under a new monarchy and temple is, while a ghastly reality for those who experienced it, a dramatic fall in slow motion, a fall in miniature, that we can observe. The salvation from exile, therefore, however politically expressed, is but a miniature of the salvation from sin, and all the language of redemption must be interpreted as metaphorical of that greater reality.

By the end of Luke's Gospel it has emerged that it is this greater reality of human sin that Jesus has come to deal with for us. The redemption he has won has only become possible because of the cross, and the core Christian message is therefore that 'The Messiah (was) to suffer and to rise from the dead on the third day, and that repentance and forgiveness (*aphesin*) of sins is to be proclaimed in his name to all nations, beginning in Jerusalem.'[30] In other words, Luke takes this one term and makes it central to his description of Jesus' ministry, as prophesied by Isaiah and Simeon. But he simultaneously shows that oppression and forgiveness are not to be understood politically or metaphorically, but as the very language by which the terms 'blind' and 'poor' are to be redefined. Jesus' principal ministry was to bring forgiveness of sins to the world by his death on the cross, and his life and teaching before that are to be seen in the light of it, rather than to be examined separately. It is illegitimate to twist Luke's agenda into a political one, because that ignores both his use of the text in the Gospel and his (correct) understanding of the context in Isaiah.

As Jesus' ministry is continued through Acts,[31] the international sweep of the post-exilic vision is realised. Acts 1:8, programmatic for the book, records Jesus' commissioning the apostles to go as witnesses of his resurrection to 'Jerusalem', the city of the Davidic King, 'all Judea and Samaria', that is, to the two halves of the divided nation of Israel reunited under his kingship, 'and to the ends of the earth', that is, to the whole of humankind, in line with the Abrahamic covenant.[32] Similarly, of the two main speeches which are programmatic for the book, Peter's in Acts 2 focuses on this gospel of Jesus' messiahship going to 'all Israel'[33] and James' in Acts 15, to 'all the Gentiles'.[34] All this is predicated upon the apostles being 'witnesses' of Jesus' resurrection (1:8, 21–2), and that must mean the resurrection of the incarnate Jesus. In other words, they must witness that Jesus' incarnation has continued beyond the grave to his heavenly throne.

To put it systematically rather than exegetically, in theology every topic is ultimately related to all others, but some are more intimately connected than others; the incarnation and the cross being a clear example. Is it possible to talk about what Jesus did without talking about who he was? I doubt it. At least, if by 'did' we mean his focal ministry on the cross, and if by that we mean a sin bearing, wrath appeasing, penalty paying, law satisfying, substitutionary death, I doubt it. In order for the cross to be effective in that sense, the incarnation of the Messiah must be operative, and in order for that gospel to be preached to the world, the incarnation of the risen Messiah must be operative. It is not possible to talk in an orthodox way about Jesus' work without talking in an orthodox way about his person. They are inseparable.

The charge, of course, is that what Jesus 'did' is so much broader in scope than his dying, and that orthodoxy is wrong – even its creeds – in leaping from his birth to his death. To turn the charge round, though, I wonder if it is a rationale for wanting to do the opposite, namely, to want to discuss the life without the death, and to find inherent meaning in Jesus' life merely as such.

To take one example from many, consider Henri Nouwen's very powerful and sensitive bestseller, *The Return of the Prodigal Son*,[35] which is a book-length exposition of Rembrandt's painting of the Prodigal Son. It is a very moving and disarming work, because it takes the painting of the parable as the key to understanding the gospel, which Nouwen understands as an acceptance and welcome of people as they are. With disarming clarity he says,

> Here is the God I want to believe in: a Father who, from the beginning of creation, has stretched out his arms in merciful blessing, never forcing himself on anyone, but always waiting; never letting his arms drop down in despair, but always hoping that his children will return so that he can speak words of love to them and let his tired arms rest on their shoulders. His only desire is to bless.[36]

Neither sin nor atonement is mentioned here, and repentance is read as a form of remorse. Nouwen dislocates the parable from its trajectory in Luke, which from 9:51 onwards has been heading towards Jerusalem, and heaven beyond that, and treats it as a complete and final summary of the Christian message. Thus he has produced a gospel without the cross, repentance or forgiveness. And a gospel without the cross, as classically defined, is no gospel at all.[37]

Jesus' continuing incarnation and his continuing ministry
The New Testament further describes the result of Jesus' ministry as that promised renewed nation, monarchy, priesthood and

legislature, but in terms which show how he has advanced and purified those terms. The kingdom of God that Jesus inaugurates has non-geographical boundaries, non-racial membership, non-hierarchical priesthood and non-political leadership.[38] This means that the tension in the Old Testament over whether Israel should be inward or outward facing, centripetal or centrifugal in its approach to the nations, can be resolved in one direction only. The kingdom of God is now an inevitably outward-facing movement that must involve the destiny of all nations.

This move is shown clearly in the closing scenes of Matthew's Gospel. The whole of chapter 28 can be read as an extended series of answers to the question, 'Where is Jesus now?' The first and most obvious answer is that he is not in his tomb. As the representatives of the most powerful army on earth proved themselves incapable of even guarding a corpse, and instead experienced a personal earthquake and 'became like dead men',[39] Jesus (note the name, for the continuity of the person-hood of Jesus in physical resurrection is crucial here) has moved on. Instead he shows himself to be with the women as they are converted and commissioned,[40] giving a model of conversion for what will follow. As the backdrop to the Great Commission, Matthew describes a 'shadow' Great Commission to tell lies about the resurrection,[41] and then gives two further answers to the question. Jesus is seated on his throne in heaven, thus fulfilling all the promises about a Son/King/Son of Man/Glorified Servant from the Old Testament, and he exercises that authority first in commanding his disciples to make disciples for him 'of all the nations',[42] baptising them in the name of the Trinity. It is as they obey him in making disciples that he promises to be with them.[43]

Jesus is therefore not in his tomb but risen, and seated on his eternal throne he demonstrates he is with people as they are converted, and with his disciples as they make other disciples, for all nations – indeed the whole of creation – belong to him. He fills the earth and subdues it.[44] This scene therefore sits at the apex of a series of Old Testament expectations, and shows how the complex monotheism of the Old Testament, married to its hopes for a renewed creation with an eternal king, is met in the eternal ministry of the crucified and risen Son.

Incarnation and the Missionary Mediator

The emphasis on the continuing and glorified incarnation at this point can be seen in the preaching in Acts on at least two defining moments. The first will be considered in this section, the second in the next.

Acts 2

In the first evangelistic address, Peter structures his material to demonstrate that Jesus is the inheritor of the promises inherent in the Old Testament's monarchy. He first makes a universal claim for the significance of what has been seen and heard, because it demonstrates the incoming day of judgement. Rescue on that day is only possible in one way, for 'everyone who calls on the name of the Lord will be saved' (Acts 2:21, NIV). Who, then, is this Lord over the heavens and earth?[45] At this point Peter introduces 'Jesus of Nazareth, a man attested to you by God with deeds of power, wonders and signs'.

Jesus, then, is the *man* who is the agent of God's eschatological acts. That is Peter's base line. He then argues on the basis of Jesus' physical resurrection that Jesus is the one whom David promised as both Lord[46] and Messiah[47] and therefore the one who can rightly give God's Spirit. His conclusion brings together his argument, combining Jesus' genuine humanity, death, resurrection and reign. By repenting and being baptised in Jesus' name they will s*ave* themselves.[48] In other words, Peter reveals that the 'name of the Lord' by which Joel had said people will be 'saved'[49] is Jesus. And '(t)his Jesus God raised up, he is exalted at the right hand of God'.[50] The evangelistic work in Acts is predicated upon the incarnation, continued through the glory of the resurrection and ascension.

Jesus our brother

Nor is this a uniquely Lukan stress. As David Peterson has shown in chapter 3, the argument of Hebrews collapses without the physical humanity of our eternal high priest, just as much as it collapses without the physical humanity of the once-for-all sacrificial victim. And our present encouragement is also drawn from his glorified humanity, for we must,

> run with perseverance the race that is set before us looking to Jesus (again, note the personal name of the Incarnate Son which

continues into his heavenly ministry) the pioneer and perfecter of our faith, who for the sake of the joy that was set before him endured the cross, disregarding its shame, and has taken his seat at the right hand of the throne of God.[51]

Drawing all three of those strands together, the writer asserts that:

> since the children share flesh and blood, [Jesus] himself likewise shared the same things, so that through death he might destroy the one who has the power of death, that is, the devil ... For it is clear that he did not come to help angels, but the descendants of Abraham. Therefore he had to become like his brothers and sisters in every respect, so that he might be a merciful and faithful high priest in the service of God, to make a sacrifice of atonement for the sins of the people. Because he himself was tested by what he suffered, he is able to help those who are being tested (Heb. 2:14–18).

The current work of Jesus as our mediating priest requires us then to see the incarnation as a still necessary element of his person, and it is wrong to see him handing over his mission to the disciples as if they replace him. For though they represent him to the world, and that still remains to be examined below, he continues to represent them before the Father, and his mission continues. Building on that, if this is the eternal and essential mission of Christ, then we cannot divide his mission from the Father's, or talk as if the Father has a mission which is somehow larger and more affirmatory that the justifying mission of Christ. The eternal plan of God is for human beings to enter into the life of the Trinity. To put it in Pauline terms, the mission of God is that we may 'gain Christ and be found in him'.[52] The mission of God, put simply, is for people to become Christians, and that is identical in every respect, without addition or remainder, with the mission of Christ.

Just as the incarnation and atonement are indivisible, and to seek a theology of one without the other is doomed to failure, so it is with incarnation and the ascension, reign and return of Christ. That is why Calvin's theology of the incarnation is correctly read as prophet, priest and king, because to stop short of those three titles is to have a truncated view of incarnation.

Incarnation and the Missionary Message

Acts 10

The second moment in Acts when the incarnation is crucial for the developing plan is at the conversion of the Gentiles, because it provides the justification for a truly global missionary enterprise. The first clear occasion is the conversion of Cornelius,[53] and the incarnation is required for Peter's message 'of peace by Jesus Christ – he is Lord of all'.[54] The ground for what Peter is about to do is the international implication of the particular ministry of Jesus, who by virtue of his death and resurrection has been installed as 'judge of the living and the dead'[55] and who therefore is authorised to send his Spirit on the Gentiles.

This link between Jesus' present enthronement and his future coming in judgement as God's vicegerent provides the impetus to the evangelistic effort in Acts, and the link gains its strength from precisely the point that it is a resurrected man who is seated on the throne and who will judge. As Paul argued in Athens, God 'has fixed a day on which he will have the world judged in righteousness by a man whom he has appointed, and of this he has given assurance to all by raising him from the dead'. It is because of this that God 'commands all people everywhere to repent'.[56]

Jesus' resurrection thus confirms that he is the one who will be God's eternal Son,[57] and that God's reign of justice will be exercised through him. Because this is an issue which tracks back to the rebellion of humankind, and relates to the issue of God's exercising justice while yet fulfilling his promise of a glorious destiny for humankind, we should read here that faith in the risen Jesus is the only hope for all humanity. Everyone will be raised for the day of judgement,[58] but now we have proof of those various elements: that it will happen, that there is a possibility of a favourable outcome, and that the only ground for that favourable outcome is faith in the crucified and risen Jesus.

Communicating this message of future judgement and resurrection, then, should be the centre ground of the church's witness to Jesus, and we should not shrink from it because of embarrassment. Such embarrassment, though, is widespread and can be variously located. For some it is the physical nature of the resurrection, for others the reality of judgement, for others, and this is less commonly noted, it is embarrassment at the physical nature of the ascension and reign of Christ. For more radical feminists it is the notion of a continuing and glorified *maleness* that is the difficulty. But is always a refusal to jump that fence which causes the problems inherent in *Lux Mundi* and its theological descendants, and which leads to finding alternate ways of dealing with the continuing work of Christ. Frequently, it is that the church assumes the office and work of the mediator, in her sacraments, her Spirit-filled nature, her witness, her accepting grace, or her servanthood. She becomes Christ's substitute, the only possible outworking of Christ's continuing physicality. The church is somehow the continuation of the incarnation, *Christus prolongatus*.

If, however, Christ's humanity continues, glorified in heaven, then that lifts the burden of being the continuing form of the Messiah from us. True, the Church is called 'the body of Christ' on numerous occasions, but it is with two referents, either with respect to the relationships between the members or in relation to its head.[59] It is never so described in relation to the world as a continuing form of witness or servanthood, or as a substitute for Christ. Such necessary tasks have different theological origins. Further, the fact that 'body of Christ' language is not 'replacement' language but presupposes the continuing and differentiated incarnation of Christ, who dwells among us by means of his Spirit, means that such language can only ever be closely analogical. Christ's glorified body and our sinful bodies (physical and ecclesiastical) continue in parallel until he 'will transform our lowly bodies so that they will be like his glorious body'[60] at the final resurrection.

Incarnation and the Missionary Mandate

We have begun to suggest that this plan of salvation is grounded in the eternal counsel of God. That guards it from being a mere afterthought of God, a Plan B that was invented because Plan A failed. It is also a useful clarification, because it makes evident that even though we may begin our discussion of mission with the Great Commission, that is merely for convenience or presentation. Theologically, it begins not only further back but deeper in, not merely as an expression of God's eternal plan, but most profoundly of his person. We need to explore in what ways God is 'a missionary

God', as a common phrase puts it. We shall also need to clarify what the word 'mission' might mean.

The mission of God

The idea of God's mission (in the Latin phrase *Missio Dei*) was used by the early Church Fathers in the precise sense of referring to the incarnation of the eternal Son: he was the one who was *sent* by the Father to accomplish the mission of salvation.[61] In that understanding, God's mission is identical with Christ's saving mission, for 'God did not send his Son into the world to condemn the world, but in order that the world might be saved through him.'[62] That sending was the fulfilment of the international and interracial promises made by God throughout the Old Testament.[63]

Working backwards, then, the Father eternally sent the Son and the result of that sending was the incarnation. So we should ground this mission in God's person rather than just his plans because this sending happens from within the Trinity. The sending of the Son into the world is the expression in space and time of the eternal generation and obedience of the Son. To that extent, we can distinguish between the *Missio Dei* (God here being God the Father, rather than the Trinity) and the *missio Christi*, because we are talking of the different poles of a single relationship. They are distinguishable but inseparable.

That, though, is not how the phrase *Missio Dei* is used in much missiological literature, principally flowing from the International Missionary Council's conference in Willingen, Germany, in 1952. It was the second-to-last IMC conference, and much of its activity and thought was transferred across to the newly emerging World Council of Churches. The principal contribution of Willingen was to locate the origin of mission in the character of God rather than in the church. That sounds unobjectionable enough, for the church did not emerge by spontaneous generation but by the creative act of God. But two strands flowing into Willingen actually meant the thought was angled rather differently, and this has had huge implications for contemporary theology and practice.

The German missiologist Karl Hartenstein had introduced the concept *Missio Dei*, the mission of God, to show that just as Barth had located theology as God's work rather than ours, so too missiology had its focus in God's word rather than human endeavour. What was left unclear was whether the *Missio Dei* is everything God is towards us in creation, or whether it is his salvific plan. Hartenstein obscured the distinction between saving and common grace. Simultaneously, the Dutch missiologist Johannes C. Hoekendijk identified the result of God's mission as the establishment of *shalom*, the overarching kingdom of God. The means to that kingdom are various, including social and political change, and including (but not identified with) the Church's task of proclamation. 'Where a liberation to a rightful humanization is taking place … the *Missio Dei*, once again, has reached its goal.'[64] The church can thus witness to and contribute to the *Missio Dei*, but it must not confuse its role with that of the much larger picture. On this understanding *Missio Dei* is grounded in the character of God, for it is a kingdom of love, joy, peace and so on, but it is much larger than the task of the church, and can in many places supersede it. The theology and language of Willingen continue to be influential, and it is worth underlining that the way the term *Missio Dei* is used is a further example of *Lux Mundi*'s tendency to sound orthodox but be unorthodox.

So what, then, is mission? The problem, of course, is that it has proved an almost infinitely pliable term, especially compared with incarnation, which is precise and defined. 'Incarnation and mission' is an unequal coupling of different kinds of terms. And the term mission may be referring to the mission of God the Trinity, or some aspect of the work of the Father, the Son, or the Holy Spirit, or to how any of those bears on the task of the church. What is immediately clear is that different people are using words to mean wildly differing things, although the similarity of the vocabulary may mask that. A number of people may agree with Vatican II's statement that 'the pilgrim church is missionary by her very nature'[65] and yet completely miss each other's meaning. In particular, it is clear that the positions flowing out of a position similar to that of *Lux Mundi* are at radical odds with the theology of evangelicals, and so, we would claim, with the Bible itself and therefore with God himself.

Two related distinctions should be made between these different understandings. First, the initial description we offered is that the *Missio Dei* should be grounded in God's eternal triune person rather than merely his character. That means that the defining focus of mission should be the redemptive sending of the Son rather than a vague God-being-for-us-ness. Secondly, because it is so grounded, it is a mistake to separate the *Missio Dei* from the *missio Christi*, because that is to separate the persons of the Trinity and their intentions. In other words, in classic orthodox theology the *missio Christi* explains and exhausts the *Missio Dei* without any remainder.

It is also clear that to talk of 'the theology of evangelicals' does not adequately represent the variety of views on offer, even among those who will take a staunchly orthodox view of the incarnation and see it as the touchstone of how mission is to be interpreted. This needs to be developed.

Incarnation and the Missionary Model

Lausanne 1

For evangelicals, the clearest and most important explanation of the link between incarnation and mission came at the first International Congress on World Evangelisation, held at Lausanne, Switzerland, in 1974.[66] It has won widespread, but not universal, acceptance.[67]

In a series of Congress addresses subsequently published as *Christian Mission in the Modern World*,[68] John Stott articulated what was to become the standard (although not the only) conservative evangelical view. He had once taught that 'the mission of the church, according to the specification of the risen Lord, is explicitly a preaching, converting and teaching mission'[69] but now he would express himself differently. Distancing himself from the twin error of identifying mission with either evangelism or social action exclusively, and refusing to see social action as a mere 'consequence' of the Great Commission, he wrote, 'The actual commission itself must be understood to include social as well as evangelistic responsibility, unless we are to be guilty of distorting the words of Jesus.'[70] The relationship between the two therefore is of a partnership, originating in love for suffering humanity. It is not an equal partnership to be sure, for Stott quotes approvingly the Lausanne phrase 'in the church's mission of sacrificial service, evangelism is primary'.[71] Nevertheless, they are inseparable partners.

The biblical basis for this is paramount, and for Stott it is rooted in the Great Commission, and particularly the Johannine form:

> The crucial form in which the Great Commission has been handed down to us (though it is the most neglected because it is the most costly) is the Johannine ... (D)eliberately and precisely (Jesus) made his mission the *model* of ours, saying '*as* the Father sent me, *so* I send you.' Therefore our understanding of the Church's mission must be deduced from our understanding of the Son's.[72]

Safeguarding the unique mission of Jesus as our Saviour, Stott maintained that Jesus' mission was one of service (Mk 10:45, Lk. 22:27) and therefore in a derived way ours is too. Again, Stott quoted Lausanne: 'We affirm that Christ sends his redeemed people into the world as the Father sent him, and that this calls for a similar deep and costly penetration of the world.'[73]

This understanding has become normative, such that the second Lausanne Congress, held in Manila in 1989, could assume it even though it went beyond it in its Manila Manifesto:

> True mission should always be incarnational. It necessitates entering humbly into other people's worlds, identifying with their social reality, their sorrow and suffering, and their struggles for justice against oppressive powers. This cannot be done without personal sacrifices.[74]

The crucial form?
In a brief written debate with the eminent missiologist David J. Hesselgrave,[75] Stott has more recently clarified and underlined his view. Pressed on the centrality of the Johannine commission, Stott wrote:

> I acknowledge that I exaggerated when I described the Johannine form of the Great Commission as its 'crucial' form. What I mean was that we are given the Great Commission in two main forms, first in its Synoptic form (Matthew, Mark and Luke-Acts) which emphasizes preaching and witnessing, and then in its Johannine

form (John 17:18; 20:21) which emphasizes our being sent into the world like Christ. The reason why the latter seems 'crucial' to me is that it is largely neglected by us evangelicals, not least because of its costliness ... I am unwilling therefore to go back on my conviction that authentic Christian mission is incarnational mission. It necessitates entering other people's worlds, as Christ entered ours, and giving ourselves in service, as he did. There is certainly room for debate regarding the forms this service will take, but not (I believe) regarding the principle that we are called to sacrifice and service like him.[76]

Various observations need to be made at this stage. No one, I think, says that the only task Christians have in the world is evangelism. We may differ over whether action to be taken includes agitating for political or economic change, over the relative priorities given to various groups, or over the rightness of supporting various claims for just wars or pacifism. We may differ over whether the best economic tools are libertarian or directed, whether the action should be taken by individual Christians, by congregations or by denominations, whether it is conceivable to set up a Christian political party, and if so whether it should be of the left, right, centre or some other way, over the proportion of money given to support aid over evangelism, or a multitude of other issues. But the core claim of Christ to be Lord, and therefore for all human institutions to bow the knee to him, and of the need for our love of neighbour to have tangible form, no one can doubt. Christians who take their Bibles seriously should be involved in both evangelism and some form of loving action.[77] This is agreed ground.[78]

That said, how adequate is it to ground this double action in the twin forms of the Great Commission and in particular the incarnational model from John? The separation between the two forms of Great Commission disappears as soon as it is applied. It looks neat to say that 'its Synoptic form ... emphasises preaching and witnessing, and ... its Johannine form ... emphasises our being sent into the world like Christ',[79] but the neatness is deceptive, for the consequent argument does not follow. In particular, to demonstrate what kind of incarnational ministry the Johannine Jesus has, Stott quotes Mark and Luke.[80] This is illuminating, because it breaks down the distinction. On the one hand, the Synoptics have a much broader expectation of what will happen when people are taught 'to obey everything that I have commanded you',[81] because it will involve the full range of things Jesus expects in those Gospels. Crucially, however, they do not make the incarnation the model for that action, and they make that action an inevitable result of obeying the theologically prior gospel. John, on the other hand, who does draw some parallels from the incarnation, does not present us with a Jesus who is actively involved in a political, social or liberation programme. The 'works' of Jesus in John are the sign-works that point to his exclusive Messiahship. The distinction between the two Commissions, and the grounds on which one is 'crucial' appear neat, and are emotionally compelling, but it misrepresents the text.

The text must be read in context. Either side of the Johannine commissioning is the phrase 'Peace be with you', tied with his showing them his hands and side.[82] It seems clear, then, that peace with God (as Thomas calls Jesus in Jn. 20:26) is only possible because of the cross and resurrection. Because Jesus has shown them his resurrected body (in a way that emphasises his crucifixion wounds), they are now witnesses who tell others and who are to be believed (Jn. 20:25, 27, 29). Moreover, the explicit outworking of that peace with God is that Jesus 'breathed on them and said, "receive the Holy Spirit. If you forgive anyone his sins they are forgiven; if you do not forgive them, they are not forgiven"' (Jn. 20:22–3, NIV). As forgiven people, they receive the Spirit to tell others of the message of forgiveness through the death of Christ. This is exactly the logic we find in the Synoptics.[83] John, like the other three Gospels, explains the content of being 'sent' as preaching and witnessing.

None of this undermines at all the costliness of Christ's being sent, nor the costliness of our being sent into a world, which is simultaneously loved and hated by God, and which hates the one who loves it, and hates his servants. But although that language is Johannine, the thoughts are not uniquely his, and can easily be found elsewhere. Indeed, Stott himself lists various actions, saying that Jesus,

> served in deed as well as in word, and it would be impossible in the ministry of Jesus to separate his works from his words. He fed

hungry mouths and washed dirty feet, he healed the sick, comforted the sad and even restored the dead to life.[84]

The Synoptic-Johannine distinction does not work. That means we do not need to ground either the cost or the sending on the incarnation. It also allows us to remove 'words and works' from that same trap of neat apparent balance and ask hard questions about their relationship: do they stand as equal partners, or is one senior, or even the cause? Given that they are both mandated, do they stand in equally balanced proportion? Given that both are important, are they equally important? And given that Jesus mandates them both, are they mandated in the same way, for the same purpose, for the same reason?

Sending and Sonship
A further observation arises here, because of the close relationship between Jesus' sending and ours. Does it demonstrate that our mission is in some sense 'incarnational'? On the surface, John 17:18, 'As you have sent me into the world, so I have sent them into the world' and John 20:21, 'As the Father has sent me, so I send you', would seem to be conclusive. The incarnation is the primary model of costly mission to our world.

In various articles and books, Andreas Köstenberger argues differently. In his work, the language of 'sending' in John is a precise theological term that relates not so much to the overarching and general movement of Jesus in the world in obedience to the Father, but is only linked to his work in his title role of 'Son'. Being 'sent' is not a concept that can bear an infinite number of meanings.

> In the context of the larger themes of Jesus' obedience and dependence, the following emphases of sending terminology in the Fourth Gospel can be identified. Generally, the sent one is: to bring glory and honour to the sender (5:23; 7:18); to do the sender's will (4:34; 5:30, 38: 6:38–9) and works (5:36; 5:23; 7:18); to speak the sender's words (3:34; 7:16; 12:49; 14:10b, 24) and to be accountable to the sender (especially chapter 17). He is to bear witness to the sender (5:36; 7:28 = 8:26), to represent the sender accurately (12:44–5; 13;20; 15:18–25), to exercise delegated

authority (5:21–2, 27; 13:3; 17:2; 20:23); and finally the sent one is to know the sender intimately (7:29; cf. 15:21; 17:8, 25), live in close relationship with the sender (8:16, 18, 29; 16:32) and follow the sender's example (13:16).[85]

We should note, too, that this is an irreversible relationship, and there is no sense in which the Son 'sends' the Father; the relationship is one of obedience to and dependence on a higher authority.

If Köstenberger's description is adequate, then it follows that in John 20:21 our relationship with Jesus is worked out in terms of intimacy, dependence and glory. However, some of his conclusions are worth stating more closely:

> The fact that Jesus shows to his disciples his pierced hands and his side (cf. 20:19), as well as his commission to forgive or retain sins, ties the disciples' mission to Jesus' death (cf. chaps 18–20; cf. also 17:4 and 19:30). Jesus' mission is unique, irreplaceable, and fundamental for the church's mission. His sacrifice makes the disciples' mission possible ... While the disciples share in the likeness of Jesus' sending from the Father – with no direct implications as to Jesus' divine nature and thus his unique revelatory or redemptive work – and thus in the manner of his sending, they share only mediately in the purpose of Jesus' mission by being his instruments of further extending it. *Jesus' mission itself is never rescinded or abandoned in the Fourth Gospel. Jesus is still, through the Spirit and his disciples, carrying out his mission, though now from heaven. The disciples do not replace Jesus.*[86]

And what is particularly instructive for our subject,

> Perhaps one can compare and contrast the relationship between the missions and sending of Jesus and the disciples this way: while the ways in which they are sent contain elements of analogy, their missions are still distinct. If the missions of Jesus and the disciples were identical the disciples could replace Jesus. But since important distinctions remain, the disciples merely enter into Jesus' mission (cf. 4:38).[87]

One further consequence of Köstenberger's analysis bears thought. The comparison between the two sendings in the Johannine Great Commissions lies simply at one point: the one being sent is sent to do a task. It is not possible to read into those verses every aspect of Jesus' incarnation and read them across to us, nor even to narrow that range down to a more acceptable but still powerful combination, as we have seen Stott has done. Those verses simply say that Jesus was sent and he obeyed, and now he is sending us and he expects us to relate to him in the way of obedient love that he relates to his Father. Whatever other grounds may be provided for the sacrificial love of neighbour, they cannot be provided by the Johannine Great Commission, and it is potentially misleading to use the incarnation as a model in this generalised way.

Incarnation and Missionary Method

We have observed the primacy of the doctrine of the incarnation for missiological thinking from a number of angles, from conservative evangelical through to the World Council of Churches. We have noted too how this agreement may be more apparent than real, given the different meanings given to 'incarnation' and 'mission'. Nevertheless, it is clearly the case that across the whole spread of missiological thinking there is a continuing move to place the incarnation as the defining centre, with only occasional voices of dissent.[88]

There are two main benefits that this move has been seen to provide, which will be examined below, but one undergirding assumption should be noted at the outset. It is that the defining model for missionary work is the messianic ministry of Jesus. Hence, the frequency of 'kingdom' language, which is typically, though not uniquely, associated with Jesus' ministry,[89] and within that his pre-crucifixion ministry, often in a fairly loose way.[90] This sounds unexceptional until we note the corollary that the defining model is therefore not the apostolic ministry of Paul, mirrored in the ministries of Timothy, Titus and so on.

This is problematic from the outset, because Paul manifestly holds up his ministry, rather than Jesus', as the one that is to be emulated, despite the shame that such emulation would cost the missionary. In fact, he links emulating his ministry with being loyal to Jesus when he says, 'Do not be ashamed, then, of the testimony about our Lord or of me his prisoner, but join with me in suffering for the gospel.'[91] To be ashamed of Paul is to be ashamed of Jesus, and in the context of 2 Timothy being ashamed of Paul means being ashamed of his pattern of ministry. Dividing the two, and then shifting the focus from Paul, with his self-evident strategy of evangelising, church planting and training, to Jesus means that core elements which the New Testament plainly gives us as the norm for pastoral and missionary service have been diluted. Whatever gains there are in making the incarnation central as the model to be copied, and Paul does use the incarnation as a model for his ministry in part, there are huge weaknesses inherent in leaping from Jesus to us and avoiding the apostolic norms.[92]

What, then, are the two main benefits that the shift to the incarnation is alleged to have won? They are that mission is *embodied* and *encultured*.

Embodied mission

One aspect of seeing the incarnation as a model of cross-cultural method is a network of ideas that crystallise around the claim that the incarnation was in some sense a benefit to God himself. It is alleged that without the incarnation, God would be incomprehensible, and that the gospel requires him to become like one of us for us to understand and know him.[93] This obviously has massive implications for our expectations of patterns of ministry today, of which two are the most striking.

The dumb God

The first implication is that God is somehow unable to communicate with us unless he is embodied. He cannot adequately show us the depth of his love by mere words. Now there is a truth here that needs to be guarded, because it is unquestionably the case that God could not save us by mere words. There was no other way than by a bloody corpse on a gibbet, however many alternatives Jesus may have wanted to take.[94] That truth needs to be stated carefully and not misunderstood, because there is a significant difference between saying 'God could not *save* us without the incarnation' and 'God could not *be known* by us without the incarnation'. It is that second statement which undermines the power of words, and ultimately the power of God.

Take, for instance, a pet dog being told off by its owner.[95] It is quite difficult, if not impossible in most circumstances, to communicate to the dog the precise grounds on why it is being disciplined. On a small group of frequently reinforced matters, the dog gets the general drift, but on a good many occasions it simply wags its tail and grins inanely. The communication problem is evident, but we shouldn't get it wrong. It is not that the human is so infinitely and transcendently removed from the dog's way of communication that two-way understanding is impossible. The problem is that the human being is *not transcendent enough*. An infinitely wise and powerful God, who made all the neurones in the dog's brain, would be able to communicate with it with no loss of understanding. So it is with God and us. The very idea that he has to become a man in order to communicate with us is absurd, because such a God would not be God. The God of the Bible could speak, write, question and even design a building to its precise proportions without becoming a man. Clearly there is an issue of communication involved in the incarnation, for it is the Word who becomes flesh, but the issue cannot be that God could not speak without it. After all, it is the Incarnate one who describes the Old Testament as what God 'said'.[96]

The implication of this for mission and ministry is clear: if God could speak with perfect clarity through his Word before the incarnation, so he is able to do it after the incarnation, or rather after the ascension. It is the glorified Incarnate one who speaks through his word to his people[97] and he needs no second, mirroring incarnation to make that communication possible. He is not dumb.

The dumb Jesus

A second implication of the assumption that God needed to become like one of us in order to communicate with us is that words, which God has access to and uses throughout the Bible, are downplayed because they are evidently inadequate for 'real' communication, which is 'being with' people.

Again, there is a truth here that must not be lost. 'Mere' words are the subject of scathing attacks by Jesus[98] – but 'mere' words for him are words that are not acted on, not words in and of themselves. That is, Jesus is not attacking words, but insincerity. Indeed, Jesus' ministry shows the very centrality of words and teaching.

To take one obvious example – but one which is central to the entirety of Jesus' ministry from the start – in Mark 1:32–9, after a series of healings and exorcisms, a crowd has accumulated around the place where Jesus was expected to be. He is not there, but praying, and it is presumably because he is facing a decision over the nature of his ministry. Peter was deputed to find him, and when he did, challenged Jesus with an accusation that Jesus was shirking his duty and failing to live up to the extravagant expectations he had raised: 'Everyone is looking for you.' Jesus' response is telling, for it reflects on the precise issue of his ministry, and 'being with' people. Rather than return to Capernaum, he said, 'Let us go somewhere else – to the nearby villages – so that I can preach there also. That is why I have come' (Mk. 1:38, NIV). The normative issue for Jesus was his teaching, his words.

Now that obviously needs expansion, for he cannot teach unless he is with people, and it is a self-evident entailment of his teaching that healings and exorcism follow as the next verse shows, and the content of his teaching was about himself and his death. Nevertheless, we must see that the heart of Jesus' ministry, even in the Gospel that is most commonly thought of as the 'action' Gospel, is to teach people rather than merely to be with people. As Mark 1:38 shows, he even abandoned some people whom he had taught so that he could go to teach others.

Again, the implications for mission and ministry are clear but profound, even on that single but central passage. Jesus did not come into the world to 'be with' people; he came to teach them, and that should be our expectation of our own missions and ministries today. The reason why this is so necessary to articulate in our theological context is the downplaying of words in our missionary thinking. Sometimes it is heard in the phrase that is attributed to Francis of Assisi, 'Preach the gospel, use words if you have to', or it is articulated along the lines that 'Being with … is itself an expression the gospel.'[99] The rock that both those ideas stumble on is that actions on their own are open to misinterpretation, *and that was as true of Jesus as of anyone else.*[100]

The crowd, the Jewish leaders and his disciples constantly misread Jesus' actions. Just 'being with' people is insufficient for adequate communication, and although Jesus did spend time with people it was so that when he spoke he would be heard, and often hated in consequence. Jesus did not come to 'be' but to act and explain his actions so that people might put their faith in him.[101] Actions and signs are in themselves ambiguous,[102] and require authentication and explanation by the spoken word. If that was true of Jesus' perfect signs,[103] how much more will we need to speak of him to make our sinful actions point to him.

Encultured mission

Cross-cultural mission requires a 'bridging' movement between the two cultures of the missionary and the culture where the work is to be done. So that the gospel can be heard, words, concepts, applications and even lifestyle must be translated so that the hearers hear the gospel as clearly in their language as did the first Christians. This process is variously called 'enculturation', 'indigenisation' or 'contextualisation', and the basic point is easy to grasp. Human knowledge of God is always embodied or incarnated in a culture, to the extent that it is impossible to have pure, non-cultural knowledge of him.

The extent to which this process should be taken is a matter of some debate, because of the differing perspectives on mission. For some it means simply ensuring accurate Bible translation so that today's hearers correctly hear the message in their own culture. For others it is that the requirement that missionaries are not mere visitors to the place where they work but live, belong and identify with the people there, together with their concerns. For yet others it will be standing with the poor and dispossessed and seeking justice and good news for them. There are quite clearly major theological disagreements along that spectrum, but the common element seems to be that genuine transmission[104] of the gospel requires a contemporary incarnation of the gospel.

The incarnate Paul

That position can be derived from Paul, of course, in his outlining of this aspect of his ministry:

> Though I am free and belong to no man, I make myself a slave to everyone, to win as many as possible. To the Jews I became like a Jew, to win the Jews. To those under the law I became like one under the law (though I myself am not under the law), so as to win

those under the law. To those not having the law I became like one not having the law (though I am not free from God's law but am under Christ's law), so as to win those not having the law. To the weak I became weak, to win the weak. I have become all things to all men so that by all possible means I might save some (1 Cor. 9:19–22, NIV).

The 'law of Christ' is central to his argument here, and it occurs in the midst of a heated defence of his freedom to become like different people in order that they may hear the gospel, and the problems that his practice caused to some believers who held he was breaking 'God's (i.e. Old Testament) Law'. What, here, is the 'law' of Christ which Paul claims he obeys? It seems to be not so much a command or a teaching but a principle, which is as valid a way of translating the word *nomos*. The principle would seem to be that just as Christ became like us in order to win us, so Paul tries to become like others to win them. The incarnation is a model for mission, to this extent.

But we should be careful to note what can and cannot be derived from that. Notice first that Paul did not adopt the habits and practices of an alien culture in this 'becoming'. He was a Jew, and he was also a Roman citizen. He was thus already at home in both worlds. True, as a Jew he would not have moved with personal ease in a Gentile setting, and he certainly would not have been taken for a Gentile. Everything in his appearance and lifestyle would have marked him. Nevertheless, under that most important rubric he was a Roman citizen with the inherent advantages, languages and access to culture. After his conversion he was committed to losing the national and racial markers, and to live as a Gentile to win the Gentiles, but the move was one he was prepared for to some extent by his dual status even if not by his theology.

So while it is true to say Paul practised flexibility and cultural relevance, it says too much too quickly to suggest he was engaged in what we would call cross-cultural mission. This is not to say that he *would not* have engaged in the task, for he clearly believed that the gospel was for all the world, nor is it to say that we *should not* engage in it, for that is the only way the gospel will spread to the unreached nations. It might suggest, though, that there are more issues to be discussed in cross-cultural mission than the mere transference of an idea. Notice, by the way, that Paul's reason for becoming like people was to 'preach', 'win' and 'save'.[105]

The incarnate Jesus

If that is true of Paul, it is even more so of Jesus. As the Incarnate One, it is commonly stated that he is the great exemplar of cross-cultural incarnational mission, for he became like us. In standing alongside the poor he showed us the true nature of incarnational mission, which is in life rather than merely in words. We must find ways to re-express this incarnation today. The youth work specialist, Pete Ward, reflects this when he writes:

> The Christian faith rests on the belief that God became human in Jesus Christ. Jesus is 'the Word' become flesh; God's revelation within human history and human culture. When God chooses to communicate his message he does so using the language, customs and social relationships of a particular group of people in a particular time and in a particular place. Jesus was therefore a Jew born into a Jewish family. *This means that the content of the 'good news' as we see it in the Gospels is intimately connected to the social, political and spiritual context within which Jesus grew up and began to minister.* The location of the Word of God within culture must be taken seriously by any Christian seeking guidance from the life of Christ. For while we may want to assert that God reveals himself in the life of Jesus, we must also acknowledge that this life was lived out in a time which was quite different to our own. The fact that the Word of God was incarnated within culture brings God closer to us*, but it also creates a cultural distance for us.*[106]

The difficulty is that, again, this proves too little. The incarnation was the moment when the God of all nations, tribes and languages became one individual man. But it was that transcultural, supreme God who acted. This God would have been equally at home, and at ease, in any human culture. He did not cross any cultural boundaries to become a man. More than that, he came to 'his own',[107] the people he had called and saved, and whose worship he had created and whose hopes he had fashioned in order to point at his coming. To put it more strongly, God had created the culture into which he was to be born, so that he would be understood. If ever there was an example of 'in-cultural' mission this was it.

This distances us from Ward, who correctly understands the corollary of his position. 'The fact that the Word of God was incarnated within culture brings God closer to us, but it also creates a cultural distance for us.' By implication, the very 'content' may have to change.[108] Ward has taken us back to Lessing's famous 'ugly ditch that I cannot get across, no matter how often and how earnestly I have tried to make the leap',[109] and to the background setting for *Lux Mundi*. As Gore wrote in another work, 'It was only in fact by His ceasing to be remembered as historically He was, that he could be serviceable for the generations to come.'[110] There is therefore no aspect of the gospel which may be fixed, or which might act as the touchstone by which the veracity of other interpretations might be corrected. One interpreter might say this while holding a clear Chalcedonian understanding of the incarnation, but it is not necessary to do so – and, indeed, removes its necessity.

Instead, we should insist that the particularity of the incarnation is its strength, because God created that culture precisely so that it would be possible to communicate the gospel *with absolute clarity to all subsequent cultures*. It is careless to think as if there are two cultural contexts to consider, Jesus' and ours, each equally time bound and limited, and that our task is to extract a timeless gospel from that culture and reincarnate it today. That is not only impossible, for there is no way of speaking which is not an aspect of culture, but more importantly it is unnecessary, because of the way God fashioned the culture into which he spoke.[111]

From another perspective, though, this view proves too much. Consider the massive gap that needed bridging – creator and cremation, eternal God and time-bound people, infinite and finite, and above all, holy and sinful. From that perspective, the task of becoming incarnate is so impossible that only an omnipotent God can achieve it. To move with ease in such a different mode of being requires being God in human form, and no human today is capable of the slightest echo of such an infinite work.

To put those observations together, Jesus' incarnation was a perfect incarnation, and before any lessons can be derived from this 'law' or principle,[112] the differences between Christ and us must be carefully and reverently drawn. If by becoming incarnate we mean the full Chalcedonian understanding of the words, then copying this model, and even adopting it as our own, should be seen as impossible. Perhaps we should relieve our missionaries of guilt on this issue. Because Christ came to 'his own' we should stop making them think that what we require of them in cross-cultural mission is in some way easy, obvious, or a necessary step in discipleship. Conversely, because it was the 'Word of God' who came to 'his own' we should stop making them think that becoming incarnate in another culture will ever be possible for them.

We must rightly locate Jesus within his first-century culture, but we must not do so in a way that locks him into it, unable to speak to different times and cultures. Over-emphasising the particularity of Jesus' incarnation in a first-century culture will inevitably weaken him. Subsequent generations then have to become the means by which Christ becomes 'real' or incarnate in their day. The church then inherits his messianic task. But correctly seeing that it is the one, great eternal and infinite God who became man at one place and time relieves us of this impossible demand. The particularity of the incarnation safeguards its reality, because it must mean that Jesus was a specific Jewish (not Gentile) man (not woman), who really ate, slept and wept, with a height and weight that could be measured and an accent that could be discerned. But that it was the eternal and infinite God who acted in this way safeguards its cross-cultural relevance, and Jesus' once-and-for-all words and actions are never locked into first-century ways of thinking or speaking which demand revision in the light of later understanding. They were perfect and complete, for all times and places.

Above all, we should cease making Jesus' messianic ministry our own, as if we replaced him in the world as God's agent for transforming human society into the kingdom of God. The post of Messiah is wonderfully and eternally occupied, and evangelicals should be the first to filter Jesus' ministry through the God-given interpretative grid of the remainder of the New Testament, particularly in their expectations of pastoral and missionary leadership.

Conclusion: Incarnation and Mission

The primary focus of the incarnation is the achieving of eternal salvation, and only the cross and resurrection of the incarnate

Messiah can bring that. Although Jesus' ministry appears to have a wide focus, it gradually becomes clear that everything in his ministry preceding the cross can only have meaning when seen in the light of the cross. Indeed, Paul argues that it is the cross that should be the method and model for our ministries.[113]

Because the incarnation was eternally intended as redemptive, we should note the plight of humankind from which we needed to be redeemed. In Paul's phrase, without Christ we are 'without hope, and without God in the world.'[114] It is wilful, then, to see the incarnation as somehow affirmatory of our spiritual or social progress, as if God were delighted in his sinful children, if occasionally mildly irritated by their foolishness. The seriousness with which evangelicals take the sinfulness of the human heart must mean that we could never see our social actions as anything but broadly preventative, and certainly not as a substitute for salvation. The theology that sees the Fall as a Fall upwards, and the incarnation as an inevitable stage on our spiritual pilgrimage is a quite different religion from the one which sees the Fall as a Fall into God's curse and the incarnation as a marvellous and utterly undeserved breaking-in of grace. They are two religions with two different Gods and two different creeds.

The mission of Christians, then, modelled in a secondary way on the mission of the apostles, is to witness to the lordship of Jesus and call others to repentance and faith in his redemptive work. Our changed lives should demonstrate that we are under a different Lord, and our concern for the poor should be exemplary. But that concern and its outworking in action must not be confused with our mission. 'Word' and 'deed' are not to be held in some creative tension or delicate balance, but both held in their proper, but different, relations to the Lord Jesus. The ground for a theology of social involvement needs to be established robustly, but perhaps the incarnation is not quite the organising principle it first appears. Because evangelism and social action are distinct, they must not be confused, as if engaging in one allowed one not to engage in the other. They are both mandatory, for different yet equally biblically driven reasons. What we are 'sent' to do is to bear witness to the Incarnate Son of God, the crucified and risen judge of all.

Notes

1. M. Ramsey, *From Gore to Temple, the Development of Anglican Theology between Lux Mundi and the Second World War* (London: Longmans, 1960), p. 27. At the time Ramsey wrote this important book he was Archbishop of York, and became Archbishop of Canterbury a year later.
2. *Lux Mundi* (10th ed.; London: John Murray, 1890).
3. From J.R. Illingworth's seminal essay, 'The Incarnation and Development', in *Lux Mundi*, pp. 152–3.
4. 'Laissez-fairism and socialism, racism and antiracism, segregationism and desegregationism, militarism and pacifism, imperialism and anti-imperialism, Marxism and evolutionary socialism, social engineering and eugenics – surely they cannot all legitimately claim descent from the same ancestor. Yet, like the evolutionary tree itself, with its many branches and offshoots, they are all related – not directly to each other but to the parent doctrine.' G. Himmelfarb, *Victorian Minds* (Chicago: Elephant 1995), p. 327. Himmelfarb correctly traces this Social Darwinism through to Teilhard de Chardin (p. 330).
5. Ramsey, *From Gore to Temple*, p. 7.
6. S. Mott, *Biblical Ethics and Social Change* (Oxford: Oxford University Press, 1982), p. 194.
7. Although with a post-millennial optimism that was a major contributor to the familiar American optimism and 'can-do' mentality. Both sit uneasily with most British evangelicalism, although it is debatable whether that is for theological or cultural reasons.
8. J. Piper, *Let the Nations be Glad* (Leicester: Inter-Varsity Press, 1993), p. 49.
9. Agreed, moreover, on a theology that was credally orthodox, and therefore not that of *Lux Mundi*.
10. See *Institutes*, Book 2, Chapters 12–16.
11. Ibid., chapter 12.5.
12. Bishop Samuel Wilberforce, who took the brunt of the attack for his disagreement with Charles Darwin and debate with Thomas Huxley, and who is therefore still an example of 'naïve fundamentalism', was at the tim Vice-President of the British Association for the Advancement of Science, and an eminent and published scientist himself.
13. D. Bosch, *Transforming Mission* (New York: Orbis, 1991), p. 512.
14. Borne out by both their doctrinal assertions and the continuing fascination with Jesus in the Gospels. The twentieth century ended as it

had begun, with international evangelical best-sellers on the life and ministry of Jesus. A. Edersheim's *The Life and Times of Jesus the Messiah* (first published 1900) and A.B. Bruce's *The Training of the Twelve* (first published 1871) are both still in print. P. Yancey's *The Jesus I Never Knew* (Grand Rapids: Zondervan, 1995) won Gold Medallion Christian Book of the Year award in 1996 by the evangelical Christian Publishers Association. See too the important counter arguments laid out by Michael Ovey in his two papers in this volume.

[15] See, in particular, J.R. Illingworth, 'The Incarnation in regard to Development' ch. 5.

[16] *Lux Mundi* (10th ed.), p. ix.

[17] I strongly suspect that evangelicals in some other denominations would recognise this pattern and methodology, although they would not use 'Catholicism' in the title.

[18] Dt. 6:4.

[19] E.g. W.C. Kaiser, *Mission in the Old Testament* (Grand Rapids: Baker, 2000).

[20] E.g. A.J. Köstenberger and P.T. O'Brien, *Salvation to the Ends of the Earth* (Leicester: Inter-Varsity Press, 2001).

[21] Gen. 1:26, italics added.

[22] Ps. 2.

[23] Ezek. 37:14.

[24] Isa. 59:1.

[25] See L.W. Hurtado, *One God, One Lord; Early Christian Devotion and Ancient Jewish Monotheism* (London: SCM, 1988), and R.T. France, 'The Worship of Jesus: a neglected factor in Christological debate', in *Christ the Lord; Studies in Christology presented to Donald Guthrie*, H.H. Rowdon (ed.), (Leicester: Inter-Varsity Press, 1982).

[26] As a summary, Lk. 7:24.

[27] Lk. 1:77, 3:3; in both cases using *aphesin*.

[28] The 'blindness' could be a simple reference to helplessness (29:18; 35:5) or refer to Israel's failure to be a light to the Gentiles, with the new promise that would come with the Servant. It is striking, though, that upon captivity King Zedekiah, typifying the nation and its hopes, was blinded (2 Kgs. 25:7). Giving sight to the blind might then have a strongly exilic context and, as with the other three terms, be a metaphor for the return to the land under a renewed monarchy.

29. See W.J. Dumbrell, *The Search for Order; Biblical Eschatology of Focus* (Grand Rapids: Baker, 1994). The current wave of interest in Biblical Theology amongst evangelicals finds its intellectual roots at Moore Theological College in Sydney (where Dumbrell taught), and it is worth remembering that the Biblical Theology course there began as a search for the biblical basis for mission.
30. Lk. 24:47.
31. On the assumption that the two works, although discrete, form a literary and theological whole (cf. Acts 1:1).
32. Gen. 12:2–3.
33. Acts 2:36. 'All Israel' can refer to Israel in totality in assembly (Dt. 1:1, 5:1, etc.), but crucially to the nation before its division (see especially 2 Kgs. 9:14). Subsequently it means the Northern Kingdom, but the hopes of reunion were tied to the Exile (e.g. Ezek. 37:15–28).
34. Acts 15:17.
35. H.J.M. Nouwen, *The Return of the Prodigal Son* (London: Darton, Longman and Todd, 1994).
36. Ibid., p. 95f.
37. As I say, this is one example among many. One might also think of the practice in many contemporary liturgies of basing our assurance of forgiveness in the fact that we are truly sorry, or that God is one who shows mercy, rather than explicitly on the cross itself.
38. 'Then give to Caesar what is Caesar's, and to God what is God's' (Lk. 20:25).
39. Mt. 28:4.
40. Mt. 28:9–10.
41. Mt. 28:11–15.
42. Mt. 28:19.
43. Mt. 28:20.
44. Cf. Gen. 1:28.
45. Acts 2:19.
46. Acts 2:23–8.
47. Acts 2:29–35.
48. Acts 2:40.
49. Acts 2:21.
50. Acts 2:32–3.
51. Heb. 12:1–2.
52. Phil. 3:8–9.

The Incarnation and Mission 147

[53] Acts 10:1–48. Although some would argue that the Ethiopian eunuch in the preceding story is the first Gentile convert, Luke uses Cornelius's conversion to deal with the inclusion of the Gentiles explicitly and theologically.
[54] Acts 10:36.
[55] Acts 10:42.
[56] Acts 17:30–1.
[57] Here 'Son' refers not to Jesus' eternal ontological Sonship, but his role as Davidic King, which he assumed at the incarnation.
[58] Dan. 12:1–2.
[59] 'Head' in this instance is not primarily a biological but a political metaphor, in the sense of 'chief' or 'ruler'. Jesus is not merely a superior member of the body, *primus inter pares,* but in a distinctive ruling position with relation to it. 'Head' and 'body' are therefore two metaphors, not one.
[60] Phil. 3:21.
[61] See, for instance, Augustine *De Trinitate* Bk. 4 ch. 20 para. 27; or Hilary, *De Trinitate* Bk. 3, ch. 12 and Bk. 5, ch. 11. Both Augustine and Hilary stress that the Son is co-equal with the Father, but that because of his eternal nature *as Son* it is proper that he should obey the Father and become Incarnate. For both the thought and the above references I am indebted to Michael Ovey.
[62] Jn. 3:17. cf. Jn. 5:30, 11:42, 17:18.
[63] Gen. 12:1–3 is the obvious starting point, and Is. 66 an obvious climax.
[64] The essence of the theology issuing from Willingen can most accessibly be grasped in N. Thomas (ed.), *Readings in World Mission* (London: SPCK, 1995), pp. 103–4, 124, 305–6.
[65] This was the first of the Doctrinal Principles of the Decree on Missionary Activity of the Church, 'Ad Gentes Divinitus', para 2. in *The Documents of Vatican II* (trans. J. Gallagher; ed. W.M. Abbott; London: Geoffrey Chapman, 1966), p. 585.
[66] The papers were subsequently published in J.D. Douglas (ed.), *Let the Earth Hear His Voice* (Minneapolis: World Wide, 1975).
[67] For a strong critique see J. Woodhouse, 'Evangelicals and Social Responsibility', in B. Webb (ed.), *Christians in Society, Explorations 3* (Homebush West: Lancer 1988), p. 9.
[68] J. Stott, *Christian Mission in the Modern World* (London: Falcon, Church Pastoral Aid Society, 1975).

69 Ibid., p. 22, referring to his three biblical expositions to the World Congress on Evangelism in Berlin 1968, published in the conference papers, C.F. Henry and W.S. Mooneyham (ed.), *One Race, One Gospel, One Task* (Minneapolis, MN: World Wide, 1967), vol. 1, pp. 37–56.
70 Stott, *Christian Mission*, p..23.
71 Ibid., p. 35.
72 Ibid., p. 23, italics Stott's.
73 Ibid., p. 25.
74 The papers from Lausanne 2 were published in *Proclaim Christ Until He Comes* (Minneapolis, MN: World Wide, 1990), this quotation from p. 30.
75 Hesselgrave published in *Trinity World Forum*, Spring 1990; Stott responded in *Trinity World Forum*, Spring 1991.
76 *Trinity World Forum* (Spring, 1991), p. 1.
77 Even to say 'social action' implies a party-political or socially controlling action that some (who would wish to limit a Christian's action to private charity) might be unhappy with. Nevertheless, for the sake of this point it is enough that even they consider private charity toward the poor a necessity for obedient Christians.
78 It is noteworthy that Stott's presentational technique requires him to reject two errors at the extremity and then position himself between them. Leaving aside the questions of why there are always two errors to avoid, and whether finding truth midway between two errors is wise, and whether truth may not be found at the extreme, he has to find someone who states that evangelism is all we do, with no social action. His example is, as he himself admits, eccentric and is increasingly dated, although the counter position that we do mission without words is still easy to illustrate. Perhaps the naïve lack of social awareness with which we are charged, and to which Stott feels obliged to plead guilty, is a chimera.
79 Ibid.
80 *Christian Mission in the Modern World*, p. 24.
81 Mt. 28:20.
82 Jn. 20:20, 21.
83 Lk. 24:47–9.
84 *Christian Mission in the Modern World*, p. 24.
85 A.J. Köstenberger, *The Missions of Jesus and the Disciples according to the Fourth Gospel* (Grand Rapids: Eerdmans, 1998), pp. 107–8. His ideas are summarised in Köstenberger and O'Brien, *Salvation to the Ends of the Earth*, ch. 8.

The Incarnation and Mission 149

86 Köstenberger, *The Missions of Jesus and the Disciples*, pp. 195–6, italics added.
87 Ibid., pp. 196–7.
88 Bosch talks of 'the recent emphasis on the significance of the incarnation – which has been accepted into the ecumenical movement at least since the 1980 Melbourne CWME conference' (*Transforming Mission*, p. 513). We have already noted David Hesselgrave's discussion with John Stott. See too his review of *Changing the Mind of Missions: Where have we gone wrong?* by J. Engel and W. Dyrness (Downers Grove: InterVarsity Press, 2000), published in *Evangelical Missions Quarterly*, July 2001.
89 The theology of 'the kingdom' is important to both Luke-Acts and Paul, and must not be ignored. A theology of the kingdom *from Luke's Gospel alone* will distort his meaning. Acts is structured around teaching on the kingdom (1:3, 6 and Acts 28:23, 31) with references at key points of conversion (8:12; 19:8) and building up churches (14:22, 20:25). This must inform what he means by the term in the gospel as he continues to define his meanings. Similarly, a theology of the kingdom *from the Gospels alone* will be a distortion. Paul uses and clarifies the concept of 'kingdom' (Rom. 14:17; 1 Cor. 4:20; 6:9, 10; 15:24, 50; Gal. 5:21; Eph. 5:5; Col. 1:12; 13; 4:11; 1 Thes. 2:12; 2 Thes. 1:5; 2 Tim. 4:1, 18). He was unembarrassed about the term and, while he invests it with no new meaning, maintains its eschatological core.
90 As, for instance, in the widespread use of 'kingdom' as an adjective to make a behaviour sound plausibly biblical.
91 2 Tim. 1: 8. On the pattern of Paul's ministry in 2 Timothy, see C. Green, *Finishing the race; reading 2 Timothy today* (Sydney: Aquila, 2000).
92 One wonders if it is precisely because Paul rarely uses the language of 'kingdom building', 'Shalom' or 'gospel for the poor' that he has been sidelined as the norm. Or it might be because of his profoundly unfashionable views on gender and sexuality. Whatever the cause, it must be noted that to be 'ashamed' of Paul is *ipso facto* to be ashamed of Jesus.
93 It is also alleged that being Incarnate gave God access to the world of human experience, and in particular to the experience of emotion, suffering and risk, without which he would be incomplete and the gospel inauthentic. See the very illuminating T. Weinandy, *Does God Suffer?* (Edinburgh: Clark, 2000), which shows in particular that the

classic orthodox view of God does give him full access to all emotions at full force, but without in any way exposing him to change or risk.

94. Lk. 22:42.
95. This illustration is Peter Adam's, and is an enduring witness to his deep love for his poodle, Poppy.
96. Mt. 19:5.
97. Rev. 1:12–20.
98. Mt. 7:24–7; Lk. 6:46.
99. P. Ward, *Youthwork and the Mission of God* (London: SPCK, 1997), p. 95. This idea seems particularly influential in current youth work.
100. There are other rocks the idea stumbles on, of course, the most obvious being that Jesus commands us to teach with propositional content.
101. Jn. 20:30–1.
102. Mk. 13:22.
103. Jn. 3:2–3.
104. I have used a deliberately vague word, as 'communication' might seem too exclusively verbal for some.
105. 1 Cor. 9:14, 19–22.
106. Ward, *Youthwork*, p. 90f., italics added.
107. Jn. 1:11.
108. Ward, *Youthwork*, p. 90f.
109. *Lessing's Theological Writings* (trans. H. Chadwick; Palo Alto, CA: Stanford University, 1955), p. 5.
110. Quoted in Ramsey, *From Gore to Temple*, p. 173.
111. This is obviously a huge issue, and is in some ways at a tangent to the subject. But the implications of the God-created nature of the cultural context into which he came would shape a quite different approach to, say, the common view of hermeneutics in which the task of the reader is to extract a timeless principle from a time-bound text. Once the incarnation's context and ours are placed on a theologically integrated ground, in which the culture at the time of the incarnation was uniquely shaped to be comprehensible to all other following cultures, interpretation becomes much less problematic. God sovereignly foreknew all possible interpretations of the gospel that would be needed to save people. So we are not obliged to go into the hermeneutical minefield where one person's timeless principle is another person's time-bound text, nor to fuse two

increasingly distant and mutually incomprehensible horizons. The Bible does not become more difficult because we live in 2003 as opposed to 1003, nor will it become so in 3003. See V. Poythress, *God-Centred Biblical Interpretation* (Phillipsburg: Presbyterian and Reformed, 1999), pp. 69–94.

[112] 1 Cor. 9:21. See above.

[113] 2 Cor. 1:5, introducing dominant themes for the first half ('sufferings') and the whole ('comfort') of the letter.

[114] Eph. 2:12.

5. The Incarnation and Scripture

Timothy Ward

> God's Word, incarnate and inscripturate, is God in communicative action. The might of God's speech is hidden by the divine lisp as the might of God's saving act is hidden in Christ's cross. God's power is revealed in weakness; this applies to God's speech-acts too.[1]

Introduction: The Word and the Words

The classical doctrine of Scripture
Orthodox Christian believers have traditionally claimed that the Bible is God's Word written. That is, they believe that whatever the Bible can be found to affirm as true is in fact what God says. It is not that God never speaks except through the words of the Bible. Rather, only the Bible can be said itself to be directly the Word of God, needing no weighing or testing to discern whether or not God is speaking in it.

The Church Fathers uniformly regarded the Bible this way.[2] Clement of Alexandria wrote: 'He then who of himself believes the Lord's Scripture and his actual voice is worthy of belief ... Certainly we use it as a criterion for the discovery of the real facts.'[3] In so saying he did not distinguish between the content of the Bible and God's 'actual voice'. For Augustine, the Bible sufficiently contains all that God wants to say to us: 'among the things that are plainly laid down in Scripture are to be found all matters that concern faith and the manner of life, – to wit, hope and love.'[4]

The concept of 'the rule of faith' was important to the Church Fathers as a summary of orthodox faith, by which teaching could be evaluated. It only functioned this way insofar as it was a summary of biblical teaching. As R.P.C. Hanson observes:

The Incarnation and Scripture 153

The idea of the rule of faith as supplementing or complementing, or indeed adding anything whatever to, the Bible, is wholly absent from their thoughts; indeed, such an idea would be in complete contradiction to their conception of the relation of rule to Bible.[5]

Similar statements about the Bible can be found throughout the writings of medieval theologians. Thomas Aquinas, for example, asserts:

> Those things which flow from the will of God alone beyond all that is due to creatures can come to be known by us only to the extent that they are handed down in sacred Scripture, which makes God's will known.[6]

It is true that Aquinas, like other medievals, speaks in other contexts of the authority of the teaching of the church, but for him church teaching, if it is to be certainly true, is to be derived directly from Scripture:

> [holy teaching's] own proper authorities are those of canonical Scripture ... It has other proper authorities, the doctors of the church, and these it looks to as its own, but for arguments that carry no more than probability.[7]

As one writer has pointed out, it would never have occurred to Aquinas that church teaching could be in disagreement with biblical teaching.[8]

John Calvin, typical of all the Reformers and their orthodox successors, regarded the Bible in the same way, making even clearer, over against claims for the authority of church teaching, that it is through the Bible that God's Word is to be heard: 'daily oracles are not sent from heaven, for it pleased the Lord to hallow his truth to everlasting remembrance in the Scriptures alone.'[9]

Thus, for a truly evangelical and orthodox view of Scripture, it is not the case that the Bible sometimes is the Word of God, and sometimes is not, depending on whether or not the reader accepts it as the Word of God. It is not that the Bible contains the Word of God, or even that it bears witness to the Word of God, pointing completely away from itself. The Bible simply is the Word of God.

Objections to this classical doctrine

However, it has been argued that this view of the Bible detracts badly from the unique identity of Jesus Christ as the Word of God. The Bible reveals that Jesus is himself the Word of God (Jn. 1.1). Implicit in these biblical statements is the idea that he is *uniquely* the Word of God. Therefore, it is claimed, if we say of the biblical words which declare Christ to be the Word that they themselves are also God's Word, then we necessarily compromise Christ's position as God's unique self-communicating and self-revealing Word. And that is just another form of idolatry.

In the end, it is argued, that this is an issue which evangelicals like to avoid, but must face up to: you cannot serve two divine Words. You either serve the Word incarnate or the Word written – a choice must be made. To treat Scripture as itself directly and permanently God's Word written, it is feared, may lead us into the kind of obsession with the details of scriptural texts which characterised the Pharisees of Jesus' day, and which made them unable and unwilling to become his disciples.

The fundamental question, then, is this: what is the relationship between the Word of God and the words of Scripture? It is the question of the incarnation and the Bible – of Christ the Word of God and the Bible as the Word of God. It is a question of the Word and the words.

This overall objection to the classical, evangelical view of the Bible has two distinct aspects. The first is *devotional*. The biblical scholar John Barton expresses the objection simply and clearly:

> it is not primarily the Bible that is the Word of God, but Jesus Christ. I do not think one could find a single Christian who would dissent from this proposition, for to do so would plainly be to commit what is sometimes called bibliolatry: the elevation of the Bible above Christ himself ... Christians are not those who believe in the Bible, but those who believe in Christ.[10]

Barton's claim is a strong one, and in many ways compellingly true. It is with good reason that we are called *Christ*ians, not 'Biblians'. The heart of our faith is a person, not a book. We are called by God to be devoted to a crucified and risen Lord, not to books and sentences and grammar. Barton is arguing that the classical doctrine of Scripture leads inevitably to the Bible taking some of the ground that only Christ should occupy in the lives of Christian believers. The Bible becomes a rival with Jesus for our devotional and religious affections. If he is right, then the classical doctrine of Scripture inevitably leads people into idolatry – as he says, into the particular sin of 'bibliolatry'.

Evangelicals are often charged with 'bibliolatry', but without much thought of what 'bibliolatrous' practice might actually look like. Barton himself defines it as 'the elevation of the Bible above Christ himself', but does not give any examples of how someone might actually commit the sin of bibliolatry. What actual bibliolatry might involve, and whether or not the classical evangelical doctrine of Scripture necessarily leads to that form of idolatry, is a topic to which we will return at the end. At this point in the discussion the reader may have some sympathy with Barton's point, or may already have a head full of objections to his arguments. For the moment, what is important is to feel the force of the serious devotional objection Barton levels at the classical identification of the Bible directly with the Word of God.

The second aspect of the objection to the classical view of the Bible is *theological*. In the last hundred years, this objection has been expressed most thoughtfully (and certainly at greatest length) by Karl Barth. For Barth, as is well known, the Bible is God's Word only as and when God speaks through it: 'The Bible is God's Word to the extent that God causes it to be His Word, to the extent that He speaks through it.' This is something we accept 'in faith and not in unbelief, and therefore precisely not in abstraction from the act of God in virtue of which the Bible must become again and again His Word to us.' For Barth, only Jesus is directly revelation from God. The Bible is not itself God's Word, but can become the Word of God for us by his power. Barth compares the Bible becoming the Word of God in this way to the pool at Bethesda becoming a means of healing when the waters were stirred. Barth concludes: '[w]e thus do the Bible poor and unwelcome honour if we equate it directly with ... revelation itself.'[11]

Barth fears that the classical doctrine of Scripture has God identify himself permanently with an object (the Bible) in human history in a way that compromises God in his transcendence. God in his free transcendence has chosen permanently to identify himself with humanity only in the hypostatic union of divine and human natures in the person of Jesus Christ. Because God has chosen to take on human flesh in Christ in this way, to worship Christ is to worship God in truth. However, to say of anything human, *other than Jesus Christ*, that it simply is divine, is to detract from the choice God made to unite the divine and the human uniquely in the incarnate Christ. To do so is to turn God into an idol, into an object that we can know and study like any other:

> What God and His Word are ... is something God Himself must constantly tell us afresh ... In this divine telling there is an encounter and fellowship between His nature and man but not an assuming of God's nature into man's knowing, only a fresh divine telling.'[12]

For Barth the stakes here are high. The direct identification of Scripture with the Word of God introduces, he argues, a disastrous self-reliance on human abilities, since it offers 'a tangile certainty [of knowledge of God], not one that is given and constantly has to be given again, a human certainty and not a divine, a certainty of work and not solely of faith.'[13] Barth thus implies that the classical Protestant doctrine of Scripture therefore undermines one of the key principles of the Protestant Reformation.

Barth correlates Christ, who simply is the Word of God, and the Bible, which can become the Word of God, in the following way:

> The personalising of the concept of the Word of God, which we cannot avoid when we remember that Jesus Christ is the Word of God, does not mean its deverbalising. But it (naturally) means awareness that it is person rather than thing or object even if and in so far as it is word, word of Scripture and word of preaching.[14]

Barth says two things here. First, he argues, the concept of 'the Word of God' is fundamentally *personal* – it refers fundamentally to the person Jesus Christ. Second, however, Barth also knows that the concept of the 'Word of God' must in some sense be verbal. It cannot refer *exclusively* to Christ – it must somehow refer to the words of Scripture (and, he adds, the words of preaching). However, he insists, when it comes to the Word of God, even when we are talking about *words* (the words of the Bible), we must not forget that what we are really talking about is a *person*. For Barth, the idea of 'person' conveys the very characteristic that he rightly wants to ascribe to God's Word, including its written form. This is something that we cannot control, which addresses us and acts upon us from outside ourselves. It seems that he cannot conceive of words in themselves having that character, for they can be studied and comprehended like any other human object in the world. If God's Word is to be a standing challenge to us, and not domesticated by us, as it must, then for Barth it *must* be really be a person.

This, then, is the heart of Barth's theological objection to the classical doctrine of Scripture. He fears that it ultimately describes *a second incarnation*: the Word became flesh in Jesus Christ – and the Word *also* became words and paper and ink, being incarnated in the body of a written text. This is for him not only unbiblical, but also encourages believers idolatrously to domesticate God. We cannot grasp hold of the person of Christ (that is, we cannot control him and cannot fully comprehend him), but we can grasp the words of the Bible. We can hold the book in our hands, we can study and comprehend its language, syntax and grammar, and we can imagine that in so doing we grasp God.

Responding to these objections
These two common objections to the classical view of Scripture are similar, although Barton has a devotional thrust, and Barth a theological one. These objections need to be taken seriously, for they are neither cheap nor frivolous. Moreover, they are becoming increasingly attractive to people who call themselves evangelicals, or who are called evangelical by others. In what follows, three lines of response will be offered, in defence of the classical understanding of Scripture: one biblical, one philosophical and one theological.

A Biblical Response: God, Christ and Words in the Bible
The heart of our response to these two significant objections to the classical doctrine of Scripture will be to outline a biblical theology of the relationships between God, Christ and words, as

Scripture bears witness to these relationships, either directly or indirectly. I will argue that there is a much closer interrelationship between God and Christ, both as regards their personhood and their actions, and the human words in and through which they speak to us, than the objections to the classical doctrine of Scripture acknowledge.

As we trace the means by which God reveals himself to us, we will find, with regard to the Old Testament, clear and surprising relationships between God in his personhood, his actions, and the words of human speakers and writers in and through which he speaks. Similarly in the New Testament, definite relationships emerge between Christ's person, his actions, the human words which he spoke while on the earth, and the human words of some of his followers, through which he continues to speak. The permanent hiatus between the human language of the Bible and God's actions and personhood, which the objections to the classical doctrine of Scripture attempt to identify, cannot in fact be sustained from the Bible's testimony to the character of these relationships.

God's action and his words
First, it is a commonplace to note that God's words and his actions are intimately related in the Bible. To say of God that he spoke, and to say of God that he did something, is often the same thing. Some examples may be given here, deliberately drawn from a variety of different literary genres in the Bible, in order to show the extent of the identification in Scripture of God's words and God's action. That identification means that God's word can be described as true.

In the Old Testament
One of the most obvious examples is found in the biblical creation accounts. According to the Bible, God creates by speaking: 'God said, "Let there be light"; and there was light' (Gen. 1:3).[15] It seems that here God's expressing the wish that light exist, and the coming into existence of light, are one and the same thing. In Genesis 1:6 God says, 'let there be a dome in the midst of the waters', and verse 7 adds, 'so God made the dome'. In light of verse 3, verses 6 and 7 do not appear to be describing two different actions. It is

not the case that God first expresses verbally his desire to create and then actually forms creation wordlessly. A more natural reading is that verses 6 and 7 give two different aspects of the single divine act of creation. The rest of Genesis 1 follows the same pattern. Either God's act of speaking is simply sufficient for an act of creation, with no additional account of God 'making' or 'creating' (vv. 9, 11), or his creative words are followed by a summary description of what that act of speech has achieved ('God made/created', vv. 14–16, 20–1, 24–5, 26–7).

This linguistic character to God's activity is not restricted to the initial act of creation. The same relationship between God's action and his words can be found, for example, in 1 Kings 13. This chapter recounts at some length the strange and sad events which took place immediately after the division of Israel from Judah under Jeroboam, in which a prophet came from Judah to Israel, but was deceived into disobeying the words which God had already spoken to him. Thus, the chapter begins:

> While Jeroboam was standing by the altar to offer incense, a man of God came out of Judah by the word of the LORD to Bethel and proclaimed against the altar by the word of the LORD, and said, 'O altar, altar, thus says the Lord.' (1 Kgs. 13:1–2)

'(By) the word of the LORD' becomes the great refrain of the chapter (vv. 5, 9, 20, 21, 26, 32), such that it is the word which emerges as the main agent in driving the narrative forward. One commentator judges that '[t]his is a story about the word's power to get itself done'.[16] Words on their own, though, can of course get nothing done. The word of the Lord only has the power to do anything because it is the Lord who sends it. Therefore, the ascription to it of the ability to perform certain actions, turning the word itself into an agent, is a particular way of talking about God himself performing certain actions. For this chapter to say that an event happened 'by the word of the LORD' is synonymous with saying 'God acted by means of language' in order that it should happen.

The same equation of God speaking and God acting is evident in Psalm 29. A central theme of this psalm is the power of God's voice:

> The voice of the LORD breaks the cedars;
> the LORD breaks the cedars of Lebanon …
> The voice of the LORD shakes the wilderness;
> the LORD shakes the wilderness of Kadesh. (Ps. 29:5, 8)

The poetic parallelism of each of these verses equates God performing an action by means of his voice, and God simply performing that action himself. Each half of each verse is a different way of talking about the same divine reality. A classic passage in this regard is Isaiah 55:10–11:

> For as the rain and the snow come down from heaven, and do not return there until they have watered the earth, making it bring forth and sprout, giving seed to the sower and bread to the eater, so shall my word be that goes out from my mouth; it shall not return to me empty, but it shall accomplish that which I purpose, and succeed in the thing for which I sent it.

The transcendent God here describes his word as the means by which he acts in the world. God and his word share the divine ability infallibly to perform their purpose. Human words often fail to perform their intended purpose, but God's words do not. Thus, there is no difference between saying that God's word has performed an action for which he sent it, and saying that God himself has performed an action.

In the New Testament

Two examples from the theology of the New Testament may be given. First, orthodox Protestant theology has identified a moment in the divine act of salvation in which God *declares* the sinner to be righteous in his sight (cf. Lk. 18:14; Rom. 3:21–4:25; 5:8–9; Phil. 3:7–9). This point has traditionally been developed under the heading of justification, with the aim of making clear that God restores us into proper relationship with himself prior to, rather than subsequent to or simultaneous with, any actual change in our spiritual state. God declares a fundamental change in our standing before him, before he effects, by the sending of the Holy Spirit, a real change to our sinful state. There is a clear parallel here with the accounts in Genesis of God's acts of creation discussed above.

God did not declare his intention to make us holy before him, and then get on and make us so. He spoke, making us by that declaration to be justified in our relationship with him, and then he went on to bring about in our lives, by an increase in holiness, the necessary and natural effects of that change in our standing before him.

Second, Protestant theology has often discerned in New Testament soteriology God's 'effectual calling'. This is an act of God by which he calls us to be saved, and in which the very action of calling itself brings us to salvation (e.g., Rom. 8.30; 11:29; 1 Cor. 1:23–4; 1 Pet. 2:9). God can choose to call people to himself in such a way that it is appropriate to say that the call itself brings about in the person's heart the very thing God intends, namely that they respond in saving faith. In other words, God speaks not just to *describe* salvation to us, or to *encourage* us to come to him to be saved, although he certainly does both these things. God *speaking* is an integral part of God *acting* to save. Thus, in biblical language and theology God speaking and God acting are often one and the same thing.

God's person and his words

Second, we need to consider the relationship between God's person and the words he speaks. God establishes a relationship between his person and his words most crucially in the covenants which he establishes between himself and his people. God initially establishes his covenants not by negotiation with human beings but unilaterally: 'I will establish my covenant with you' (Gen. 6:18; also Gen. 17:7; Ex. 6:4–5). The heart of the covenant promise is expressed in the formula, 'I will be your God, and you will be my people', and related statements (for example Gen. 17:7; Ex. 6:7).

The unilaterally established covenant does, however, place obligations on the people whom God has chosen to bring into covenant relationship with himself. It is at this point that the covenant became a two-sided matter. God promises his people blessings if they obey the stipulations for their behaviour laid down in his covenant, and he promises the withholding of those blessings if they disobey him. A classic extended statement of this aspect of the covenant is found in Deuteronomy 28. Two further points follow, reflecting on what the covenantal nature of God's relationship with his people suggests about God's own relationship to the words that he speaks.

First, in and through the words of the covenant which he speaks to his people, God makes himself knowable to humanity. We come to know other people by living over time in relationship with them, listening to them speak about themselves and others, and watching them act. God graciously allows us to come to know him the same way. Thus, he identifies himself for his people as the God of Abraham, Isaac and Jacob, the God who makes and keeps his covenant with his people. God promises Abraham's offspring that he really is the God who presents himself to them in the covenant that he establishes between himself and them. The covenant is not a means by which God deals with his people, as it were, at arm's length. God's covenant is not a form of mediation, transaction or negotiation that takes place between essentially separate persons; it is not a relationship in which God remains fundamentally absent. Rather, the covenant, and therefore the human words in which it is given expression and enacted, are the means by which God elects to be God in relationship with us; it is the very means by which he comes to be God for us.

Thus, when Abram hears and obeys the divine command to leave Haran and go to the land that the Lord will show him, he comes directly into relationship with God. To trust God's covenant promise is not to enter into an agreement with an absentee God – it is to trust God. There is, then, a complex relationship between God and God's actions, expressed and performed through God's words. It seems that God's actions, including his verbal actions, are a kind of extension of him.[17]

Second, God cannot meaningfully establish his covenant with us – he cannot make his promise to us – without using words. God's covenant promise is a complicated affair, in which God has to refer to himself, to the relationship he is establishing between himself and his people, to what is now required of his people, and to the future, promising a future of blessing if his people keep the covenant, and warning of a future of cursing if they disobey. None of this is possible without words. God chooses to use words as a fundamental means of relating to us, because the kind of relationship he chooses to establish cannot be established non-verbally. Moreover, the words he uses need to be words which human beings can comprehend, since only if the covenant promise is given in such words is it a covenant to which we can respond.

Thus, words, including human words, do not necessarily obscure a relationship with God, somehow getting in the way; they are a necessary medium of a relationship with God. To put your trust in the words of the covenant promise that God makes to you is itself to put your trust in God – the two are the same thing. Communication from God is therefore communion with God, when it is met with response from us.

This is not to say that words are everything, that speaking and being spoken to exhausts our relationship with God. There are and should be varieties of wordless contemplation of God, and wordless resting in his presence. Yet it remains true that, if the God with whom we are in relationship is to be the true God and not an idol, our only access to the kind of depth of relationship with God at which words sometimes fall away is precisely in and through words which God speaks to us. If that were not true, then we could not know that the God whom we contemplate wordlessly is the true God, the covenant-keeping God of Abraham, Isaac and Jacob. Even what we contemplate wordlessly therefore cannot contradict what God has revealed in Scripture.

It is, of course, a fatal mistake to assume that the words by which God chooses to establish his relationship with us exhaust God. There is much that remains mystery, because it remains unsaid by God. However, the necessary focus on God as mystery must not be allowed to obscure the extraordinary act of grace by which he speaks to us human words of promise, such that for us to trust them is an act of trusting God himself.

God's words and human words
The third relationship to consider is that between God's words and human words. The Old Testament regularly assumes that God can and does speak in and through human words, such that those words can truly be said to be his words. This is particularly true of prophetic speech, and the point is given general expression in Deuteronomy 18:15–20: 'I will put my words in the mouth of the prophet' (v. 18). The words that the prophets speak are words that come directly from God.

The opening of the book of Jeremiah provides a good example. God says to the prophet:

> Now I have put my words in your mouth. See today I appoint you over nations and over kingdoms, to pluck up and to pull down, to destroy and to overthrow, to build and to plant. (Jer. 1:9b–10)

Jeremiah is appointed by God to have power over nations and kingdoms, but this power comes only from the divine words which God has put in his mouth. Only God has this power over nations. Jeremiah, as his deputised speaker, is given the same power only in that he speaks words given him by God – words which can therefore perform what God intends them to perform. Jeremiah will speak ordinary human words in an ordinary human language – God doesn't put special magic formulae or secret heavenly words into Jeremiah's mouth – but those words will also be God's words. Jeremiah's words are ordinary human words, but they are not any less divine for also being fully human.

This identification of human and divine words extends beyond actual prophetic speech, and also covers written texts. Gordon McConville, in particular, has argued this point recently with regard to the book of Jeremiah.[18] He points out how Jeremiah 36 allows for the word once given to the prophet to be written down and to be effective as God's speech beyond Jeremiah's life and beyond the circumstances in which the word was first given to him.[19] Regarding the non-prophetic aspects of the book, McConville argues that Jeremiah's experiences – his suffering reflects God's suffering over Israel's unfaithfulness – 'all in some sense mark the involvement of God in Israel's history, in a way that may be called "incarnational"'. In adding both this theme and the clear hope of a new covenant to the wider Old Testament canon, the book of Jeremiah as a whole becomes part of God's speaking through Scripture.[20] The non-prophetic, prosaic parts of the book are therefore woven intricately together with actual prophetic speech in a form which subsequent communities receive *in toto* as canonical.

It is worth summarising the biblical argument of this section so far. When we encounter certain human words, we are in direct contact with God's words, which is itself a direct encounter with

God's activity, especially his covenant-making activity. And an encounter with God's covenant making, communicative activity is itself an encounter with God. We turn now to consider the relationship of the words spoken by the Word incarnate to God's action and person.

Christ's words and God's action and person

Christ, as the Word incarnate, comes as the fulfilment of the Old Testament theology of 'word'. If we want to hear God speaking, we now listen to Christ speak. If we want to see God in action, we now look to Christ's deeds. If we want to encounter God himself, we need to encounter Christ.

This theme is especially prominent in John's Gospel: 'Whoever has seen me has seen the Father' (Jn. 14:9). This principle of course applies to Christ's person and his action – to see him raise Lazarus from the dead, for example, was to witness the reality of God's power over death. It also applies to the words that Christ speaks: 'I do nothing on my own, but speak these things as the Father instructed me' (Jn. 8:28b, also 12:49–50; 17:8). To listen to Christ speak, using ordinary human language, is therefore to hear the Father speak. Christ is here making the straightforward but extraordinary claim that God the Son, the Word incarnate, speaks to us in ordinary human words the very things he has heard God the Father say within the eternal life of the Trinity.

Although extraordinary, this claim can also be seen to follow naturally from Christ's biblical depiction as 'Word'. The disciples picked this up, stressing that God's coming to earth in Christ referred both to his words and actions, as well as to his flesh: 'We declare to you what was from the beginning, what we have heard, what we have seen with our eyes, what we have looked at and touched with our hands' (1 Jn. 1:1). Even those who met Christ in the flesh needed from him words of teaching about his identity, and words interpreting for them the actions he performed.

God's words, Christ's words and human words

By definition, of course, Jesus' earthly ministry is limited in time and space. The Word is made flesh in one individual, to live one actual human life and to die one death. That is inherent in the means of salvation which God foreshadowed in the Old Testament and brought into effect in Christ. His Spirit can subsequently be poured out universally on all believers, but his first appearing on earth is necessarily limited. It turns out, then, that human words will still be necessary to communicate the gospel of the Word-made-flesh through time and space.

Jesus implicitly taught his disciples about this in the last week of his life, praying to his Father: 'the words that you gave to me I have given to them ... I ask not only on behalf of these, but also on behalf of those who will believe in me through their word' (Jn. 17:8, 20). Jesus has given words from God the Father to his disciples in ordinary human language. They are to be passed on through the words of the disciples. Those who never met the Word incarnate, but who hear the words of Christ from the disciples, encounter the words of the Father and of Christ, who in those words present themselves as a covenant making God who is to be trusted.

It is noteworthy that this theme is not just typical of the Christology of the Fourth Gospel. It is also prominent, for example, in Matthew's Gospel. As he sends out the Twelve, Jesus tells them:

> If anyone will not welcome you or listen to your words, shake off the dust from your feet as you leave that house or town. Truly I tell you, it will be more tolerable for the land of Sodom and Gomorrah on the day of judgement than for that town ... Whoever welcomes you welcomes me, and whoever welcomes me welcomes the one who sent me. (Mt. 10:14–15, 40)

To reject the disciples' words is to reject God, and so to be liable for condemnation. It cannot be that God has established an arbitrary test, as if his decision was nothing other than to condemn all those who do not accept the proclamation of the gospel of Jesus. Rather, God has identified himself both with Jesus Christ and with the passing on by disciples of the words that Jesus brought from the Father, such that to reject those human words simply is to reject God.

The same point is made in the Parable of the Sheep and the Goats (Mt. 25:31–46). Here, the Son of Man saves or condemns people on the basis of kind deeds they have done for 'the least of these my brothers'. The key question in this parable is whether this phrase refers to suffering humanity in general, or to Christian disciples, especially those who come bringing the gospel of Christ in often hostile circumstances. A study of that phrase and similar phrases throughout Matthew's Gospel suggests the latter restricted sense.[21] In this parable, too, the rejection of those who come speaking Christ's words is itself a rejection of Christ. It is therefore not the case, as is sometimes argued, that human language is simply inadequate to speak of God and his work. Human language can never render God exhaustively, but it is an adequate vehicle, in the mouths of Christ and his ordinary human disciples, for God to present himself to us in the proclamation of the covenant through which he chooses to relate himself to us.

Thus, the coming of the Word incarnate does not alter the fact that, for all who come after Christ, human language is the essential medium by which God acts in relation to us and presents himself to us as the Father whose Son is the Word incarnate for us. The final step of this argument will be to relate the human language through which God speaks through the words of the Bible.

God's words and the Bible

So far we have had in view not the Bible in particular but the general proclamation of the words of Christ and of the covenant. Why equate God's words (and all that that entails theologically) supremely with the human words of the Bible? It is common for theologians to be happy to speak of the proclamation of the gospel as God's speech, but to refuse, as we have seen, to make a permanent identification of the Bible as God's Word.

Since our only substantive access to Christ and his words is through the content of the Bible, the common strategy for such writers is to discern a canon within the canon, that is, a section of Bible, or some strands of its content, which for them expresses the true gospel *over against* other parts of the Bible.[22] This involves more than seeing that some parts of the Bible do not tell the whole truth, for example because they only foreshadow a reality which has not yet come; it involves identifying certain things that the Bible affirms as in fact only human and not at all divine. Once this 'canon within the canon' has been identified, it can be used as the basis of an 'inner-canonical criticism' of other parts of Scripture, effectively distinguishing between biblical words through which God does choose to speak, and biblical words through which he does not speak directly, because they are in no way expressive of the gospel.

Wolfhart Pannenberg outlines this strategy especially clearly. He insists that the Bible is God's word only to the extent that it gives expression to the apostolic gospel, and that it does so unevenly:

> the authority of scripture rests on that of the gospel and its content – the saving presence of God in the person and history of Jesus Christ. Only insofar as they bear witness to this content do the words and sayings of scripture have authority in the church ... How far this is true must be tested for each writing and each saying in each writing.[23]

Elsewhere he judges that the New Testament writings can be regarded as inspired Scripture 'only insofar as those writings witness to the Pauline gospel of God's saving activity in Jesus' death on the cross and in his resurrection'.[24]

The problem with this strategy is that, since our only substantive access to the gospel of Christ is through Scripture, it is impossible to identify an unambiguous and non-arbitrary principle of inner-canonical criticism, by which we may discern which of the Bible's words are God's words and which are not. Bruce Metzger, writing on the New Testament canon, asserts that:

> New Testament scholars have the responsibility as servants of the church to investigate, understand, and elucidate, for the development of the Christian life of believers, the full meaning of every book written within the canon and not only of those which may be most popular in certain circles and at certain times. Only in such a way will the church be able to hear the Word of God in all its breadth and depth.[25]

It has been widely observed that all critical reconstructions of the historical Jesus produce a Jesus made in the image of the observer. Similarly, critical reconstructions of the gospel tend to result in the selection of those parts of the New Testament which most appeal to our sensibilities, or which most reflect our spiritual experience of Christ. Given the inevitable inadequacy of the latter, and the culture-bound character of the former, any search for an inner-canonical critical function based on either or both of these is always arbitrary and often dangerous. A significantly better approach is to acknowledge that our only access to the words that the Father gave to the prophets and to his Son, and to the words that Christ gave to his first disciples, is through the Bible as a whole. If this is an 'uncritical' approach, it is in no way thoughtlessly and blindly so.

The biblical argument of this first section can be simply summarised. God chooses to present himself to us, and to act upon us, in and through human words. When we encounter those words, God is acting upon us, paradigmatically in the making of a covenant promise to us. God identifies himself with his act of promising in such a way that to encounter God's promise is to encounter God.

The supreme form in which God comes to encounter us in his covenant promise is through the words of the Bible as a whole. I say 'through the Bible as a whole' because the Bible's positive statements, once interpreted within the context of the canon as a whole, cannot without arbitrariness be set over against each other. The Bible therefore witnesses to such a close relationship between God, Christ and (human) words that there is no necessary competition between God and Christ, on one hand, and the biblical words through which they speak on the other. To pay proper attention to the latter is to encounter the spiritual reality to which God intends his words to point.

A Philosophical Response: Persons, Actions and Words

The chief characteristics of the relationships between God and Christ, and their words and actions, are not unique to God, but are true of all persons. The above arguments are not a case of special pleading in the case of God, in order to defend a now widely rejected doctrine of Scripture. Rather, the fundamental relationships between persons, actions and words are the same, whether the speaker is human or divine.

Philosophers have tended to think of the primary purpose of language as being to describe states of affairs or to state facts, an activity in which one mind communicates information to other minds. If that is our basic conception of language, then God's actions as a speaker can indeed look unique, for his words do far more than just communicate information – they create, establish relationships, build up and tear down. God's 'word' then appears to be a significantly more personal and dynamic entity than the 'word' spoken by human beings, and the equation of Scripture with the word of God consequently appears to be a declension from the basic identity of the person of Christ with the word of God. However, more recently it has been argued by a number of philosophers of language that the primary task of all language is not to describe or to state, but to perform actions. When we speak we perform the action of warning, ordering, promising, informing, and so on. The Oxford philosopher J.L. Austin provided the impetus for this view of language,[26] and John Searle and others have developed it under the overall heading 'speech-act theory'.

Nicholas Wolterstorff has explored the implications of this view of language as action in a particularly fruitful direction. What is actually going on when someone speaks? Wolterstorff's fundamental answer is that moral relationships between people are created and altered. If I make a promise to you, simply in uttering the words of the promise I acquire the moral responsibility (other things being equal) to keep that promise. (Wolterstorff calls this the ascription to speakers of 'normative standings'.) You, as the addressee, acquire the responsibility to trust that I will keep my promise (unless you have good reason to suspect that I am untrustworthy, or will be unable to keep my promise).

It is relatively easy to make this case for language with the example of a promise. Wolterstorff argues that it is also true even of assertions, when all that the speaker might seem to do is to communicate information:

> Asserting that so-and-so introduces into human relationships the (prima facie) right to be taken at one's word that so-and-so. We say, 'It's your own fault; you should have accepted what I said.'[27]

He concludes:

> Speaking introduces the potential for a whole new range of moral culpabilities – and accomplishments. At bottom, it is our dignity as

persons that requires that we be taken at our word, and take ourselves at our word.[28]

When we reflect about our experiences of actually using language, Wolterstorff's account can seem all too obviously true. Part of his argument is that for a long time this obvious truth has not impacted the philosophy of language in the way it should have done.

Wolterstorff's point can be expressed in a way that makes its relevance to this essay clear. A person is identified with his actions, and therefore with his words (since in uttering words we perform actions), to such an extent that for the hearer to respond to those words simply is to respond to the speaker. Again, the example of a promise will help. If I utter the words of a promise to you, I have identified myself with those words. I have taken to myself the responsibility to keep that promise; I have become in relationship to you the person who is now obligated to keep my promise. You, as the recipient of my promise, are now in a position whereby, in order to relate to me, you must relate to the words I have spoken. If you respond in trust that I will keep my promise, we might ask whether you are trusting me, or my promise, or my words? It does not seem possible to draw a distinction: to trust me, or my promise, or the words in which it was uttered, amounts to the same thing.

To those unaccustomed to the philosophy of language, even a brief discussion like this can seem to be a laborious exercise in stating what is obvious to anyone on a moment's reflection. However, because we use language so often, because it is such a part of the fabric of our being, its actual nature is often not obvious to us, unless it is spelt out for us in the kind of detail we have just noted. Our conclusion, emerging from these details, is that the actions a person performs are a complicated extension of that person (e.g. philosophers have great difficulty working out where a person stops and his or her action starts). Since it is by means of words that we perform many of our actions, our words can also be said to be a complex extension of our selves. This point is counter-intuitive, because we often think of words as life-less, dictionary-bound things. Wolterstorff's analysis, though, argues strongly that it is by words that we as persons engage with and act in relationship to other persons, identifying ourselves with the words we say. We may not be what we eat, but we are what we say.

It is worth noting that the general view of persons and language put forward here is not unique to Wolterstorff and the small band of professional speech-act theorists. It is true that much philosophy of language and philosophical hermeneutics in the last century has called into question the power of language, the stability of the self, and consequently our ability to perform actions through language (most notably post-structuralism and the early career of Jacques Derrida). Yet it is also the case that some of the most significant hermeneutical theorists and philosophers of the last century have to some extent attempted to put the moral necessity to listen and to respond to the other at the heart of their account of personhood and language.[29] Thus, the overall proposals of this essay can draw on much wider support than simply the branch of the philosophy of language called speech-act theory.

However, no illicit smuggling of general philosophy into a fundamentally theological discussion is taking place here. We deliberately began with a section on the Bible's own witness to God, Christ and language. The purpose of this philosophical section is twofold. First, overall concepts for language and personhood have been suggested which enable the reader to discern more clearly the relationships between God, Christ and words to which Scripture actually bears witness. Secondly, however, questions of personhood and language inevitably touch on general philosophical questions, and some thought must be given to these if the particular doctrine of Scripture that this essay defends is to seem more plausible in relation to the incarnation.

So far the discussion has referred to speakers and listeners, not to writers and readers. To what extent may we legitimately regard written texts as speech-acts? It is, of course, important to consider this, if Wolterstorff's account of language is to contribute to our basic conception of the Bible in its relation to God. One significant writer dissents from the view that texts can be treated in the same way as person-to-person speech. Paul Ricoeur argues that writing and reading are not like speaking and answering, because the former 'is not a relation of interlocution, not an instance of dialogue'.[30] In particular, says Ricoeur, the action performed by an utterance is less 'inscribable' than its propositional meaning, because writing lacks 'mimicry and gesture', the 'nonarticulated aspects of discourse', on which face-to-face speech often relies.[31]

Kevin Vanhoozer has defended the view of texts as speech-acts in detail. He argues that Ricoeur has ignored a characteristic which writing possesses and speech does not: literary genre. The author's choice of a literary genre performs the equivalent role that gesture and expression perform in speech: 'precisely because writing does not assume a shared situational context, genre creates the possibility of a shared *literary* context.'[32]

Thus, a writer expresses the action he is performing in authoring his text by choosing to write narrative, or prophecy, or apocalyptic. Readers come to discern that intention by becoming more skilful at recognising each of these genres, and interpreting texts accordingly. This is not a straightforward and easy process, but it can and does take place as readers submit themselves to reading the text as it is, not as they at first take it to be, or would like it to be. This is not a purely technical skill, but is part of readers' redemption and discipleship, as they become better able to deny themselves and their own prejudices, in order to listen clearly to the voice of another speaking through what they are reading.[33] Vanhoozer's fundamental definition of a written text is therefore that it is 'a communicative act of a communicative agent fixed by writing'.[34]

Barth's particular understanding of Scripture as the Word of God can helpfully be brought into the discussion here. Hans Frei judged, very perceptively, that 'Barth's discussion [of revelation] in [*Church Dogmatics*] I/1 and I/2 can be understood as an analysis, without benefit of J.L. Austin and his successors, of the logic of performative utterances.'[35] Barth does not say a great deal about language in general, but he does seem to think of language in terms which accord very well with Wolterstorff's view:

> How much wrong is continually being perpetrated, how much intolerant obstruction of human relationships ... has its only basis in the fact that we do not take seriously ... the claim which arises whenever one person addresses a word to another.[36]

Barth insists on a fundamental and exclusive personification of the Word itself, identifying Christ and not Scripture as the Word, except and to the extent that God takes up Scripture and chooses to speak through it. He does so because he fears that anything other than such a rigorous personification will lead us not to take God's claim on us seriously, and will cause us to obstruct our relationship with him.

However, if a text is an extension of a person, there is no reason not to identify it simply as that person's word. It is true that when persons extend their selves in order to encounter others by writing texts, they run the risk that readers will abuse that act by treating the text as something different. For example, readers may not seriously consider that this was a text written to them by someone, or they may get so lost in the minutiae of the text that they never get as far as encountering the author's personal act of communication. Yet such abuse is not inevitable. Readers can and do focus on the details of texts in order to grasp and be grasped better by the single act of personal communication which the text as a whole represents.[37]

Scripture, we may say, is the Word of God in a secondary sense to Christ as the Word of God. Scripture serves Christ, in that, as the semantic part of his action in the world, it is that part of his extension of himself by which we may come to know and name him as the promised, crucified, risen, ascended and coming Lord. Yet it need not follow that the Bible cannot without danger to Christ be directly identified with the Word of God. Scripture as the Word of God is secondary to Christ as the Word of God only in the same sense in which a promise I utter to you is secondary to me. It nevertheless is and remains permanently my promise, just as Scripture is directly God's promise to us.

This identification of the Bible with the Word of God is sometimes thought to lead to certain inappropriate ways of treating the Bible. It is alleged that it leads Bible-readers to abstract individual verses from their canonical and historical context – what Colin Gunton calls 'wring[ing] equal meaning out of every text'.[38] In fact, though, the permanent identification of the Bible with the Word of God should lead readers to be even more attentive to and respectful of the literary form, and literary, historical and theological contexts in which God gives each part of his written word to us. Nor need it lead Bible-readers, as is sometimes alleged, to miss the spiritual reality to which God intends Scripture to lead them, for close and careful reading of the words of Scripture shows that it is a word which demands to be lived, to be embodied, in communion with God.

The Incarnation and Scripture 175

A Theological Response: Scripture and Spirit

In the foregoing discussion of Karl Barth, one question that has clearly been begging is that of the Holy Spirit. In the biblical response to the two objections to the classical evangelical view of the Bible, we noted that the inherent space-time limitations of the incarnate Word's earthly ministry raise the question of how the incarnate Word can continue to reveal himself through space and time. We have privileged the Bible itself as the means by which this ongoing revelation takes place, but this clearly does not happen without the accompanying activity of the Holy Spirit. It is important to address this issue, because it is by means of the Holy Spirit that the Word himself continues to speak in and through the written word. The on-going relationship between Christ incarnate and his word is therefore at the heart of any discussion of Scripture and Spirit.

There are two common suggestions, of which we should take account, for the prime location of the Spirit's on-going activity in relation to the Bible. Neither locates the Spirit's work as being normatively in and through Scripture. In each case, however, it will be suggested that the Spirit's activity through Scripture is logically prior to the other suggested location for his prime activity.

The first common suggestion for the prime site of the Spirit's activity is the *individual believer*, personally in-dwelt by the Holy Spirit, as he or she reads the Bible. This conception of the Holy Spirit's activity in relation to Scripture is probably more practised than it is consciously articulated. Most church ministers, whether evangelical or not, regularly hear people say of a particular Bible-text, 'What this means to me is …' The comment that follows is often not one of personal application of a textually given meaning, but a reading that the text itself, in its historical, canonical and theological context, cannot possibly bear. Those who make such comments assume, or at least are logically implying, that the Holy Spirit can change the meaning of the biblical texts he once inspired.

In fact, many people who regularly interpret the Bible in this way remain largely faithful to the overall teaching of Scripture. They only do so, of course, because they have been clearly taught the correct meanings of countless Bible passages, and have become convinced of their truthfulness. Their orthodox biblical theology means that the meanings they wrongly ascribe to a biblical text are nevertheless right biblical meanings – they just happen to be given elsewhere in Scripture. Believers who lack such a background of biblical-theological teaching as a safeguard often fall into error. The determining factor in a person knowing the meanings that are and are not given in Scripture is the activity of the Spirit speaking those meanings to him in the present, and having spoken those meanings in the past to previous generations who have passed them on and taught them to him. Thus, the action of the Holy Spirit in and through the Bible is theologically prior to his work in us.

It is sometimes thought that the orthodox Protestant doctrine of Scripture necessarily leads to individualistic appeals to the Holy Spirit speaking through Scripture, to justify eccentric interpretation of biblical texts. Particularly in view here is the Reformation principle of *sola Scriptura*. However, this principle is often misrepresented, both by its critics and by many of its keenest proponents. Keith Mathison recently presented this case, at length.[39] He argues that the main Reformers were calling the church back to the view which it held for the first three centuries: not an autonomous ignorance or rejection of tradition and the rule of faith, but a subordination of them to the supreme authority of Scripture. Scripture is the only source of revelation, but it is to be interpreted within the communion of saints and the context of the rule of faith.

After the Reformation there developed, though, 'the radically individualistic Anabaptistic version of *sola Scriptura* (or more properly called *solo Scriptura*)', and this blossomed quickly in the ground of 'Enlightenment rationalism and American populism'. Many contemporary evangelicals are defending, and many Roman Catholics and Orthodox are attacking, not *sola Scriptura* but '*solo Scriptura*'.[40]

The second common suggestion for the location of the Spirit's on-going revelatory activity is the church – not the church apart from the Bible, but the church as it reads the Bible. This sounds like a distinctively Catholic argument, but in fact it is has been argued recently by a number of Protestant theologians. A good example is the American theologian Stanley Hauerwas. Commenting on the disciples who failed at first to recognise the risen Christ on the Emmaus road at the end of Luke's Gospel, Hauerwas points out that their problem was not that they did not know the Old Testament, whose aim was to point them to Christ. Instead, he says, '[t]heir problem was that they did not know how to find Jesus in it. They had not received the training that would instill in them a whole set of practices that would give the text a whole different reading.'[41] His point is that the Spirit has to work through the church, turning converts into active, faithful disciples before they can find Christ speaking to them in Scripture.

However, it seems that this kind of biblical-theological reasoning glosses over the fact that the Bible remains theologically prior to the church, as the location of the Spirit's primary activity. Hauerwas supposes that the church provides a context in which people become Christian converts and then become active, faithful disciples – and when it is properly living out its calling, that is exactly what the church does. This, though, begs the question of how the church knows what its proper calling is, and how that calling should be properly lived out.

What is the right direction in which to point people in conversion? How does the church come to know what kind of active discipleship to encourage, and which behaviours and beliefs it must warn converts to shun? How does the church come to be the kind of community which can foster true discipleship? The church's life has only come to be shaped in these ways because in repeated acts of grace the Spirit has already taken many of the words of Scripture, and moulded the life of the church in faithful obedience to them. It is the Spirit himself, working through the words of Scripture, who enables us to grow as a community of disciples who can shape other disciples.

Hauerwas is certainly right to assert that the more we have been formed as Christian disciples, the better able we are to discern Christ clearly in Scripture. In this, he is in accord with Keith Mathison's construal of *sola Scriptura*. Yet it is not the case, as Hauerwas thinks, that Christian interpretation of Scripture creates meaning through a creative interaction between the text and a set of community practices, such that if those practices did not exist, that meaning could not be said to exist. Instead, as the church is more deeply marked by the beliefs and practices which Scripture prescribes for it, so the church is better able to discern clearly the meaning that is already there. It is at this point that Hauerwas parts company with the kind of construal of *sola Scriptura* that Mathison offers.[42] The evangelical theologian Stanley Grenz has pointed out this priority of the Bible in forming the church as the body of Christ: 'By looking to the biblical story as constituting our own identity, we become the contemporary embodiment of Jesus' narrative, and hence we are indeed "the body of Christ."'[43]

The particular ongoing role of the Holy Spirit in relation to the Bible is therefore, first, not to create new meanings, but to press on our hearts the meaning that is already there through his inspiration in the words of the Bible. As Vanhoozer puts it, the Spirit does not change the meaning for us, but ministers it to us, convincing us that this is a meaning that is true, and that is true *for us*.[44] This becomes self-evident once we are clear that to use language, in speech or in writing, is to perform an action. We cannot undo an action that has been performed and remake it as something else: if a promise has been made, or a warning given, then that act remains what it is. Subsequent interpreters may disagree over what in fact did happen, and even radically alter their interpretations of an act performed in the past, but they are still trying to establish what in fact happened. If Scripture is made up of countless individual speech-acts, which together perform God's speech-act to us, then the reader's initial proper role can only be to determine the act which the writer in fact performed in authoring the text.[45]

Secondly, Christ, by his Spirit, through his Word, is re-creating us as Christ-centred creatures. This again is Stanley Grenz:

> Just as God created the world 'in the beginning' through the act of speaking the Word, so also God creates a world in the present by the Spirit speaking through Scripture. And what the Spirit now constructs is a world centered in Jesus.[46]

The world of the Bible comes to life in Christians – Scripture is embodied in us, as we live lives of faithful obedience in response to its commands, and following in the normative patterns of its narratives. For the church to be identified as the body of Christ on earth is therefore not to give the church any kind of 'incarnational' precedence here and now over Scripture. It is rather to say that the church must be continually formed and reformed by the action of the Spirit of Christ through the word of Christ, so that it may embody the Scriptures in which Christ comes to us.

Conclusion

We return to the two common objections to the classical identification of the Bible with the Word of God with which we began. Karl Barth seems fundamentally to fear that the identification leads to heresy, in that it treats the Bible as a kind of second incarnation, a second hypostatic union of divine and human natures. That, however, is not what the classical identification proposes. Christ, as the Word incarnate, can say of himself uniquely, 'if you've seen me you've seen the Father'. A second incarnation would claim the same for the Bible: 'if you've seen this book, you've seen God'. That, however, is not what the classical evangelical view of Scripture is proposing.

The uniqueness of the incarnation lies in the union of God with a particular flesh-and-blood human being. However, the unique divine character of the Bible has nothing to do with its various manifestations in paper and ink.[47] The unique divine character of the Bible has to do only with the speech-acts which God performs through its words; it has nothing to do with any particular material incarnation of those words.

The classical doctrine of Scripture should not be rejected on the basis that, when not fully expounded, it can sound roughly like a second incarnation. God has given warrant for the *apparent* theological risk of challenging the uniqueness of the incarnate Christ by the very verbal means in which he has chosen to reveal himself and to relate himself to us. As we have argued throughout, for us to say 'I trust Christ' and to say 'I trust the words that Christ speaks in Scripture' is effectively to say the same thing. We therefore have no choice but to develop a doctrine of Scripture which will raise some concerns that the uniqueness of revelation in Christ is being compromised. Only a very carefully delineated doctrine will make clear that Christ's incarnational uniqueness is not threatened, but actually served and made knowable by the permanent identity of Scripture with the Word of God.

Of course, the problem is not unique to Scripture, since many true aspects of Christian teaching can seem to run dangerously close to heresy, when not fully expounded. Petrine talk of participating in the divine nature (cf. 2 Pet. 1.4), which sails close to the winds of Platonism and mystery religions, is just one biblical example.

The question of christological heresy also arises in the common accusation that the classical doctrine of Scripture is analogous to a docetic view of Christ, treating the Bible in practice as only apparently human. It has been argued here that the classical view of Scripture should lead readers to take full and careful account of the literary, linguistic and contextual features of the Bible. All these are very real human aspects of Scripture. In that sense, the classical doctrine of Scripture proposes that the Bible should be read and interpreted in the same way as any other text. A docetic view of Scripture, by contrast, would be one which treats Scripture as a book of magic divine formulae or as a divine codebook.

Secondly, John Barton fears that the classical doctrine of Scripture leads to bibliolatry, that is, to the worship of the Bible alongside or even in place of Jesus. Bibliolatry, in the most obvious strict sense of the word, would be worship of a particular copy of the Bible – pointing to one individual paper-and-ink form of the Bible and saying, 'Behold your God'. Such idolatry can happen, but usually not in churches which confess the identity of Scripture with the Word of God. Certainly, nothing of this sort is entailed by the classical evangelical doctrine of Scripture.

A different kind of misuse of Scripture could also conceivably be called 'bibliolatry', in an extended sense of the word. Some evangelicals can practise a form of biblical interpretation that delights in the details of Scripture, to the ignorance of its overall function of leading us to Christ and fostering our discipleship of Christ. This misuse of Scripture is probably what is often in mind when the accusation of 'bibliolatry' is made.

However, 'bibliolatry' is an analytically poor term with which to describe this particular form of mistreatment of Scripture. This is so because it is a fault of Bible reading which cannot be rectified by somehow paying less attention to Scripture and more attention to Christ, for that is a false dichotomy. Instead, it can only be rectified by an even closer attention to Scripture's own testimony to its Christ-focused nature and purpose. Thus, those who hang on every word of the Bible, interpreting it canonically, theologically and contextually, are not 'bibliolaters'. Rather, in engaging with the words of Scripture, they will encounter God, and will, if responding in faith to God's action in and on them through the words of Scripture, have their lives shaped by God in obedience to Christ.

Notes

1. K. Vanhoozer, 'God's Mighty Speech-Acts: The Doctrine of Scripture Today', in P.E. Satterthwaite & D.F. Wright (eds.), *A Pathway into the Holy Scripture* (Grand Rapids, Michigan: Eerdmans, 1994), pp. 143–81, at p. 180.
2. See G. Bray, 'The Church Fathers and their Use of Scripture', in P. Helm and C. Trueman (eds.), *The Trustworthiness of God: Perspectives on the Nature of Scripture* (Leicester: Apollos, 2002), pp. 157–74.
3. Clement of Alexandria, *Stromateis* VII.16, Library of Christian Classics 2 (London: SCM Press, 1954).
4. Augustine, *On Christian Doctrine, Nicene and Post-Nicene Fathers* (ed. P. Schaff; Grand Rapids: Eerdmans, 1956), II.9.
5. R.P.C. Hanson, *Tradition in the Early Church* (London: SCM, 1962), p. 126.
6. Aquinas, *Summa Theologiae* (Blackfriars, 1964–), III, q.1 a.3.
7. Aquinas, *Summa Theologiae*, I, q.1 a.8.
8. H. Schüssler, *Der Primat der heiligen Schrift als theologisches und kanonistisches Problem im Spätmittelalter* (Wiesbaden: Franz Steiner Verlag, 1977), pp. 51–2.
9. J. Calvin, *Institutes of the Christian Religion* (Library of Christian Classics 20–21; trans. Ford Lewis Battles; ed. John T. McNeill; Philadelphia: Westminster Press, 1960), 1.7.1. See also R.S. Wallace, *Calvin's Doctrine of the Word and Sacrament* (Edinburgh: Scottish Academic, 1995), pp. 96–9.
10. J. Barton, *People of the Book? The Authority of the Bible in Christianity* (Louisville, Kentucky: Westminster/John Knox, 1988), pp. 81, 83.
11. K. Barth, *Church Dogmatics*, (ed.) G.W. Bromiley and T.F. Torrance (Edinburgh: Clark, 1956) I/1, pp. 109–12.
12. Barth, *Church Dogmatics* I/1, p. 132.
13. Barth, *Church Dogmatics* I/2, p. 524.
14. Barth, *Church Dogmatics* I/1, p. 138.
15. As Francis Watson shows, while God does more than simply speak in creating, his acts of speaking are fundamental to his accomplishing of

creation. Cf. F. Watson, *Text, Church and World: Biblical Interpretation in Theological Perspective* (Edinburgh: Clark, 1994), pp. 137–53.

[16] R. Nelson, *1 & 2 Kings Interpretation Commentary* (Louisville: John Knox, 1987), pp. 84–5.

[17] The philosophical aspect of this point, applied both to human and divine persons, their actions and their language, will be developed further below.

[18] G. McConville, 'Divine Speech and the Book of Jeremiah', in P. Helm and C. Trueman (eds.), *The Trustworthiness of God*, pp. 18–38.

[19] McConville, 'Divine Speech and the Book of Jeremiah', pp. 25–6.

[20] Ibid., pp. 32, 37.

[21] See, for example, D.A. Hagner, *Matthew 14–28* (WBC 33B; Dallas, Texas: Word, 1995), pp. 744–5. For a consideration of this reading of the parable, in comparison to the more universal interpretation of 'brothers' (which he favours theologically and hermeneutically), see F. Watson, 'Liberating the Reader: A Theological-Exegetical Study of the Parable of the Sheep and the Goats (Matt. 25.31–46)', in F. Watson (ed.), *The Open Text: New Directions for Biblical Studies?* (London: SCM, 1993), pp. 57–84.

[22] J. Goldingay, *Theological Diversity and the Authority of the Old Testament* (Grand Rapids, Eerdmans, 1987), pp. 122–7, gives a very lucid analysis of the different ways in which the phrase 'canon within the canon' has been used.

[23] W. Pannenberg, *Systematic Theology* 1 (trans. G.W. Bromiley; Grand Rapids: Eerdmans, 1991), p. 463.

[24] W. Pannenberg, 'On the Inspiration of Scripture', *Theology Today* 54 (1997) pp. 212–15, at p. 213.

[25] B.M. Metzger, *The Canon of the New Testament: Its Origin, Development, and Significance* (Oxford: Clarendon, 1987), p. 282.

[26] J.L. Austin, *How To Do Things With Words* (2nd ed.; Oxford: Oxford University, 1975).

[27] N. Wolterstorff, *Divine Discourse: Philosophical Reflections on the Claim that God Speaks* (Cambridge: Cambridge University, 1995), pp. 83–5.

[28] Wolterstorff, *Divine Discourse*, p. 94.

[29] Paul Ricoeur, Emmanuel Levinas, Hans-Georg Gadamer, and even, some would argue, Jacques Derrida, in his later writings.

[30] P. Ricoeur, *Hermeneutics and the Human Sciences: Essays on Language, Action and Interpretation* (trans. & ed. J.B. Thompson; Cambridge: Cambridge University, 1981), p. 146.

The Incarnation and Scripture 183

31 P. Ricoeur, *Interpretation Theory: Discourse and the Surplus of Meaning* (Fort Worth, Texas: Texas Christian University, 1976), p. 27.
32 K.J. Vanhoozer, *Is There a Meaning in This Text? The Bible, the Reader and the Morality of Literary Knowledge* (Leicester: Apollos, 1998), p. 339.
33 This kind of hermeneutical spiralling towards true understanding has been variously described. N.T. Wright calls it a hermeneutics of agape, in which we treat the text as we should another person, to be listened to on its own terms. Cf. N.T. Wright, *The New Testament and the People of God* (London: SPCK, 1992), p. 64. Vanhoozer talks about a hermeneutics of the cross, and a hermeneutics of humility and conviction (Vanhoozer, *Is There a Meaning?*, pp. 452–68). Gadamer famously speaks of a fusion of the horizons of text and reader as the way in which understanding takes place (although whether or not that fusion brings understanding of the text, or an understanding of the text on the reader's own terms, is debated). Understanding does not of course entail agreement with everything we read in every text – some texts must be judged immoral.
34 Vanhoozer, *Is There a Meaning?*, p. 225.
35 Referred to in G. Lindbeck, 'Barth and Textuality', *Theology Today* 43 (1986) pp. 361–76, at p. 368.
36 Barth, *Church Dogmatics* I/2, p. 465.
37 See further on this: T. Ward, *Word and Supplement: Speech Acts, Biblical Texts, and the Sufficiency of Scripture* (Oxford: Oxford University, 2002), pp. 106–36; K. Vanhoozer, 'God's Mighty Speech-Acts: The Doctrine of Scripture Today', pp. 143–81.
38 C. Gunton, *A Brief Theology of Revelation* (Edinburgh: Clark, 1995), p. 66.
39 K.A. Mathison, *The Shape of Sola Scriptura* (Moscow, Idaho: Canon, 2001).
40 Mathison, *The Shape of Sola Scriptura*, pp. 346–7.
41 S. Hauerwas, *Unleashing the Scripture: Freeing the Bible from Captivity to America* (Nashville: Abingdon, 1993), p. 56.
42 Hauerwas falls victim to the non-realism that affects a great deal of contemporary (theological) hermeneutics. Similar to his work is S.E. Fowl's sophisticated *Engaging Scripture: A Model for Theological Interpretation* (Oxford: Blackwell, 1998). Fowl argues that we should be more interested in what Scripture does, and what we do to it, than in theoretical or doctrinal statements about what kind of a thing it is. However, our use of Scripture must be demonstrably grounded in its

intrinsic nature, if that use is to be ethically appropriate. We cannot side-step doctrines of Scripture with community-based hermeneutics in this way (see Ward, *Word and Supplement*, pp. 190–3).

[43] S. Grenz and J. Franke, *Beyond Foundationalism: Shaping Theology in a Postmodern Context* (Louisville, Kentucky: Westminster/John Knox, 2001), p. 80.

[44] Vanhoozer, *Is There a Meaning?*, p. 413.

[45] For a rich and robust defence of this as the reader's primary moral duty, see Vanhoozer, *Is There a Meaning?*, pp. 367–452.

[46] Grenz and Franke, *Beyond Foundationalism*, p. 78.

[47] That is why Christians do not generally consider it irreverent to drop a Bible on the floor, or to let a Bible become dog-eared through use.

6. The Incarnation and the Lord's Supper

Carl Trueman

> I say that although Christ is absent from the earth in respect of the flesh, yet in the Supper we truly feed on his body and blood — that owing to the secret agency of the Spirit we enjoy the presence of both.[1]

The Lord's Supper: A Neglected Gift

There would seem to be little doubt that neglect of the Lord's Supper or the Eucharist is one of the hallmarks of contemporary evangelicalism. With the exception of the conservative tradition of Highland Presbyterianism, which still maintains its practice of infrequent communion seasons, and evangelical Anglicanism, with its liturgical practices, the Lord's Supper is not a particularly important part of evangelical church life.[2] Many attend churches where the sacrament is little more than an addendum attached to the end of the main Sunday service; and a glance at basic theology primers for evangelicals reveals a dramatic neglect of the theology of the Lord's Supper in the litany of what are otherwise considered to be evangelical essentials and distinctives. Thus, for example, in John Stott's recent manifesto for evangelical unity, the Lord's Supper is scarcely touched upon except for a couple of lines in the section on the cross of Christ.[3] But such has not always been the case in Protestantism. Indeed, at the Reformation, the Protestant consensus was shattered at precisely this point, when Lutherans and Reformed failed to reach agreement at the Colloquy of Marburg in 1529 and set up a division within the ranks which persists to this day.[4] If we equate modern evangelical values and attitudes with those of the Reformers, then such a breach becomes incomprehensible; it is a dispute about trivia. If, how-ever, we return to our roots and see the Lord's Supper in terms of the theological dimensions of the Reformation itself, we can see both why the breach took place and how impoverished we ourselves have become through our contemporary indifference to the practice of communion in the contemporary church. The Lord's Supper is a gift of God; the Reformation's most brilliant sacramental theologians, men such as Calvin and Cranmer, clearly understood it as such; and thus we neglect it only to our own detriment.

How and why this neglect has come about is not easy to discern. Possible reasons include the inherent emphasis upon individual rather than corporate activities as the gauges of spiritual health within the evangelical church. Emphasis upon quiet times, individual Bible reading etc. rather than upon gathering as believers would be one sign that this is the case. Theologically, the frequent failure of evangelicals to have any real doctrine of the church is also almost certainly part of the problem. At another level, the failure of church leadership within evangelicalism to provide a solid rationale for sacramental activity within a theological tradition committed to justification by faith has undoubtedly eroded Eucharistic practices. Then, at the level of sheer pragmatism, the ecumenical difficulties involved in any sacramental discussion by a movement that is, in essence, transdenominational no doubt militate against the kind of sharp drawing of boundaries in which Luther and Zwingli indulged. The reasons are probably manifold and complex; the result is rather simple – in general, evangelicals neglect the Lord's Supper.

My approach in this paper will be twofold: first, I will lay out the incarnational aspects of the Reformation debates surrounding the Lord's Supper between Lutherans and Reformed (and, for the sake of argument, I used 'Reformed' here not in any sense of modern church politics but in terms of that Reformation tradition represented by such as Zwingli and Calvin); and, second, I will explore how and why the Eucharist was significant for the Reformers and how their vision might be renewed today. I must, of course, lay my own cards on the table at the very start. I write not as an Anglican but as a Presbyterian; yet, in honour of my immediate context and as a symbol of the fundamental catholicity of the evangelical faith, I intend to interact closely with the writings of the great Thomas Cranmer, a man for whom neglect of the Lord's Supper within the life of the church would have been inconceivable.

Luther versus Zwingli: The Lord's Supper as Incarnational Problem

Lying behind the sacramental breach between Luther and Zwingli were both differing views of salvation and differing views of incarnation. At the most basic level, Luther regarded the incarnate Christ as the only context in which God could be encountered as gracious; and this required Christ's humanity to be really present in the Eucharistic elements.[5] Zwingli, however, felt no such need to find God gracious only at the point where divinity and humanity coincided and thus had no need to find Christ's humanity within the elements. For him, the Lord's Supper was more of a memorial and a ritual of horizontal significance between believers.[6] This is why there could ultimately be no compromise between them. For Luther, mere spiritual presence of Christ, or, even worse, complete absence of Christ, turned the Lord's Supper into law rather than gospel, into a message of judgement rather than of good news and grace.

Underlying these soteriological concerns was a fundamental disagreement over the nature of the incarnation itself and it is important that we grasp this in order to see that Protestant understandings of the Lord's Supper were at their inception intimately related to understandings of incarnation. For Luther, the need to maintain a real presence of the whole Christ, both divine and human, in the Eucharistic elements led him, in the heat of controversy to argue for the general ubiquity of Christ's flesh. His arguments on this issue represent a remodelling of philosophical notions about presence inherited from his Occamist background.[7] He is indeed careful to distinguish Christ's corporeal presence from a crude spatial and circumscriptive presence, whilst yet maintaining the reality of that presence in the elements. To do this, he is driven to argue for a direct communication of properties between the two natures in Christ.[8] Thus, the human nature becomes infinite through its contact with the divine. One consequence of this is that Christ's human nature becomes ubiquitous. However, it must be stressed that this in no way relativises the sacrament, or Christ's presence therein, since Luther regards as crucial the fact that Christ's presence in the sacramental elements is presence joined to a promise, thus giving a different significance to the presence in the elements than, say, in the ink and paper of this essay.[9]

Zwingli, however, holds to an understanding of the communication of properties whereby the properties of the two natures are communicated indirectly in the person of the mediator. Thus, while Christ the one person can be described as infinite, this is according to his divine nature, not according to his human nature. There is, therefore, no need to argue for the presence of Christ's humanity wherever one finds the divinity, a position now commonly known by the later Lutheran pejorative term 'the extra-Calvinisticum'. This is actually not an innovation, but a position held by such luminaries as Athanasius, Gregory of Nyssa and Thomas Aquinas, which became normative for the later Reformed tradition.[10] This Christology finds its expression in the linguistic convention of *alloiosis* where, as Zwingli defines it, 'what applies to one of the natures is predicated of the other.'[11] This, in turn, allows him to understand the phrase 'This *is* my body' in a non-literal sense as 'This *represents* my body'. Indeed, he has to do so, for to do otherwise would lead him into what he would regard as a Christological absurdity – a literal, physical identification of Christ's body with something that is patently not so.[12]

Enough has been said regarding the Eucharistic dispute between Luther and Zwingli, and then between Lutheran and Reformed traditions as a whole, to demonstrate that underlying these disputes were important, irreconcilable differences over the nature of the incarnation. There is not time in this paper to thrash out in detail all the ramifications of the two approaches, but it seems clear to me at least that the Reformed position on the communication of properties is both closest to the mainstream patristic and western medieval tradition of the church and the one which most clearly preserves the balance of natures and personhood which is expressed in the Chalcedonian definition of Christ's incarnation. Perennial Lutheran accusations of Nestorianism aside, the Reformed position would seem to preserve the integrity of the two natures in the one person in a way in which the Lutheran position simply does not. While it must be conceded that the exalted humanity of Christ after the resurrection possesses properties not generally associated with our humanity (such as the ability to pass through solid walls), it is a long way from these references in Scripture to the ubiquity doctrine, even in the refined form in which later Lutheranism held to it.[13]

The Positive Function of the Lord's Supper in Reformed Theology

Christian assurance
The conflict between Luther and Zwingli is instructive for seeing the historic connection between views of the incarnation and of Christ's presence in the Lord's Supper, but it is somewhat less helpful in constructing a positive Eucharistic doctrine for evangelicals today. This is because, whatever the virtues of Zwingli's Christology, his understanding of the Lord's Supper is highly reductionist, rooting its usefulness almost exclusively in its power to recall to mind the death of Christ and as a corporate pledge binding believers together like some communal oath.[14] I suspect that this aspect of Zwinglianism is the default position of many evangelicals, not because evangelicals are at all noted for profound reflection upon the metaphysics of incarnation but for a more prosaic reason: it is so easy to understand relative to the alternatives (Lutheran or Reformed). Indeed, in many evangelical churches, the Lord's Supper becomes an opportunity simply to sit in silence and reflect upon Christ's death in the service, with the sacramental action itself being entirely accidental to what is going on. Some evidence that this is in fact the case is provided by John Stott's book to which I referred earlier. Talking of preaching as calling to mind the cross in the minds of those who hear, Stott parallels this with the function of the Lord's Supper:

> This is also what the Lord's Supper or the Eucharist does. The technical word for it is *anamnesis*, or remembrance, as word and sacrament together dramatize verbally and visually the unique, epoch-making event of the cross.[15]

The problem with such a view is, of course, that it dramatically relativises the Lord's Supper and begs the obvious question: what do we get here that we cannot get better through better preaching

– or, even, any preaching? Furthermore, this memorialism presents a much narrower understanding of the Eucharist than that contained within classic reformation documents. Take, for instance, the Anglican Article 28, which says the following:

> The Supper of the Lord is not only a sign of the love that Christians ought to have among themselves one to another; but rather is a Sacrament of our Redemption by Christ's death: insomuch that to such as rightly, worthily, and with faith receive the same, the Bread which we break is a partaking of the Body of Christ; and likewise the Cup of Blessing is a partaking of the Blood of Christ.

Now, this article, which is good, solid Reformation theology, clearly goes beyond the kind of mere memorialism that lies at the heart of Zwinglian, and of later popular evangelical, approaches to the Eucharist. Whatever else the Eucharist is in Anglican theology, it involves more than just the mere remembrance of Christ's death upon the cross.

We need not, however, restrict ourselves simply to official Anglican documents on this issue. A glance at the Westminster Confession of Faith reveals a similar cultural divide between our evangelical forebears and our own church theology and practice. Chapter 19 of the Confession opens with the following paragraph:

> Our Lord Jesus, in the night he was betrayed, instituted the Lord's Supper, to be observed in his church, unto the end of the world, for the perpetual remembrance of the sacrifice of himself in his death; the sealing all benefits thereof unto true believers, their spiritual nourishment and growth in him, their further engagement in, and to, all duties which they owe unto him; and to be a bond, and pledge of their communion with him, and with each other, as members of his mystical body.[16]

Though the emphases are perhaps a little different, once again the importance of the Lord's Supper as more than mere remembrance is brought out clearly. This sacrament seals the benefits of Christ's death to us (i.e. is one part of our assurance of salvation), nourishes us spiritually, and encourages us to, and strengthens us for, greater devotion to Christ. The implications of neglect of the Lord's Supper from a Westminster perspective are thus both obvious and devastating.

The language of the Westminster Confession at this point clearly indicates that the Westminster divines considered the Lord's Supper to have a significant role in the matter of Christian assurance. Indeed, this is a constant theme in the writings of the Reformed at the time of the Reformation, reflecting their interest in asserting the reality of Christian assurance over medieval Catholic denials of the doctrine. This concern regarding the Eucharist is central to Cranmer's masterful exposition of Eucharistic doctrine, his *Defence of the True and Catholic Doctrine of the Sacrament of the Body and Blood of our Saviour Christ*.[17] Cranmer's argument regarding this issue is summed up in the following quotation from this work:

> [A]lthough, in the truth of his human nature, Christ be in heaven, and sitteth at the right hand of God the Father, yet whosoever eateth of that bread in the supper of the Lord, according to Christ's institution and ordinance, is assured of Christ's own promise and testament, that he is a member of his body and receiveth the benefits of his passion which he suffered for us upon the cross.[18]

This is classic Reformed theology: the emphasis upon the localised presence of Christ's body in heaven, the identification of the right hand of God as a place rather than a metaphor for divine power, and the language of promise and assurance all locate Cranmer on the Reformed wing of the Reformation. More important for us is the clear connection he makes between partaking of the Eucharist and assurance of faith. The Eucharist is not simply a memorial which allows the believer an opportunity in the service to remember Christ's death; it is also an important aspect of a healthy, assured Christian life, a belief Cranmer shared with, among others, John Calvin.[19]

We might say, therefore, that Reformed Eucharistic theology of the Cranmer variety was profoundly pastoral in its orientation towards Christian assurance. This particular point is made in a firm yet beautiful fashion in the liturgy of Cranmer's Prayer Book. The structure of the service is a masterpiece of pastoral relevance and simplicity. After prayer comes the reading of the law, by which all hearts should be convicted; then shortly thereafter we have the readings from Scripture, the Creed, the sermon, intercessions, exhortations to attend communion worthily, prayer of confession, words of comfort, the prayer of humble access, the consecration and partaking of the elements; and finally an extended opportunity for thanksgiving and prayer. The whole thrust of this service is towards underlining the sinfulness and unworthiness of the communicants and the overwhelming grace and mercy of God in providing his Son, Jesus Christ, for their salvation. The desired result is exactly what Cranmer argued for in his *Defence*: the assuring of weak consciences.

The question now arises, of course: how does it do this? The basic negative point we can make in this context is that it does not do it by way of being in any sense an offering or a sacrifice to God. The focus in the service is on what God has done for the communicant, not on what the priest is doing for God on behalf of the communicants. Several factors serve to undergird this. First, there is the obvious christological issue. Reformed Christology provides a basic axiom for understanding the nature of the Eucharist in that it stresses that Christ's humanity is now ascended to heaven, sits at the right hand of the Father, and will not return until the Second Coming.[20] This means that Christ's humanity cannot be present in the Eucharistic action in a manner which would be required by anything approximating to the medieval Catholic notion of the sacrificial nature of the Mass.[21] Thus, from a Reformed perspective, there is nothing on offer to God in the Eucharist. Second, the commitment of Cranmer to the doctrine of justification by grace through faith means that assurance is a reality for the believer only because of the action of God in Christ for humanity, not because the believer has done something for God.[22]

This is why it is somewhat unfortunate in the latest Anglican liturgy, *Common Worship*, that a certain ambiguity slips into the language of Holy Communion. In Eucharistic Prayer G, for example, we have the following words:

> Father, we plead with confidence
> his sacrifice made once for all upon the cross;

we remember his dying and rising in glory,
and we rejoice that he intercedes for us at your right hand.
Pour out your Holy Spirit as we bring before you
these gifts of your creation;
may they be for us the body and blood of your dear Son.[23]

The prayer starts well, by pointing participants unambiguously towards the sacrifice of Christ as the basis for salvation but then, and quite out of step with the theological flow of the prayer, we have this unfortunate statement about bringing before God these gifts of his creation, in this context clearly the elements of bread and wine. While these words can probably be given a harmless meaning from an evangelical perspective, they are nonetheless unfortunately ambiguous, particularly against the background of the historic debates about the significance of the Eucharist. While the traditional language of the Book of Common Prayer focused exclusively on what God had done for the communicants, here we suddenly have hints that the communicants may themselves be doing something for God. There is no exegetical basis for taking the Lord's Supper as any kind of offering to God with regards to the elements. If anything is being offered, it is Christ's body and blood to us by God, not to God by us; and if we offer anything at all, it is ourselves, our praises, our thanksgiving and our loving response to God's prior grace in Christ as shown forth in the action of the Lord's Supper. The ambiguous language is, therefore, unfortunate. One might also add at this point that to take something which is meant to work for assurance and to turn it into something we offer back to God is pastorally extremely cruel – as cruel as typical evangelical neglect of the sacrament – depriving congregations of the full joy and benefit of God's gift of Holy Communion by turning it into yet another work.

If the understanding of incarnation and of justification restrict the understanding of the Eucharist in a negative sense by telling us how it does not offer us assurance, we can now turn to the positive construction which the Reformed give to the Eucharist, and that focuses on the true (as opposed to real) presence of Christ. Hear what Cranmer has to say in his *Defence*:

[T]he bread and the wine be not so changed into the flesh and blood of Christ, that they be made one nature, but they remain still

> distinct in nature, so that the bread in itself is not his flesh, and the wine his blood, but unto them that worthily eat and drink the bread and wine, to them the bread and wine be his flesh and blood; that is to say, by things natural and which they be accustomed unto, they be exalted unto things above nature. For the sacramental bread and wine be not bare naked figures, but so pithy and effectuous, that whosoever worthily eateth them, eateth spiritually Christ's flesh and blood, and hath by them everlasting life.[24]

Cranmer's language here is quite dramatic, and reflects the systematic underpinnings of the Book of Common Prayer and the Anglican Articles, both of which talk about eating Christ's body and drinking his blood. This language has profound implications. If the worthy are really eating Christ in some sense, then Christ must be really present in some sense. Thus, while Cranmer rejects the real presence as understood in Catholic and Lutheran circles, his language yet carries him beyond a mere memorialism which roots the efficacy of the sacrament in its function as a mere prompt to the remembrance of Christ's death.[25] The crucial qualification for Cranmer is provided by faith. Take, for example, the language used when the element of bread is distributed:

> The body of our Lord Jesus Christ, which was given for thee, preserve thy body and soul unto everlasting life. Take and eat this in remembrance that Christ died for thee, and feed on him in thy heart by faith with thanksgiving.

This language reflects the theology of the Article 28, which declares that:

> The Body of Christ is given, taken, and eaten in the Lord's Supper, only after an heavenly and spiritual manner. And the mean whereby the Body of Christ is received and eaten in the Supper is faith.

The key words in this context are faith, heavenly and spiritual. These are the things which qualify our understanding of what is taking place in the Eucharist. For those that believe, by faith Christ is truly present and partaken in a heavenly, spiritual manner. Here we get what we might term the subjective and objective dimensions of the

The Incarnation and the Lord's Supper 195

Eucharist coming into relation with each other, tying in with the typical Reformation insistence that the sacrament is only a sacrament in the context of the word clearly declared; and only effective in the context of that same word grasped by faith.

The result of all this is that, for all the Reformation stress upon the importance of the recipient's subjective disposition, the sacrament is not reducible in Reformed theology to mere subjectivity. Faith for the Reformers is always faith in something; it always has a specific object and a content. The emphasis upon personal religious experience at the expense of objective theological and ecclesiological factors which one finds in later pietism and evangelicalism – and which may well be another factor feeding into the decline of the sacrament in evangelical life and practice – is absent from their writings. Faith is always faith in Christ; it grasps hold of that which is presented to it in Christ; it is not simply a leap in the dark or a contentless psychological state; and the sacraments are always actions of the whole church, performed in the context of the word preached, and therefore of real benefit to the church community.[26] This is where the incarnation becomes not simply negatively significant in setting boundaries for our understanding of how Christ is *not* present in the sacrament but positively significant in determining how he is present.

Why Christ is present?

At this point, we need to be precise about exactly what sort of questions the Reformed asked about the Lord's Supper. The debate between Luther and Zwingli is focused very much upon the issue of *how* Christ is present. What is fundamentally wrongheaded about allowing the debate to get channelled in this direction is that the question of how Christ is present is really subordinate to the question of *why* Christ is present. It is quite clear in Luther, for example, that the necessity of maintaining the presence of Christ's humanity in the Eucharist is predicated upon his understanding of how God reveals himself as gracious to his people. That Zwingli's soteriology has no such need serves to explain both the Eucharistic differences between them and the ferocity of Luther's repudiation of the Zuricher's position. In other words, the metaphysics of presence are in actual fact somewhat subordinate to wider questions about the practical role of the sacraments in salvation and the life of the church. It is when the Reformed tradition moves beyond the impasse of the *how* question and focuses instead upon the *why* question that it makes its most significant contribution, and where the work of a man like Cranmer marks a significant improvement on the work of Zwingli.

The refusal to take any of these obvious options (Roman, Lutheran or Zwinglian) on the Lord's Supper is not distinctive to Cranmer but is part of mainstream, non-Zwinglian Reformed thought, and finds its finest advocate in John Calvin. It is in Calvin's writings that we can find theological moves which serve to explicate the realist language of eating and drinking in terms of incarnational theology and, more importantly, trinitarian theology. Clues to this are provided in Calvin's 1561 tract against the Lutheran polemicist, Heshusius. Lutherans, of course, objected strongly to the Reformed rejection of the physical presence of Christ's humanity in, with and under the elements of bread and wine, seeing this as leading to a real absence of Christ from the Eucharist. Calvin rejected such an accusation, and in so doing made the following comment which clearly underlines both his rejection of transubstantiation and his repudiation of accusations of straightforward memorialism:

> I say that although Christ is absent from the earth in respect of the flesh, yet in the Supper we truly feed on his body and blood – that owing to the secret agency of the Spirit we enjoy the presence of both. I say that distance of place is no obstacle to prevent the flesh, which was once crucified, from being given to us for food. Heshusius supposes, what is far from being the fact, that I imagine a presence of deity only.[27]

What is so important here is the reference Calvin makes to the role of the Holy Spirit in overcoming the problem which the Christology of the Reformed has created. To put it crudely, the spatial distance between the body of Christ in heaven and the elements of the Lord's Supper is overcome by the action of the Holy Spirit.

There are a number of issues raised by this argument which require further comment. First, we should note the direction of what we might call the spiritual movement. Christ is not brought down from heaven so much as we are raised up to heaven to feed upon him there.[28] It is indeed mysterious as to how this happens, but Calvin's thought is clearly no mere memorialism, and comports well with Anglican language of heavenly and spiritual eating. In addition, we might also note the eschatological implications of such eating: the Lord's Supper is a reminder of Christ's death; but the physical absence of Christ's humanity from the elements also serves as a reminder that he is not here in the flesh now. As the mind is lifted by the Spirit to feed upon Christ in heaven, it is also made acutely aware that this is indeed an action of faith and not sight, and that the return of Christ has not yet happened, capturing well the eschatological implications of Paul's comments on the Lord's Supper in 1 Corinthians 11:26. Our doctrine of the incarnation which leads us to emphasise Christ's physical absence from the elements draws us elsewhere to find his flesh and reminds us that he will come again.

This approach to the action of the Spirit, of course, stands in sharp contrast to the typical notion of 'epiclesis' which has found a place in modern liturgical practice.[29] There, the movement is not upward but downward, bringing Christ down through the Spirit to the elements. Recently, David Peterson has drawn attention to the epiclesis in Prayer E in *Common Worship*. The wording on which he comments, and his criticism, are as follows:

> Send your Holy Spirit, that broken bread and wine outpoured may be for us the body and blood of your dear Son.

> The idea that God should need to 'send' his Spirit upon those who already have the Spirit is unbiblical. Other verbs such as 'fill' or 'renew' make more sense with respect to the people of God.[30]

Peterson goes on to quote with approval the language of the *Westminster Directory for Public Worship*, which focuses on the work of the Spirit and the reception by faith of the body and blood of Christ without making the elements the object of the Spirit's action. The criticism of *Common Worship* at this point seems valid and, indeed, we might elaborate by saying that the kind of theology which the *Westminster Directory* represents is consistent with precisely the kind of orthodox Christology, soteriology and eschatology that provide the framework for sacramental theology but which are basically undermined by the kind of downward movement of Christ and the Spirit implied by the kind of epiclesis we find in *Common Worship* at this point.

Secondly, we should note how much of Calvin's language at this point, and of Reformed thought in general on the Lord's Supper, is incarnationally oriented. This is because underlying all of Calvin's theology of the Eucharist is his stress upon the spiritual union with the incarnate Christ which provides the basis for our enjoyment of the benefits which his incarnation and incarnate work have achieved.[31] Criticising the idea that one needs to physically eat Christ's physical body to enjoy such benefits, he says the following:

> And there is no need for us to enjoy a participation in it, since the Lord bestows this benefit upon us through his Spirit so that we may be made one in body, spirit, and soul with him. The bond of this connection is therefore the Spirit of Christ, with whom we are joined in unity, and is like a channel through which all that Christ himself is and has is conveyed to us.[32]

Cranmer expressed a similar thought, but this time with language that speaks more explicitly about the church as a whole:

> [A]s the bread and wine which we do eat, be turned into our flesh and blood, and be made our very flesh and very blood, and be so joined and mixed with our flesh and blood that they be made one whole body together, even so be all faithful Christian spiritually turned into the body of Christ, and be so joined unto Christ, and also together among themselves, that they do make but one mystical body of Christ.[33]

This, of course, brings us to the point where most evangelicals will now raise the crucial question: what do I obtain in the Eucharist that I do not obtain elsewhere? The question is a most powerful and pertinent one because it is faith in God's word which effects union with Christ and there are ultimately no degrees of union with Christ any more than there are degrees of justification. One cannot be a little bit united to Christ any more than one can be a little bit pregnant. One is either united to Christ or one is not. Then, if this is so, one already enjoys all the benefits that flow from this union and thus participation in the Eucharist cannot add to this any more than absence can detract from this. Indeed, this is the kind of argument, I suspect, that lies at the back of much evangelical neglect of the Eucharist: we are justified by faith, so why bother with the Lord's Supper? The typical response in many churches has amounted to a crude form of Zwinglianism: we do it simply to help remind ourselves of Christ's death, even though we may actually think that good preaching is in itself quite sufficient for such memorialist purposes. Given this reality, I wish to spend the rest of this paper mounting a defence of the importance of the Eucharist based upon what I have discussed so far.

Why is the Lord's Supper Necessary?
The first major reason for ascribing the Eucharist a place of importance in church life is, of course, that Christ commanded it. Thus, whether we understand the rationale behind Christ's thinking at this point or not, we have no right to consider the Eucharist as anything but important and central to the Christian life and all evangelical emphasis upon individual piety and downgrading of the doctrine of the church must be critiqued in the light of this fact.

Secondly, we need to make a careful distinction here between types of necessity. On one level, it is indeed true that all we need is faith in Christ for salvation; and on this level, we do not, strictly speaking, *need* to take the Eucharist in order to be saved. Yet this same kind of necessity applies to almost everything else which we routinely do as Christians. We do not need to pray or to read our Bibles, yet few of us would consider a Christian life where these activities are not part of our daily staple to be particularly good or helpful examples of healthy Christian living. Nor do we need to go to church on a Sunday, yet we do so because that is a basic part of a well-rounded, vibrant Christianity. What we have in the thought of Cranmer, Calvin and other Reformed theologians is a similar approach to the Eucharist. On one level, it is not necessary for salvation; but, we might add, just because something is not necessary for salvation does not mean that it is not necessary for a good, healthy Christian life. To return to my last point: the Lord's Supper is a command of Christ; therefore it is necessary; and, as Christ's command is understood by the Reformers, it is necessary not simply because of a divine whim but because it conduces to our spiritual health.

Why does it do so? The answer lies in the idea that the Lord's Supper serves to assure us of God's favour towards us. There is, of course, a tendency within popular evangelicalism to reduce the means of assurance to the word preached and this does indeed capture something of the Reformation emphasis whereby the word can be preached without the sacrament being administered, but the reverse can never be the case: the sacrament always needs the word for it to be a valid sacrament. Nevertheless, by subordinating sacrament to word in this sense, the Reformed tradition did not regard itself as having made the sacrament dispensable, as we noted above. Instead, when attached to the word of promise, the sacrament itself becomes yet another sign of God's bounteous grace in providing further means of assurance. The great Scottish Presbyterian, Robert Bruce, makes this point with power:

> The Sacrament is appointed that we may get a better hold of Christ than we got in the simple Word, that we may possess Christ in our hearts and minds more fully and largely than we did before, by the simple Word. That Christ may have more room in which to reside in our narrow hearts than He could have by the hearing of the simple Word, and that we may possess Him more fully, is a better thing ... The Sacrament assures you of no other truth than that contained within the Word. Nevertheless, because it is a seal annexed to the Word it persuades you better of its truth, for the more the outward senses are awakened, the more is the inward heart and mind persuaded to believe.[34]

In other words, while the sacrament gives us nothing that the word itself does not give us, it gives us it in a better – or perhaps 'different' – way so that we might have our hearts and minds expanded, the better to appreciate what we have and who we are in Christ.

Now, I must confess to a lack of ease with Reformed language of heavenly and spiritual eating that Calvin does so much to inject into the tradition. It is not exactly clear to me what, if we take it in anything approaching a literal sense, such language imparts. It is better, I believe to take the *intention* of the Reformers at this point to heart while perhaps leaving behind – or at least exerting some caution towards – the actual language that they use which can, unless carefully handled, create more sound than light. Their intention is, after all, quite clear – to underline the fact that the Lord's Supper is part and parcel of healthy Christian living because it plays a crucial role in assurance, because it is the meal of the New Covenant. Christ himself makes the covenant connection quite explicit in his words of institution at Luke 22:20. And what is the essence of the New Covenant? It is, to summarise Jeremiah 31:31–4 that all shall know God directly, that all will have the law written on their hearts, that there will be no need of mere human priests as mediators.

There, at the very heart of the gospel message, is assurance, a point which the Reformation brought to the very forefront of Christian life and thought; and the Lord's Supper is tied emphatically to that assurance. This is what Reformers such as Cranmer and Calvin saw so clearly. Whether language about ascending to heaven and feeding spiritually upon Christ there is the best way to express this, I am not sure; it may well be something resident in the very physical actions of hearing the promise and eating and drinking the elements which is that which helps to assure us both of the concrete reality of Christ, of his work in the past, and his present absence – an absence which is assuring precisely because it points us to his future return. There is, perhaps, a danger in reifying the language of present eating as Calvin does to the point where the reference to Christ's death in the past and his return in the future is, if you will pardon the pun, swallowed up in too much satisfaction with the present. One might say that the Eucharist's task is to feed us in such a way as to leave us hungry for real food yet confident that one day we shall receive it.

How Christ is present?

When we move from the *why* to the *how* question, we are perhaps on more difficult ground. Obviously, the incarnational theology of Chalcedon (which I would argue is probably the closest to a coherent Christology that one can get in terms of its ability to make sense of the biblical account of Christ's person), imposes certain restrictions: we are not assured by a physical eating of Christ. Nor, I would suggest, is a radically Zwinglian approach acceptable: Zwinglians will always struggle to give any rationale for the Lord's Supper at all. Something approximating the Reformed position, which takes seriously Reformed concerns, would seem to be the way forward. Thus, is the sacrament necessary? Well, strictly speaking, no, in the way that prayer and reading the Bible are not strictly necessary. But is the sacrament something which we neglect to our own disadvantage? Yes, for in doing so we cut ourselves off from one of the two basic media by which God makes known to us the reality of our union with Christ. And, just to anticipate the objection that I have here quoted a Scottish Presbyterian, let me turn once again to Cranmer to demonstrate that the thoughts expressed so beautifully by Bruce stand in basic continuity with those of Cranmer, pointing us, incidentally, to the catholicity of the Reformed tradition. Writing in his *Defence*, Cranmer says the following:

> [O]ur Saviour Christ hath not only set forth these things most plainly in his holy word, that we may hear them with our ears; but he hath also ordained one visible sacrament of spiritual regeneration in water, and another visible sacrament of spiritual nourishment in bread and wine, to the intent that, as much as is possible for man, we may see Christ with our eyes, smell him at our nose, taste him with our mouths, grope him with our hands, and perceive him with all our senses. For as the word of God preached putteth Christ into our ears; so likewise these elements of water, bread, and wine, joined to God's word, do after a sacramental manner put Christ into our eyes, mouths, hands, and all our senses.[35]

Here, Cranmer drives home his belief that the sacraments make Christ more real to us by appealing not simply to our disembodied intellects but to all our senses. Cranmer instinctively grasps that human beings are physical creatures and that the very physical nature of the sacraments thus reinforces faith by bringing Christ to us not simply via the auditing of words but by the smelling and tasting of the elements. In fact, we can probably broaden Cranmer's own approach here and say that the whole sacramental action, including the visual impact of the breaking of the bread, serves this purpose of reinforcing the word in the public worship of the church.

In a recent essay, Melvin Tinker has argued that Calvin's view of the Lord's Supper can be understood using the categories of speech-act theory. Picking up on the Reformed tradition's analogy of the sacraments to seals, he argues that, for Calvin, the Lord's Supper does not add to the knowledge we have of Christ given in the gospel but, like the seal or signature at the bottom of a degree diploma, gives a certain force and public validity to the thing to which they are appended.[36] This would seem to be consistent with the picture I have drawn above, and as applicable to Cranmer as to Calvin. Understood in this way, the elements back up the word, reinforcing its message. As we eat the bread and drink the wine, our minds are drawn by the Spirit through the transformation of the signifying power of the elements by the word of God to that heavenly feeding upon Christ's body which we do by faith and which is the instrument of our salvation. This is neither the magical hocus-pocus of an *ex opere operato* understanding of the real presence of Christ, nor is it merely a recollection of Christ's death. It is rather an action performed by the church community which has a much richer and more dynamic role to play in our Christian lives than either of the other two options. It serves to dramatise God's word before us and thereby to strengthen our confidence in its truth; and, as we grasp both word and sacrament by faith, we become more conscious of that heavenly feeding upon Christ which is our very lifeblood.

Conclusion

What, therefore, are the conclusions which can be drawn from these brief observations?

First, our understanding of the Eucharist is inevitably closely related to our understanding of the incarnation. Doing full justice to Christ's humanity would seem to require that we understand his body to be now in heaven and not here on earth, and certainly not in the Eucharistic elements. To place the human Christ there is to do violence to his human nature and to indulge in an over-realised eschatology that actually undermines the purpose of the Lord's Supper as something to be performed, in part, as a reminder that he has not yet returned in his humanity to claim that which is his own.

Secondly, we must not allow mere memorialism to remain the default position for evangelicalism. That it is easy to understand, that it seems to sit so comfortably with justification by faith, and that a word-based religion seems to have little space for the Lord's Supper being anything other than a convenient slot in the service to cast our minds back to Calvary, are none of them adequate reasons for taking this option. The theological reflection of the church on this point indicates that mere memorialism is scarcely an adequate basis for maintaining the necessity of the sacrament which Christ's own command imposes upon us. We need to tap once more into the riches of our Eucharistic heritage, and reflect upon the significance of the Lord's Supper as a New Covenant meal, with all of the theological and existential significance that possesses.

The Lord's Supper is not incidental to our lives as Christians – it is something commanded by the Lord and something which has reference to the past, the present and the future. The Eucharistic action as a whole serves to bring home a whole variety of truths to the believer about Christ, about union with him, and about the corporate nature of Christianity. In a day where 'everyone does what is right in his own eyes', these are aspects of Christian life we can scarcely afford to ignore. We may not find the quasi-mystical language of Calvin and his colleagues to our taste; we may regard their theology as somewhat obscure at this point; but I believe we must acknowledge that, at the very least, the current tendency for mere memorialism in the Eucharist, which takes little account of the Eucharistic action itself, is somewhat inadequate, and a richer understanding of the signifying power of the Eucharist, which takes into account the whole of the Eucharistic action, its context as a New Covenant meal, and its symbolic references both to Christ's death and to our vital union with him, must be part of our sacramental testimony today.

Thirdly, we must ensure that whatever liturgy we use (be it of the formal or informal variety) emphasises that the Lord's Supper is gospel, not law: namely, it is about God doing something for us, not about us doing something for God. Any attempt to make it into an offering to God strikes at the heart of the whole notion of the incarnation as God giving himself for us, and enjoys no biblical support whatsoever, however much certain branches of the Christian tradition might wish to maintain the contrary.

Fourthly, and related to the above, we must emphasise in our sacramental services that the theological 'movement' is not God coming down to us, but us being raised up to God. Calling on the Holy Spirit is right and proper – he is the one through whom we are united to Christ – but we are the objects of his activity, and he raises us to heaven by faith; he does not bring Christ down to the elements.

Finally, let us take seriously once again the role of the sacraments in assurance. We live in an age where traditional Protestantism is often excoriated for being too word-oriented and too focused on cerebral matters rather than upon taking seriously the existence of human beings as physical entities. There is a level at which there is nothing we can do in relation to this criticism: words expressing the Word are central to Protestantism and to remove the former leads to the removal of the latter. But there is also a sense in which this criticism should drive us back to our own theological heritage, to see that the Reformers themselves did have a place for drama and for the senses in Christian worship. They called this the Lord's Supper and they considered it to be an integral part of their pastoral practice. In a day when we are increasingly concerned about pastoral care, perhaps it is time to reflect upon the profound pastoral usefulness of the sacraments, especially the Lord's Supper, in our church lives. If the Reformers were right, and the Lord's Supper made the Incarnate Christ more real to those who partook of the Lord's Supper in faith, then for us to neglect the Lord's Supper or to isolate it from a deep incarnational theology and turn it into a mere memorial, is for us unwittingly to deprive our people of a vital element of healthy Christian living. Correct sacramental practice, that is, sacramental practice in the context of a careful theology of incarnation and salvation which is preached and applied to the sacramental action, is crucial to such and may well bear more fruit in our church lives than we could ever imagine that simple obedience to Christ's command could bring forth.

Notes

[1] *The Clear Explanation of Sound Doctrine Concerning the True Partaking of the Flesh and Blood of Christ in the Holy Supper to dissipate the mists of Tileman Heshusius.* Reprinted in John Calvin, *Tracts* 3 vols

(ed. H. Beveridge; Edinburgh: Calvin Translation Society, 1844–51), vol. 2, p. 502.
2. For an interesting account of the function of the Lord's Supper in Highland Presbyterianism with special reference to its connection to the rise of American revivalism, see L.E. Schmidt, *Holy Fairs: Scottish Communions and American Revivals in the Early Modern Period* (Princeton: Princeton University Press, 1989).
3. J. Stott, *Evangelical Truth: a personal plea for unity* (Leicester: Inter-Varsity Press, 1999).
4. See, for example, the agreement between the Evangelical Lutheran Church in America, the Presbyterian Church (USA), the Reformed Church in America, and the United Church of Christ, which finds much common ground between the churches yet still finds their diverse Eucharistic teachings, rooted in the language of the historic confessions, impossible to harmonise. See the statement at < www.elca.org/ea/Relationships/formula.html >.
5. See Luther's 1527 treatise, 'That These Words of Christ, "This Is My Body," etc Still Stand Firm Against the Fanatics' in *Luther's Works* (55 vols; ed. J. Pelikan; St Louis: Concordia, 1955–86), 37, esp. pp. 85 ff. On Luther's theology in general, see B. Lohse, *The Theology of Martin Luther* (Edinburgh: Clark, 2001).
6. See Zwingli's 1527 treatise, 'Friendly Exegesis,' in Huldrych Zwingli, *Writings*, vol. 2 (trans. H.W. Pipkin; Allison Park: Pickwick, 1984). On Zwingli's theology in general, see W.P. Stephens, *The Theology of Huldrych Zwingli* (Oxford: Clarendon, 1986).
7. See the comments in Lohse, *Theology of Martin Luther*, p. 174.
8. On the different ways in which language of presence can be used, see *Luther's Works* 37, pp. 214–17; on the communication of properties, see *Luther's Works* 37, p. 210; and on the elaboration of this idea in later Lutheranism, see J.T. Mueller, *Christian Dogmatics* (St Louis: Concordia, 1934), pp. 268–86; W. Elert, *The Structure of Lutheranism*, ET W.A. Hansen (St Louis: Concordia, 1962), pp. 231 ff.
9. This is clearly the burden of much of his sacramental writing: see, for example, *Luther's Works* 37, pp. 94 ff. Elert addresses this point explicitly in his work on Luther, and his comments are well worth consulting: see *The Structure of Lutheranism*, pp. 314–15.
10. See Athanasius, *On the Incarnation of the Word*, ch. 17; Gregory of Nyssa, *The Great Catechism*, ch. 10; Thomas Aquinas, *Summa Theologiae*, 3a.5.2; for the Reformed understanding, see H. Heppe,

Die Dogmatiek der Evangelisch-Reformierten Kirche (Neukirchen: Neukirchener Verlag, 1958), p.354; also E.D. Willis, *Calvin's Catholic Christology* (Leden: Brill, 1966).

[11] Zwingli, *Writings*, vol. 2, p. 320. On the communication of properties in classic Reformed theology, see L. Berkhof, *Systematic Theology* (Edinburgh: Banner of Truth, 1958), pp. 323–4.

[12] Zwingli, *Writings*, vol. 2, pp. 337ff.

[13] On this modification of Luther's position, see Elert, *The Structure of Lutheranism*, pp. 231–2.

[14] Zwingli is particularly attracted to the semantic range of the Latin word 'sacramentum' which he takes to mean 'pledge' or 'oath': see his *Commentary on True and False Religion*, (ed.) S.M. Jackson (Durham: Labyrinth, 1981), pp. 179–84; on his Eucharistic theology in general, see Stephens, *The Theology of Huldrych Zwingli*, pp. 218–59.

[15] Stott, *Evangelical Truth*, p. 98.

[16] Various editions of The Westminster Confession exist. The best is probably *The Westminster Confession of Faith* (Glasgow: Free Presbyterian, 1994), a volume that also contains, among various relevant ecclesiastical materials, the other official statements produced by the Westminster Assembly.

[17] This is reprinted in *The Work of Thomas Cranmer* (ed. G.E. Duffield; Appleford: Sutton Courtenay, 1964), pp. 45–231.

[18] Cranmer, *Defence*, p. 63.

[19] See, for example, Calvin's comments in Institutes 4.17.1.

[20] 'And with the selfsame body he forsook the world, and ascended into heaven, (the apostles seeing and beholding his body when it ascended,) and now sitteth at the right hand of his Father, and there shall remain until the last day, when he shall come to judge the quick and the dead.' Cranmer, *Defence*, p. 123; cf. Calvin, *Institutes* 4.17.12.

[21] For the official Catholic definition, which links the sacrifice of the Mass to the real presence, see H. Denziger, *Enchiridion Symbolorum* (Friburg: Herder, 1937), 424.

[22] Thus, one of the prayers after Communion thanks God that in the Supper he assures those who rightly receive, 'of thy favour and goodness towards us; and that we are very members incorporate in the mystical body of thy Son, which is the blessed company of all faithful people; and are also heirs through hope of thy everlasting kingdom, by the merits of the most precious death and passion of thy dear Son.'

23. The text is available via < www.cofe.anglican.org/common worship/resources/downloads >.
24. Cranmer, *Defence*, p. 190.
25. Memorialism is there, of course, as the words of the officiating minister make clear, but this memorialism is carefully juxtaposed to language about eating and drinking. The same theology is reflected in the words of the Book of Common Prayer:'[G]rant us … (gracious Lord) so to eat the flesh of thy dear Son Jesus Christ, and to drink his blood, that our sinful bodies may be made clean by his body, and our souls washed through his most precious blood, and that we may evermore dwell in him, and he in us.' The language of eating and drinking, and the emphasis on flesh and blood point both to the importance of the Lord's Supper as an action, and its intimate connection to the incarnation.
26. On the necessity of the Word accompanying the sacrament, see Martin Luther, *The Babylonian Captivity of the Church*; Calvin, *Institutes* 4.17.39.
27. Calvin, *Tracts*, vol. 2, p. 502.
28. *Institutes* 4.17.12 and 4.17.31.
29. The Greek word *epiklēsis* is used with reference to the invocation or 'calling (of the Spirit) upon' the elements of bread and wine or upon the participants in the Lord's Supper by the presiding minister.
30. D. Peterson, 'Holy Communion in *Common Worship*', p. 6. Paper available at < www.geocities.com/the_theologian/content/pastoralia/cw_communion.html >.
31. In the *Institutes*, Calvin prefaces his discussion of the Eucharistic presence with a section on the incarnation, linked closely to Christ's teaching in John 6: see *Institutes* 4.17.8–9.
32. *Institutes* 4.17.12.
33. Cranmer, *Defence*, p. 72.
34. R. Bruce, *The Mystery of the Lord's Supper* (ed. T.F. Torrance; Richmond: John Knox, 1957), p. 64.
35. Cranmer, *Defence*, p. 70.
36. M. Tinker, *Evangelical Concerns* (Fearn: Christian Focus, 2001), pp. 133–4.